D0723441

Date

Anxious for
Armageddon

A Call to Partnership for Middle Eastern and Western Christians

Anxious for
Armageddon

Foreword by
Fr. Elias Chacour

Donald E. Wagner

HERALD PRESS
Scottdale, Pennsylvania
Waterloo, Ontario

Library of Congress Cataloging-in-Publication Data
Wagner, Donald E.
    Anxious for Armageddon : a call to partnership for Middle Eastern and
Western Christians / Donald E. Wagner ; foreword by Elias Chacour.
      p. cm.
    Includes bibliographical references and index.
    ISBN 0-8361-3651-9 (alk. paper)
    1. Jewish-Arab relations—Religious aspects—Christianity. 2. Wagner,
Donald E. 3. Jewish-Arab relations—1917- 4. Palestine in Christianity.
5. Christians—Middle East. 6. Christian Zionism—Controversial literature.
7. Dispensationalism—Controversial literature. 8. Middle East—History—
20th century. 9. Middle East—Religion—20th century. I. Title.
BT93.6.W34 1994   94-501
231.7'6—dc20   CIP

The paper used in this publication is recycled and meets the minimum requirements of American National Standard for Information Sciences—Permanence of
Paper for Printed Library Materials, ANSI Z39.48-1984.

ANXIOUS FOR ARMAGEDDON
Copyright © 1995 by Herald Press, Scottdale, Pa. 15683
    Published simultaneously in Canada by Herald Press,
    Waterloo, Ont. N2L 6H7. All rights reserved
Library of Congress Catalog Number: 94-501
International Standard Book Number: 0-8361-3651-9
Printed in the United States of America
Book and cover design by Paula M. Johnson

1 2 3 4 5 6 7 8 9 10 00 99 98 97 96 95

To my immediate family—
    Grandpa and Grandma Nelson;
    Mom, Dad, and sister Karen;
    My wife, Drew, and children Anna, Matthew, and Jay—
    To my inlaws: Dr. Gordon and Lynn McAllister—
    Who have provided me with the love of Christ and immeasurable joy throughout my life.

And to my extended Middle Eastern family—
    Christians in the churches throughout the Middle East;
    Israeli Jews committed to peace and security based upon justice for Palestinians and Jews;
    Muslim friends who work for religious tolerance, freedom, and full human rights for all peoples, and peace based on dignity to each person as a child of the one true God.
    May God grant you many years and strength for the difficult journey which lies ahead.

Contents

Foreword

The biggest question facing present-day Christianity is how serious Christians will deal with issues of justice and human rights. The question is not "How clean are my hands?" The question is rather "How dirty did I get my hands?" How dirty did I become to "bring the good news to the poor. . . . to proclaim release for the captives and recovery of sight to the blind, to let the oppressed go free, to proclaim the year of the Lord's favor" (Luke 4:18-19)?

Serious Christians understand and live their faith in a God-made-human so that men and women can become godlike. Christians believe in a historical Lord who died and is risen from the dead.

Serious Christians understand and accept in their daily life and their relations to each other the fruits of the resurrection. According to the New Testament, these fruits include the crumbling once and forever of the dividing wall between Jews and Gentiles. All human beings are called to become adopted children of God. This God is no more seen as a regional or as a tribal God—but as the universal God whose chosen people are man and woman, created in his image with his likeness.

Everything has been given through the resurrection, but everything has not yet been received. Human beings are still called to adhere through their lives to what God has given them through the death and the resurrection of Jesus Christ, the one from Galilee. *No more Jew, no more Gentile; no more lord or slave; no more man or woman. Now all are called to become adoptive children of God.*

Eternity starts for believers on the day of their baptism. The commission entrusted to Christians by the risen Lord from Galilee is to live and to witness in a new way, with a renewed vision so that others, "outsiders" seeing their good works, may praise their Father in heaven (Matt. 5:16). It is crucial for Christians to keep in mind how and on which points they will be judged worthy or unworthy for the kingdom of heaven. What shall decide whether Christians are fit for punishment or for eternal life? Jesus' words quoted in Matthew 25:35-36 give this clear answer: "I was hungry and you gave me food, I was thirsty and you gave me something to drink, I was a stranger and you welcomed me, I was naked and you gave me clothing, I was sick and you took care of me, in prison and you visited me."

The task given to Christians by their Master should keep them busy, no matter how long or short are their days on this earth, till they depart this earthly life to eternity. How seriously, Christians should ask themselves, did they accept the call to get their hands dirty like Dietrich Bonhoeffer, Dorothy Day, Martin Luther King, Jr., Mahatma Gandhi, Oscar Romero, and of course Jesus Christ above all? How seriously did they commit themselves to show God's compassion and witness God's mercy?

If those from the household of the Lord are no more the good salt of the earth, how can we expect others to be the salt? It is not a matter of choice but a must for Christians to take the side of the oppressed, the hungry, the thirsty, the stranger, the naked, the sick, and the prisoner. It is not a matter of choice but an imperative to side with the poor, the persecuted, the downtrodden. Christians must act for the liberation of the oppressed people as God did in the exodus: God saw the suffering of his people. God was moved, God cared, God acted, and with an extended powerful arm, God did liberate the slaves from the darkness to the light of freedom.

This was apparently a political act as well. God acts politically. God sided in the Bible with the oppressed and continues to do so today. Christians should do the same.

However, siding with the oppressed should not mean one becomes one-sided or turns against the oppressor. The proper response to injustice is not merely for the roles to be switched, for the oppressed to become oppressors. The goal is to change the situation so all are freed.

If this goal is to be reached, special care must be taken to liberate oppressors from their own arrogance, their own blindness, their own corrupting power. Liberation is needed for both the oppressed and the oppressor.

The temptation of triumphalism and the arrogance of possessing the truth has often led Christians to justify domination over other nations, groups, or individuals. Christians have erroneously believed they possess the truth, even the One Absolute Truth. Thus they establish themselves as dispensers of heavenly blessings and condemnations.

The calling of the Lord to be the light of the world should not mean that Christians blind the world with the glare of their light. Often in the presence of Christian triumphalism and arrogance, the "outsiders" to the church, and especially those in more oppressed parts of the world, must hide their face with their hands. They must say, "Turn down your lights, Christians, you are blinding us with your projectors."

Christians need to speak out boldly. However, the need is not so much for a theology of liberation as for a liberation of theology. Don't we need to set God free from certain theologies, certain civilizations, certain obsessing historical events?

To set God free *means to go back to the centrality of Jesus Christ and his message.* Jesus was and is the good Samaritan. Jesus did not waste his time on earth speculating about the future. Instead he was the suffering servant of his heavenly Father. He spent time with the renowned Samaritan woman, with Nicodemus, with Lazarus, with Peter, with so many more. He now calls Christians to be his servants by healing, consoling, teaching, forgiving, reconciling—and thus witnessing for his Father.

We are to bear witness that God sees oppression. We are to bear witness that God is moved by the cries of the oppressed. We are to bear witness that God is present even if the oppressed are modern Gentiles such as Palestinians in modern Ninevahs such as Palestine.

This is exactly what Don Wagner is trying to do with his life, as I have observed since having the honor of coming to know this man of God long ago. I have always found in him a sharp concern for both the Jews and the Palestinians. Although he discovered the plight of the Palestinians and felt their unbearable burden, although he witnessed the horrors committed against the terrorized Palestinian people in Lebanon and Israel's occupied territories, Don Wagner never became anti-Jewish.

We would not have been able to remain friends had Don yielded to the unacceptable attitude of hatred and bitterness. This is not to deny that Don was angry, as is so often true of prophets of God. Don was frequently angry, asking, "Why all these atrocities? Were the concentration camps in which the Jews faced their Holocaust not enough to teach human beings the horrors of persecuting each other?"

I witnessed Don Wagner maturing in love and growing sharper in his quest for justice for the oppressed Palestinians. Often we prayed together for all of the miserable victims of the Israeli-Palestinian conflict—the Jews and the Palestinians. The first are victims of their own corrupting power; the second are victims because of their powerlessness. Don always tried to join the two ends of the conflict. In *Anxious for Armageddon*, he continues to care, expressing the need for justice and reconciliation rather than the vanity of vengeance.

Don Wagner is a person from the United States of America who speaks out courageously and eloquently. He should be happy he is not a U.S. senator; he would not survive the next election. Yet, even if he is not a politician but a disciple of Jesus Christ, he pays a price for faithfulness. For many years he lived on the edge of poverty, for instance. Don has not made a fortune addressing the Palestinian-Jewish conflict: only a few went to hear the message from his perspective. When the Palestinians were as unpopular as the Jews, Don was there to speak out for peace and justice for both conflicting parties. His contribution to mutual understanding has a healing effect on people. His courage to speak out when many do not dare gives this book a special power and an important authority.

Among other truths, Don inspires the reader with a major and often forgotten truth about God—God does not kill! Wars are simply unjust. There is no just war but always another war. Since God does not kill, no one is entitled to use biblical arguments to justify killings and murder. No one should be allowed to use biblical arguments to justify any national political oppressive entity or state. Human beings have the power to go against God's will as they did in the concentration camps, as they did in the Cambodian towns and villages, exactly as they did in the Palestinian refugee camps and occupied territories. God does not kill. We are the keepers of our brothers and sisters whom God does not kill and commands us not to kill.

Whenever I meet with Don Wagner or hear him speaking with his unique passion and eloquence, I remember a famous prayer hanging at the entrance of Prophet Elias Community College in Ibillin, Galilee. That prayer describes Don Wagner's work and especially this book, which is an act of courage and of painful truth.

> Lord, give me the courage to say the word of truth
>   at the face of mighty people.
> Give me, Lord, the courage to never flatter the poor
>   to win their applause.

This book speaks the truth of a man always keen to search for truth with a strong sense of integrity. I feel honored to write the foreword to this eye-opening and thought-provoking document.

Persons like Don Wagner, who have the courage to say the truth and to defend the unpopular victims of oppression, are the prophets of their own times and societies. Things they say or write are not always popular or easily accepted. It would have been so much better if prophets had from the very beginning spoken against the evil of the concentration camps and if the people had listened. But the horrors were not confronted until too late, when almost every evil was accomplished.

It is very late but not yet too late to decry what has happened in Israel. The Palestinians are still alive, the Israeli Jews are still uncomfortable with their militarism, movements toward peace are being made. Who will join Don Wagner in awakening blind political leaders and one-sided supporters to the urgency of pursuing justice and integrity, so all can enjoy peace and security?

—Abuna Elias Chacour
Parish Priest of Ibillin, Israel and
President, Prophet Elias Community College

Author's Preface

In 1988, my family and I spent a remarkable and inspiring nine-month sabbatical in Cyprus with extended stays in Jerusalem. Initially, I had planned to do research and write a book on Western Christian evangelical relations with Israel and various Christian Zionist groups in Jerusalem. Several welcome interruptions shifted my focus.

First, the Palestinian Intifada (uprising) began at about the time we arrived, giving expression to a new form of largely nonviolent Palestinian resistance that was both intense and organized from the bottom up. These exciting days and weeks heightened attention to the cause of the Palestinian people and their unanimous desire to make peace with Israel. The churches had a major role to play in this journey of justice, and I was able to become involved in several significant projects at once.

In addition, I found myself working full-time for the Middle East Council of Churches—as tends to happen if one is in the company of the General Secretary of MECC, Gabriel Habib. Gabi is a uniquely qualified and wise student of the troubled political waters of the Middle East as well as of the churches. I tried to learn as much as I could from this leader of the regions historic churches who became a mentor and special friend.

These exciting developments left little time for research and writing, particularly for someone like myself who leans more toward activism than research. But I began to see that my involvement in the daily events of the Middle Eastern churches and in both the Lebanese and Palestinian-Israeli cases were reshaping my ever changing focus of writing. I became convinced that the Arab churches, called "the Forgotten Faithful" or "the Living Stones," (1 Peter 2:5) as they called themselves, were a largely unknown story in the West.

My growing concern for the search for peace among Israelis and Palestinians and the role of Western evangelicals converged with the agendas of the churches. I knew little of the remarkable history, spirituality, and even existence of these amazing Christians. But worse, it was clear that they are a vanishing breed in the Middle East.

Gradually, my journey of understanding these Christian communities and the historical and political context of their contemporary lives became the focus of my concern. Perhaps God gave me new ears to hear their pleas and learn from several sides of these complicated issues.

Time after time my preference for action and organizing various programs caused me to set aside the writing. The rapid changes in the Middle East during these years—beginning with the Intifada; then the Gulf War; the failed Madrid Peace Process; the remarkable September 13, 1993, Arafat-Rabin handshake; the frustrating delays in implementing the Declaration of Principles; and then the bloody Hebron massacre and Hamas bombings—led to additional delays and inevitable updates in the text. On four separate occasions I put the manuscript on the shelf.

But finally one must bite the bullet and decide: "This is it!" Or as my wife, Drew, would say: "Are you ever going to finish that book?" So here it is, submitted in the knowledge that some items will be obsolete as soon as they are written. I beg for patience from my highly politicized friends and those from the Jewish, Muslim, or other beliefs, as you follow my personal journey as a Christian into these issues. I hope that my naive and simple journey toward understanding will also touch responsive chords in the experience of Christian friends and those I have never met.

I have attempted to organize the manuscript into five movements, all having different lengths and themes. Chapters 1-5 represent my personal journey from early childhood to my first involvement with Middle East issues some fifteen years ago.

Chapters 6-7 are my attempts to summarize various biblical arguments concerning such vital themes as the land, covenant, people, and justice. These sections are written for lay readers and are intended to be a primer rather than the last word on these issues.

Chapters 8-9 are the only sections that remain from the initial research I conducted in London and in the Middle East on Christian Zionism. Although these chapters are condensed versions of extensive notes and experiences, perhaps they will provide helpful starting points for entering this largely uncharted history (plus one contemporary illustration of the subject, the International Christian Embassy-Jerusalem).

In chapters 10-13 I deal with Palestinian history and the Palestinian Christian experience, as viewed primarily through the lens of Palestinian Christians and the community as a whole. Palestinian history since the emergence of Zionism is treated in an abbreviated manner, simply to set the context in which these "Living Stones" presently find themselves unsure of their very future as a living community.

Finally, chapter 14 and the epilogue serve to discuss the future, in terms of a viable political settlement in the Israeli-Palestinian conflict, and suggestions for Western Christians responses. I have selected various maps, documents for the appendices, and a bibliography for those who wish to go beyond my initial probings of these concerns.

Obviously, a work that took five years to complete needed considerable support, practical help, and innumerable suggestions for improvement. I have not always included the helpful suggestions and bear full responsibility for the oversights and interpretations represented here. I would like to thank my friends at the Middle East Council of Churches and those Arab Christian and Muslim friends mentioned, (and in many cases not mentioned) throughout this book. Their faith and suffering have both inspired me and given endless hours of hospitality and renewal. I express my deepest gratitude to the Lebanese, Palestinian, Israeli, Egyptian and Jordanian friends who yearn for and work for a better future. Special thanks goes out to Professor Ghada Talhami of Lake Forest College (Illinois) and Salim Tamari (Buzert University, Palestine) for their time and insights after reading selected chapters.

Several colleagues and my family in the United States made this book possible, both by their patience and practical support. George Kovats and the Stewardship Foundation provided two short-term grants that allowed me to continue writing when I was out of funding and did not know if I could feed my family. My parents, Don and Thelma Wagner, my sister Karen, and my faithful godfather, Norm Nelson, kept me going with their prayers and occasional financial support. My father-in-law, Dr. Gordon McAllister, contributed on several occasions to our family, enabling us to get through difficult financial situations.

The two organizations I serve, Mercy Corps International and Evangelicals for Middle East Understanding, have enabled me to continue in this unusual Middle East ministry. Their willingness to walk this journey as partners, often like Abraham "not knowing where we are going" (let alone how we will pay for it), have brought incredible joy and inspiration.

Michael A. King at Herald Press was a patient and wonderful editor with whom to work. Thank you, Michael, for taking a risk with me in publishing this manuscript.

Finally I thank my family—my wife, Drew, and children Matthew,

Anna, and Jay. It has been difficult living with one who cannot always find the financial resources, but you have stuck it out with me. Thank you for your patience and for being more a part of this journey than you may realize.

On the technical side, I cannot express sufficient appreciation to my wonderful assistant at Mercy Corps and EMEU, Susanne Donaghue. Her sharp eye for editing text and many hours of reworking the manuscript go above and beyond the call. Liz Stout stepped in at an important time to render assistance, as did my previous secretary, Leyla Gungor. No doubt many go unmentioned; to you I apologize hoping that the story that follows will be sufficient compensation for my oversight.

—Donald A. Wagner
May 1, 1994, Evanston, Illinois

Anxious for
Armageddon

1
Raptured: The Case of the Empty Birdcage

When I was a child, I spoke like a child, I thought like a child, I reasoned like a child.
1 Corinthians 13:11

I recall my conversion experience as if it occurred last week. My grandparents, to whom I was very close, had asked me to join them for a revival meeting on a hot July evening in rural western New York State. I was eight years old.

First let me set the stage. My mother's parents, John and Anna Nelson, were simple people, farmers who lived close to the land and close to the Lord. They lived lives of fervent daily prayer and were utterly dependent on God in every aspect of their lives. I recall how Grandpa would always respond to appointments or upcoming events with the phrase, "God willing."

Grandpa was extroverted, warm, and self-assured. A deeply spiritual Norwegian immigrant who had sown his wild oats after leaving home at age fifteen, he arrived in the United States without a cent in his pocket in 1901. His elder brother Neil arrived two years later, and they purchased a small farm near Lockport, New York, a blue-collar city approximately twenty miles north of Buffalo on the Erie Canal.

Grandma was a frail and compassionate woman. She was far more introverted and shy than Grandpa; I could see how the "opposites attract" theory applied to their relationship. Grandma lacked Grandpa's fun-loving, adventurous spirit, which may have been a trait he developed during his teenage years while roaming the seas in the Norwegian Merchant Marines.

As the eldest of seven children, Grandma carried most of the burden of childcare after her stern, alcoholic German father left the family. Although she would never discuss it, we later suspected that her father physically abused her when she was a little girl. She carried all her life the scars of a damaged right eye and unresolved emotional trauma. Although Grandma was often depressed and complained constantly about her health, she was also a very loving and compassionate person who would give her last dress to the poor and the homeless.

Grandpa always had a smile on his face and was filled with energy. I will never forget the time he walked around the farmhouse on his hands at the spry age of seventy-five. Later, as a baseball pitcher in college, I was amazed that at the age of eighty he could still throw a curveball and catch my return throws. As a small boy of three and four, I would sit on his lap in his favorite rocking chair for hours, listening to baseball games on the radio or tuning in to our favorite dramas, *The Lone Ranger* and *The Green Hornet.*

I was raised in their simple farmhouse during my first four years while my dad served in World War II. Mom needed to work two jobs, which left me free to roam eighty acres of orchards and farmland. I always looked forward to the evenings, to the baseball broadcasts followed by Grandma and Grandpa's hour of Bible study. They rarely missed this nightly discipline of prayer and study. My early love of the Bible began with these family study sessions.

Shortly after my dad returned from the war, my sister Karen was born, and we moved to the city of Lockport. I still spent several weekends on the farm, especially during the summers. One memorable Friday evening, when I was eight, we drove about half an hour to a small church in the countryside near Niagara Falls, New York. We arrived shortly after the revival began so we quietly took our seats in the back pew. Fortunately, we arrived just in time to hear the evangelist's message.

As the evangelist walked to the pulpit, I noticed he was an enormous man, well over six feet tall, weighing close to three hundred pounds. His voice had become hoarse after preaching twice a day for a week. His gravel-toned voice and highly emotional style gave his preaching an eerie quality that grew more exaggerated as the evening continued. The sermon topic for the final service of the week-long revival was "Hell and the Latter Days."

I still recall how he developed the message. He began with a detailed description of hell and the eternal punishment God had prepared for unbelievers. His description of the "lake of fire" (Rev. 19:20) particularly caught my attention. He made his point very clear. If you had not repented of your sins and accepted Jesus as your personal Savior, you were destined to suffer in hell. "The pain and agony will be beyond anything you can imagine," he screamed.

By this time the hot, humid July evening gave the message a direct physical reality. I was sweating like crazy. The evangelist mopped his brow, paused to clean his glasses, and shifted into high gear, pouring every ounce of energy into his gigantic frame.

"We have entered the final days of history," he proclaimed. "There is a terrible, bloody battle about to be waged," he added, "far worse than anything we witnessed in World War II. The Bible predicts this war will be fought at Armageddon and will involve the nation Israel against forces from the north, probably Russia. There has never been a war as terrible as the one we are about to witness. Nation will fight nation, and brother will battle brother."

"How do we know this?" he asked. "Because everything is happening just as the prophets of the Old Testament predicted. When God's people Israel return to the Holy Land to establish their own state, everything will be in order for the countdown to the end of history. The Bible says that when this occurs, the final battle will be close at hand. Just two years ago, after centuries of statelessness, the Jewish people miraculously created their nation. What an amazing opportunity! God has chosen to begin this prophetic countdown to the end of history in our lifetime."

"But the Bible warns us," he continued, "that Jesus will return before this terrible battle takes place. He will take his own from the earth. They will be spared this awful final battle, and you can be among them if you have accepted Jesus Christ as your Lord and Savior."

Then the evangelist turned to 1 Thessalonians 4:16-17.

> For the Lord himself, with a cry of command, with the archangel's call and with the sound of God's trumpet, will descend from heaven, and the dead in Christ will rise first. Then we who are alive, who are left, will be caught up in the clouds together with them to meet the Lord in the air.

"My God, what a wonderful promise!" he cried out. "But are you ready tonight to meet Jesus if he returns? If you have not accepted him as your Lord and Savior, if you have not repented of your sins, you could be left behind to perish in the final battle."

By now I was literally shaking in my shoes. At that moment the evangelist asked everyone to stand and bow their heads in prayer. I was so nervous that I had difficulty standing and was forced to lean on the pew in front of me. With every head bowed and a pianist gently playing a hymn, the evangelist cried out again, reminding us that this might be our last chance before the rapture.

I took a cautious peek around the room. My grandparents and everyone else were dutifully praying.

Then the evangelist said, "If you are uncertain about the state of your soul as you stand before God tonight, this is your moment. I want you to come forward and make that decision before it is too late."

I felt a magnetic pull almost leading me out of the pew, but I simply could not move. What was I going to do? I could not even stand, let alone walk down the aisle. In addition, I felt profoundly embarrassed, believing Grandma and Grandpa thought I was already a Christian. My skinny knees shaking, I became immobilized.

The evangelist wailed on, "Come to Jesus tonight, come now, tomorrow will be too late!"

But I was riveted in my pew. Hiding my tears, I prayed in my heart, "Oh, God, save me tonight, so I won't burn in hell and suffer forever."

This scary moment was the time I have always pointed to as my conversion as a Christian. In retrospect, I now realize that my baptism, the wonderful foundation provided by my grandparents on the farm, and the loving nurture of my parents were also God's vehicles of salvation. However, I most clearly and consciously accepted Jesus Christ into my heart on that hot Friday in mid-July 1950. Since that decision, I have never doubted my salvation for a moment—aside from an experience that took place the very next day.

The drive home was long; I sat quietly in the back seat trying to recover. I was too confused to discuss the multitude of feelings I was experiencing. After all, a good Scandinavian and German male does not reveal his feelings, especially when confusion and weakness reign.

On Saturday morning I sat alone on the porch, one of my favorite childhood places. The birdcage had been placed there to catch a rare summer breeze in the intense heat. I began to pester the canary with a stick, no doubt out of boredom and confusion. Suddenly the bird disappeared. She simply vanished right before my eyes. I ran into the dining room, pulled a chair out onto the porch, and climbed up to look for the canary. I feared I had injured the little bird and began to feel sorry. I peered in and the canary was nowhere to be seen.

Something strange was happening. I checked the door to the cage, and it had been securely fastened the whole time. I climbed back up on the chair and looked around the cage to see if there was a hole that might have allowed her to escape. It was as tight as a drum.

I looked expectantly on the floor of the cage, hoping she had reappeared. The bird had vanished, plain and simple.

I rushed into the house calling for Grandma. There was no answer. I ran out the back door, hoping she was working in the garden. Nobody was there; I began to cry. Then I rushed down the driveway to the barn, which was about five hundred feet from the house. Grandpa would often return from the fields to work on the tractor or other farm equipment. I ran into the barn calling for him, but he was not there.

My thoughts turned to the evangelist's sermon. *Oh no!* I thought. *This must be the rapture. Jesus has returned just as the preacher said, and I have been left behind.* I really panicked. I walked slowly up the driveway in tears, feeling utterly abandoned and devastated. *Have I missed my opportunity to be saved by not going forward last night?* I wondered. Or perhaps God was punishing me for hurting the little canary. My young mind ran wild with fear. I looked up into the sky and saw a few clouds, the bright sun, but no sign of Jesus. "Oh, God," I prayed, "please forgive me and don't leave me here alone." I sat in the middle of the driveway and cried.

After what seemed an eternity, I heard voices coming from next door. My grandparents were walking across the path from Mrs. Roberts' house. Wasn't it just like them? They had taken lunch to old Mrs. Roberts, who was ill. I ran to greet them, never more excited to see anyone in my life. I tried to contain my excitement and hide my tears as I ran over to give them each a hug. Grandpa put his strong arm around me and we returned to the farmhouse for lunch. The fear and confusion left immediately. I said a quiet prayer as we walked, thanking God for giving me this second chance, before the rapture took us all away.[1]

2

The Holy Land I Never Knew

What was the cause of the first destruction of Jerusalem?
Idolatry. And of the second destruction? Causeless hatred.
Rabbi Johanan, *Minor Tractates of the Babylonian Talmud*

Since early childhood I had wanted to visit the "holy" [1] land. I imagined walking where Jesus walked and sitting by the Sea of Galilee where he taught the crowds and delivered the Sermon on the Mount. Bethlehem, Nazareth, and Jerusalem were such familiar cities. I could even envision Mt. Carmel where Elijah defeated the prophets of Baal (1 Kings 18), or Mount Nebo (Deut. 34:1-8) where Moses first viewed the Promised Land. My ultimate dream was to visit Jerusalem, the city of David, where so many of the major events in the Old Testament and in Jesus' life took place.

Naturally, I grew up with the Scofield Bible, an annotated version of Scripture developed by C. I. Scofield at the turn of the century (1909). Since the day of my conversion experience, I never missed the discipline of daily Bible study until I entered seminary, ironically enough. During my childhood and high school years, I was influenced by various preachers and writers from the futurist premillennial dispensationalist tradition that one finds in the Scofield Bible. From the time I was ten I never missed Billy Graham's weekly radio program, *The Hour of Decision*, where I heard the dispensational message on a regular basis. As I studied the graphic apocalyptic chapters of the Bible, including Ezekiel 38—39, Daniel 7—12, 1 Thessalonians 4, and Revelation, I came to adopt the dispensationalist worldview.

According to the leading proponents of this school, we were living in the last days of history. They claimed that the present era was the "time of the Gentiles," when dramatic events would unfold, leading to the sudden return of Jesus. Prior to Jesus' return, however, the world would be threatened by a buildup of evil forces, which would culminate in the rise of one demonic world leader called the Antichrist.

Several dispensational authors and pastors speculated as to who the Antichrist might be. Among the candidates were Adolf Hitler, the pope, or Communism and the evil Soviet empire. I personally leaned toward the latter option, especially after watching the famous television series *I Led Three Lives,*" a weekly drama about Soviet espionage in the United States.

According to the futurist premillennial scenario,[2] once Israel became a nation in 1948, the movement toward the last days of history was set in motion. Israel would gradually attain international acclaim and become God's chosen instrument to fight the Antichrist. Each modern war won by Israel (1948, 1956, 1967, 1973, 1982) provided sufficient evidence to me that Israel was becoming a significant military power and might play the predicted role in the prelude to Armageddon.

The Armageddon scenario with which I was most familiar included a ten-member confederation, which many equated with the European Economic Community. According to this prophecy, the confederation will invade Israel and seek to destroy her. A long, bloody battle will be waged at Armageddon. Jesus will return to save Israel and establish his millennial kingdom in Israel. Born-again Christians will be raptured out of history and not pass through the several years of tribulation (views vary concerning the timing of the tribulation and rapture, with pretribulationists claiming the rapture will occur before the major warfare, midtribulationists claiming it will occur after three and a half years of agony, and posttribulationists expecting it after the warfare).

The dispensationalist arguments which appealed to me at that time elevated Israel as God's chosen instrument to oppose the satanic Antichrist. It seemed natural to equate the modern state of Israel with the biblical Israel. I accepted this interpretation and never questioned it.

I grew up with these views, which were confirmed in my daily study (the Scofield Bible and such trusted commentaries as *Halley's Bible Companion*, which I received free with my subscription to the *Hour of Decision* magazine). My Sunday school teachers (first in independent Bible churches, then the Southern Baptist Church, and later in the Christian Missionary Alliance, and Missouri Synod Lutheran Church) all taught these views.

In high school I attended an Assemblies of God midweek Bible study and Youthtime evangelistic rallies in Buffalo, New York. One evening at a Youthtime rally, evangelist Jack Wyrtzen was preaching and opened the floor for questions. I was beginning to entertain a tiny seed of doubt concerning such doctrines as the pretribulation rapture and questioned the evangelist's emphasis on the latter days. But Wyrtzen shamed me with his answer, implying I was doubting the Word of God where these teachings were plain for anyone to see.

He became angry with my question and avoided a direct answer, so I probed again, "Doesn't Jesus caution us about looking for signs of the end?"

"Look," he repeated, "the Bible is clear about these matters and tells us all we need to know. It is not your place to question it. You should get my recent pamphlet that explains these teachings. Next question!"

I sat down embarrassed but unconvinced.

In college I was exposed to the Reformed-Calvinist theology, which had no place for premillennial dispensationalist teachings. Gradually, my worldview began to change, and I gave little thought to the rapture, the Antichrist, and the timing of Jesus' return. By my initial year in seminary, I had completely abandoned the dispensationalist worldview. Within a two-year period during the turbulent mid-1960s, I had changed politically and theologically into a different person.

Despite these theological and political changes in my orientation, I remained committed to Israel and to Zionism—the political ideology supporting a Jewish state in Palestine. However, a new stream of Christian influence converged with the liberal theological authors I was reading. I became deeply interested in the Jewish Holocaust and found the efforts of Dietrich Bonhoeffer, Martin Niemöller, Karl Barth, and the Confessing Church in Germany both fascinating and inspiring.

This small movement of German clergy and laity was committed to faithful discipleship. When Hitler took control of the German churches in 1934, the above-mentioned theologians and many others formed a small but powerful movement called the Confessing Church. Their Barmen Declaration, which anchored its theology in the lordship of Jesus Christ, was a powerfully moving statement by the few Germans who stood against Hitler. In addition I read Jewish writers like Elie Wiesel and Richard Rubenstein, whose works confirmed that Jews should never again trust others with their fate and must have a state of their own—Israel. I couldn't have agreed more.

My first parish experience after seminary was an African-American congregation on the tense Newark-East Orange, New Jersey, border. The four years I spent with that parish changed my life in many ways. Interestingly, the deeply spiritual and biblically based witness of the black church drew me back to my evangelical heritage. At the same time, my newfound social activism awakened an authentic outlet in the justice and poverty issues facing our community.

During my urban experience in Newark, we learned there was a need to work on black-Jewish tensions which had peaked during the Newark riots of 1967. We began a dialogue and congregational exchanges with a large Newark synagogue, where the noted Rabbi Joachim Prinz served. With my senior pastor, Dr. Joseph L. Roberts, an outstanding preacher and pastor, we began to build bridges between the two communities.

In my second parish experience, I was able to be more intentional in implementing my concerns about anti-Semitism and the Holocaust. Called as associate pastor to a large two thousand member suburban congregation in Ridgewood (West Side Presbyterian Church) New Jersey, I discovered that our high school young people were spending considerable money on a month of summer camp. Why couldn't we turn this into a Christian education program? I wondered.

As a result, we developed a ten-week study course followed by a month of travel to Europe. We studied the Protestant Reformation, the Holocaust, the Confessing Church, and Christianity in Eastern Europe. After ten weeks of study (in Wiesel's *Night*, Leon Uris' *Mila 18* and viewing such films as *Night and Fog*), we traveled to Europe. After visiting historic Wittenberg (where Luther nailed the Ninety-five Theses to the church door) and Geneva (where Calvin led his theocracy), we went to Dachau, Terezin (in northern Czechoslovakia), and Auschwitz.

I will never forget the visit to Auschwitz. After walking through the death factory, witnessing the gas chambers, viewing bins of baby pacifiers (where the Nazis conducted experiments on children) and lamp shades made of human flesh, I was overcome with horror. Our group of thirty-five high school and college young people were in shock. We saw a film that penetrated our souls to the core as skeletal figures stared at us asking, *Why?* Corpses by the thousands were buried by bulldozers in mass graves. We returned to the parking lot and wept. We entered a time of prayer and confession, holding hands and crying as we prayed. Anna, our Polish guide and a Catholic Christian, had lost an uncle at Auschwitz.

Within months of the Auschwitz experience, I accepted a call to join the staff of a large Presbyterian congregation in Evanston, Illinois, just north of Chicago. I recall driving across the country during the 1973 October War, feeling deeply worried about Israel because they were losing the initial phase of the war. Eventually Israel defeated the Arab forces but at an enormous price in lives and financial resources. Little did the world know that the United States went on a stage IV nuclear alert during this time (stage V means the launching of an attack).

One of my first committee assignments at the new congregation was to represent the staff in the Christian education and church and society committee. One member recommended we study the Middle East conflict. This seemed a helpful suggestion to me. By then the Arab boycott was in full swing and our people, like Americans across the country, were angry about sitting in long gas lines. We thought the congregation would be interested and we could help them process and understand their anger.

I discovered during my first committee meeting that one lay member had been deeply involved in the Palestinian issue. We were on opposite sides of the debate; Bill sided with the Arabs and I with Israel. I learned that during the 1949-50 period, Bill had helped settle Palestinian refugees who had fled from their homes when Israel was established. I had never heard of such a thing, and it immediately put me on the defensive. The more he talked the angrier I became. He wanted to do a course that would bring in Arab speakers so they could relate this "untold" story.

This is outrageous!, I thought, not wanting to be overly vocal in my first committee assignment. I did, however, state clearly that there was another side of the story—that of the chosen people, Israel. We compromised and agreed to set up a ten-week course that would offer both perspectives.

Four of us met separately to plan the course. We drew up a list of names, all of them new to me. I made sure that significant Zionist organizations were represented so they could present Israel's cause in a clear and articulate manner. I also wanted to raise issues about Christian perspectives and responsibilities in this volatile region.

The course began. I arranged for the initial speaker, the Israeli Consul General for the Midwest, Shaul Ramati. He delivered a superb lecture, presenting Israel's perspective on the "Yom Kippur War," as Israelis called it. Those attending the course were pleased and so was I.

But the second session was arranged by Bill, who had a surprise for us. He brought in a Palestinian professor of political science from nearby Northwestern University, Dr. Ibrahim Abu-Lughod. The professor was a neatly dressed, gray-haired scholar who presented a remarkable case for the Palestinians. He did not fit my media stereotype of Palestinians, and I had never heard a persuasive intellectual presentation of the case before. The professor was born in Jaffa, Palestine, and received his Ph.D. from Princeton University. Most confusing was the fact that he was a member of the Palestine National Council, the PLO's parliament in exile. As a strong supporter of Zionism, I held a very low view of the PLO, considering it a terrorist organization which attacked women and children. But Abu-Lughod's presentation caused me to think more deeply about the Palestinian case.

The course continued, with a leading Chicago Zionist spokesperson the third week, an Arab the fourth, and so on. By now word had spread and the sessions were standing-room only. After the fourth session, I received a telephone call that took me by surprise. The caller asked me to stop the course because it was offensive to the Jewish community and could be interpreted as anti-Semitic. He said, "If this course continues, we will have no choice but to picket your church next Sunday."

The accusation cut me to the core. I felt sorry and guilty. But at the same time, I believed that we were presenting an honest and balanced array of viewpoints.

Actually, I was in shock. In all my years of church work and peace education, I had never run into anything like this. In the African-American community, we freely debated the difficult issues and even had Black Panthers as part of the dialogue. We did not agree with each other, but we came to respect each other. The same was true in my antiwar involvement. The issue of free speech had become important to me, and the Christian community was a vital arena in which the views and needs of those with no voice could be protected. The Confessing Church took those risks on behalf of the Jews during the Nazi era, and the body of Christ might need to do so on a number of issues.

I discussed the puzzling call with my senior pastor, Dr. Ernest Lewis. He responded, "Keep it going, and let's see what happens."

I arrived at church on Sunday, expecting to see our worshipers picketed. There was no protest, so I breathed a sigh of relief. The fifth session went on as scheduled. But on Monday morning I received another phone call, this one more confrontational and mean. The caller identified himself as a Holocaust survivor from Skokie (a predominantly Jewish community west of Evanston). If the course continued, he said, something serious would happen to me. Then he hung up.

I was not only shocked, I was angry. This was pure intimidation. Here I was, a defender of Israel and Zionism for my entire life, and these defenders of Israel were threatening me without bothering to see how fair we had been. When pushed in this manner, my deep sense of injustice was engaged. I began to question the Zionists' motives and tactics. What did these people have to hide? I wondered.

The course and the telephone threats had a lasting effect on me. Practically, they served to stimulate my interest in the Palestine question. In fact, this was the beginning of a two-year period of self-education, during which I read several historical and theological books on the issue.

In 1975, I was invited to join a group of pastors, seminarians, and professors who had returned from the Middle East. They too desired more education so we met monthly to discuss books and developments in the Middle East. The group was far more experienced than I with Middle East issues, all having toured the region. The key person around whom the group gathered was a brilliant young professor at McCormick Theological Seminary, Dr. Bruce Rigdon. He was to become a close friend and mentor on such topics as the Eastern Orthodox Church and my renewed interest in John Calvin's theology.

After three meetings, the convener of the study group accepted a parish outside of Chicago. Nobody wanted to take over his role so I accepted, simply to keep the group together. After three meetings we concluded that while the group was edifying for us, we should consider our broader responsibility to the church. We decided to organize a conference on

Christianity in the Middle East for Presbyterians in the Chicago area. By now we called ourselves the Middle East Task Force of the Chicago Presbytery.

During the next three years, I studied the Middle East vigorously, particularly the Palestine question. But I was not comfortable with how my beliefs were changing. My commitment to the Jewish people remained strong, but I had developed serious questions about the State of Israel and Zionism. I began to feel extremely guilty whenever I criticized Israel and became very sensitive about being labeled anti-Semitic.

It seems God was working in ways that I did not understand in raising these disturbing questions. The conference organized by our study group had brought four Middle East theologians to Chicago. During these sessions and in personal dialogue with Arab Christians, I began to rethink my views on such biblical concepts as the Promised Land, chosenness, prophecy, and Israel.

The two Lebanese Christian leaders who attended the conference discussed the terrible situation facing Christians in their country, where a civil war was raging. The Coptic Orthodox bishop, Samuel, came from Cairo and reflected on the rich spirituality and history of his church, which was established as a result of the evangelist Mark's missionary efforts in the first century. I had never thought about these issues. These deeply spiritual and brilliant Arab Christian leaders clarified the biblical framework for us and broadened Christian perspectives on these complicated issues.

Having gained new biblical insights and met several Arab Christian leaders, I needed to take the next step. I was ready to travel to the Middle East (concentrating on Lebanon, Israel, and the occupied territories), to gain firsthand experience with the people and the issues of these fascinating lands.

3

Journey to Beirut

My people died of hunger, and he who did not perish from
starvation was butchered by the sword; They perished from hunger in a land
rich with milk and honey. . . . they died because the vipers and sons of
vipers spat out poison into the space where the Holy Cedars and
the roses and the jasmine breathe their fragrance.
Kahlil Gibran, "Dead Are My People," from The
Treasured Writings of Kahlil Gibran, Castle Books, 1981

As my Middle East Airlines flight approached Beirut, Lebanon, I
pressed my face against the window for a closer look at the scene developing below. I could hardly believe what I was seeing—a modern city
stretching far across the horizon. The buildings appeared to be high rise
apartments and offices. There were hundreds of them. In the background
I could see beautiful mountains nestled behind the city to the east. The
western side of the city was built on the Mediterranean coastline, with
beautiful beaches interrupted occasionally by luxury hotels.

To my amazement, I could not see a sign of the massive destruction
caused by the barbaric civil war, now over a year old. I said a prayer,
thanking God for my safe arrival as the passenger jet touched down at
Beirut's International Airport. So many people had said, "You are crazy—
don't go. Beirut is a war zone." But having met my new Arab Christian
friends, nothing could dissuade me.

In some strange way I felt that the Lord was encouraging me to make this trip, despite the warnings. Two weeks prior to departure I had contacted my friend Gabi Habib, newly elected head (General Secretary) of the Middle East Council of Churches (MECC). He advised me to come as soon as possible. There was a tenuous ceasefire in the civil war which he judged would hold for a few weeks. I had saved four weeks of vacation from my pastorate and was able to leave Chicago on Labor Day, 1977.

During the summer, I had read several books on the political history of Lebanon, especially the recent civil war. But nothing could have prepared me for what lay ahead. After clearing customs I walked into the rather old and dingy airport lobby to call Gabi. I was traveling alone and knew but two words of Arabic—*marhabah* (hello), and *shukran* (thank you). Following Gabi's instructions, I changed money and found a telephone so I could ask him to come and pick me up. It was now close to ten o'clock in the evening; I was dead tired after more than twenty hours of travel and not a wink of sleep.

Gabi's home phone rang and rang, with no answer. *That's strange*, I thought. He had said he would be there. I knew one other telephone number in all of Beirut: Gabi's office. I hoped he was working late. My mind turned toward a backup strategy, such as finding a cheap hotel and simply getting some rest.

The phone was ringing at the new MECC office . . . ten, twelve, fifteen times. I was so desperate for an answer that I simply held my tired head in my hands with the phone still ringing and wondered what to do next. All of a sudden a woman's voice said, "Hello, who is it?"

I identified myself and asked for Mr. Habib. "Oh, yes," she said. "Mr. Habib was delayed out of the country. He told us to have you check into the Mayflower Hotel near our office. There is a room reserved for you, so just take a short cab ride from the airport, and you will be there in fifteen to twenty minutes." Then she abruptly hung up, leaving me with all my unanswered questions dangling on my tongue. *Oh, well*, I thought, *that's good enough. I just want to go to sleep. My body is numb, and my mind is like jelly.*

Perhaps I was in an appropriate mental state to meet the crowd gathered outside Beirut Airport. It appeared as if an unruly convention was being held. Hundreds of people were congregated outside the front door in the hot and humid tropical evening. Apparently they were not allowed inside. Waiting for arriving flights seemed to be a family, if not a neighborhood, event.

I wandered aimlessly out the door, observing the dress and other features of the people. Most of them appeared to be men in their late teens to early thirties. There were some families looking for loved ones. A young man followed me out of the airport and his family rushed over to hug him, exhibiting great joy in celebrating his arrival.

Suddenly two young men approached me and said, "Taxi?" Before I could answer, one fellow was holding my bag and the other pointed me toward a row of small taxis. "Welcome, my friend," said the man in perfect English. "Where are you from?"

"The United States," I answered gingerly, not knowing how that would be received.

"Ah, welcome," he repeated. "What city are you from?" he asked.

"Chicago!" I answered proudly.

"Oh, it is dangerous there. Al Capone and Mafia—shoot'em up, rat-a-tat-tat!" He pretended to shoot a machine gun.

How ironic, I thought. *They believe Chicago is dangerous and everyone in Chicago is advising me to avoid the dangers of war-torn Beirut.*

"Where can we take you, my friend?" he asked.

"Do you know the Mayflower Hotel?"

"Of course, everyone knows the Mayflower. It is very near the AUB campus." I knew that meant the American University of Beirut, the finest university in the Arab world, well respected for having educated several generations of Arab leaders.

I handed my other bag to the younger of the two men; he placed both suitcases in the trunk. I took a seat in the cab, and the driver turned around and said, "Do you know the Arabic word *bakshish?*"

"No," I replied.

"We had better begin your Arabic lessons with this word, because it is very important. It means 'money,' and my friend here would like something for his help."

Feeling a bit reluctant, I pulled out a couple of dollars, for which he seemed grateful. The car pulled away from the chaotic scene and drove down a long avenue. It was dark but to my left I could see the moon reflecting on the Mediterranean in the distance. Suddenly I had a burst of fresh energy, and my eyes were alert to study everything in this fascinating new world opening up to me. On my right I could not see much at all, but halfway down the airport boulevard, I began to see tiny houses crammed together.

"What is that section called?" I asked.

"That is Bourj el-Bourajneh, one of the large Palestinian refugee camps. In a minute I will show you where I live, Shatila camp. Next to it is Sabra refugee camp. These are all Palestinian camps."

"Ah, yes," I responded. " I have read about them in books." I had just finished reading *The Disinherited*, by Fawaz Turki, a well-written volume about his childhood in Beirut's refugee camps.

We turned left and were suddenly in another world, with traffic and people everywhere. Tiny shops were open, selling *falafel* and *shawerma* (like the Greek *gyros*) sandwiches. I looked at the main entrance to the camp; it was jammed with people. I could see more clearly now the tiny houses. They were made of cinder blocks and corrugated metal (held down with large stones) for roofs.

Suddenly we were brought to an abrupt stop by Syrian soldiers at a checkpoint outside the refugee camps. Two soldiers walked to our car and took the driver's papers. The driver told me to get my passport out and not to take pictures. I wasn't about to do anything to get the soldiers excited. I knew the Syrians were the primary occupying army in Beirut and had fought the Palestinians in savage battles during recent months. I wondered if my being with a Palestinian driver would arouse suspicions. The young soldier took a look at my passport, shined his flashlight in my face, scowled, and waved us on.

We drove toward the Hamra District, where I noticed less poverty and a completely different atmosphere. It was a residential area, full of new apartment buildings, offices, and small shops. We rounded a few corners, the driver paying no attention to the traffic lights except to slow down for red lights. Apparently no one paid attention to the traffic control mechanisms, and the police couldn't care less. My driver stopped in front of the Mayflower Hotel, a nicely appointed British establishment. I checked in and collapsed as soon as I touched the bed.

Gabi Habib's welcome telephone call woke me up at 9:00 the next morning. He invited me to come over to his office as soon as I could get ready, so he could introduce me to his colleagues on the Middle East Council of Churches (MECC). He also invited me to sit in on one of the first meetings of the executive committee, scheduled to begin late in the afternoon. *What an honor*, I thought. *Here I am, a nobody, and these leaders take me in as an honored guest!*

The MECC was actually formed in late 1975 but had been unable to meet due to the severity of the Lebanese civil war. MECC replaced the Near East Council of Churches, a Lebanese/Syrian and Egyptian organization that was dominated by the Presbyterian and Reformed mission churches of the region. While they are important churches there and have gained tremendous respect, due largely to their excellent record in higher education, they represented only around 3 percent of the Christians in Lebanon, and a tiny fraction of the overall population. The reorganized MECC would include the Eastern Orthodox, Melkite Catholic, Anglican, Armenian Orthodox, Coptic (Egyptian) Orthodox, and others.[1] The new makeup enabled the council to be far more representative of the Christians in the Middle East, and certainly much larger than the old council.

I greeted Gabi with a hug, and as my Arab friends reminded me, with three kisses on the cheek (one for each person of the Trinity, Christian Arabs will tell you, but Muslims do it too). Then Gabi said to me, "Look who is here!" It was my Coptic Orthodox friend, Dr. George Bebawi, who spoke at our Chicago conference the previous year and stayed with me an additional week. We greeted each other enthusiastically with the same procedure I had used with Gabi. I was feeling right at home.

After lunch the meeting began. Gabi introduced me to the executives and department chairs of each section of the Middle East Council of

Churches. I was generously introduced as the chair of an "important Presbyterian Church organization in Chicago that sponsored the conference" Gabi attended. I was hardly worthy of the introduction, but it made good copy for the executives. They conducted the meeting in English for my benefit, another expression of hospitality that astounded me.

During a coffee break, George Bebawi pulled me aside and quietly asked, "How long are you staying?"

"I'm flexible, ten days or so," I answered.

"Good. I am taking a few days of vacation here myself, and I want to introduce you to a few friends. We will get started as soon as the meeting is over."

"Great," I responded. "I want to learn as much as I can." I did not know then that he was cooking up a program beyond belief.

George is truly a character. He is a Cambridge University (England) Ph.D. and at that time was the leading young theologian in the Coptic Orthodox Church. He has a brilliant mind and is a specialist on the early church fathers (Patristics) and church history in general. He also has a keen wit and loves confrontation. I was drawn to him immediately. When he stayed with me in Chicago, we had become good friends and prayer partners. I had prayed for George and his family every day throughout the past year.

Gabi had been thinking as well about how to maximize my time in Beirut, a trait of Arab hospitality that would amaze me for years to come. In the midst of his many responsibilities for this new ecumenical body, he was asking me, "What kinds of meetings and experiences can I help you with this week?" All I could say was what I had said to George. I was ready to learn as much as I could in ten days. "Are you free for dinner tonight?" he asked. "How about me inviting a few colleagues over, and we'll sit around and discuss the situation this evening?"

"Wonderful," I said. "Let me pay for dinner then!"

Gabi laughed. "We will discuss that later, but you need to know that when you are in an Arab home, it is an insult to think about such things. You will be my guest."

The "few friends" turned out to be George, Gabi's Antiochian Orthodox priest, Father Joseph, and Tarik Metri, a brilliant young theologian who was directing the World Student Christian Federation's office in Beirut and finishing his Ph.D. at American University of Beirut. We sat on Gabi's balcony and discussed politics late into the evening, something I came to learn was a favorite Arab pastime.

In many ways I took advantage of the evening, but everyone seemed more than willing to assist in the education of this "green" American in their midst. I began with the naive question, "What are the real reasons for the Lebanese civil war? It is more than just Christians versus Muslims, as our U.S. press simplistically portrays it. What are the real issues?"

I can't recall who started it, but a brief history lesson began for my benefit. Fr. Joseph began, "Lebanon was formed out of the dissolution of the Ottoman Empire, following World War I. The British and French made a secret treaty in 1916 called the Sykes-Picot Agreement, which essentially divided the Middle East between them, despite British promises of independence to the Arabs.

"This was typical of the British, and now you Americans. When the Turks were defeated in 1918, much to Syria's dismay, the French did the Maronites a tremendous favor. They created Lebanon out of the belly of Syria, and placed it under a French mandate. The flag of the new Republic of Lebanon took as its symbol the cedar tree, which reflected the Maronites' power.

"In your reading,[2] you have probably noted that the British made a similar arrangement with the Zionist movement. The Balfour Declaration [November 2, 1917] gave the Zionists their legitimacy, and despite the fact that 90 percent of the population in Palestine was Arab, the British decided to authorize a Jewish state with no mention of the same for the Arabs."

"Syria and the Muslims were furious about the French decision, although they could do nothing about it with the French occupying Lebanon and Syria itself. But the Syrians and the Muslim majority never forgot this injustice. In fact, the Sunni Muslims in Beirut and north Lebanon, the Shiite Muslim majority in the south of Lebanon, the Druze in the Chouf Mountains, and the Orthodox Christians all resented the favoritism granted the Maronites."

"Thus were the seeds of Lebanon's conflict sown. All of the five major communities listed above had their own distinct histories, geographic districts, unique cultures, religious differences, and economic infrastructures. There were always tensions between certain communities, such as the Druze and Maronites, who had actually fought each other in the 1860s." [3]

"In 1932, the French conducted a national census, with the following results: the Maronites comprised 29 percent, Melkites 6 percent, Orthodox 11 percent, Jews and Protestants 3 percent, Sunni 22 percent, Shiites 22 percent, and Druzes seven percent. Aside from the Maronites, nobody believed the census was accurate. When Lebanon became independent in 1943, the above proportions of the population were reflected in the political formula that evolved. In other words, the Maronites were represented in the Parliament at the rate of nearly one third of the seats, and be given the offices of prime minister and defense. The Sunnis and Shiites were next, and so on." [4]

I learned that after World War II the makeup of the population in Lebanon changed dramatically, as Muslim (Sunni) and Christian Palestinians poured into the country in the late 1940s. Through the succeeding years, there were numerous attempts to form political coalitions to unseat the Maronites, but nothing came of them. Alliances shifted from time to time, creating extreme tension in the late 1950s. In 1958, for example, the Eisenhower administration landed U.S. Marines in Beirut to keep the Maronite (Christian) president Chamoun in power.

Refugees from other countries and poor Shiites from the south continued to move north to Beirut, forming the "Belt of Misery," or suburban slums that literally encircled the city. Meanwhile, the oil-rich Arab countries in the Gulf decided to make Beirut their financial center. This stimulated several industries, particularly drugs and tourism. A building boom during the late 1950s through early 1970s created extreme disparities in the population. Lebanon became a complex amalgamation of haves and have-nots, also bringing people of differing religions, cultures, and histories together to live in close proximity.

The failure to develop a more balanced political and economic sharing of power created frustrations that were doomed to explode. For example, an estimated 4 percent of the population disposed of one third of the gross national product, but the poor majority disposed of only 18 percent. The Maronites dominating Mount Lebanon controlled about 38 percent of all schools, while the south, with approximately 20 percent of the population, had only about 15 percent of the schools. Economic distribution was even more unbalanced. In 1960, Beirut had a per capita income of $803, compared to only $151 in the Shiite south.[5]

I leaned back in my chair, trying to absorb this complicated and troubled history. "Being here and listening to your explanation is so different from how the press in the United States presents the conflict. We hear that it is Christians versus Muslims. Once in a while they mention that there are significant economic and political issues involved," I added.

"Yes, it is no doubt a combination of ignorance about Lebanon's history and the U.S. tendency to simplify matters, even if it compromises the truth," George replied.

I looked out at the city from Gabi's balcony and could see rockets and tracer bullets lighting up the Beirut skyline in the distance. "I thought there was a ceasefire!" I exclaimed, half in jest and half in bewilderment. Everyone laughed, although I did not catch the humor. "This goes on every night," said Gabi.

"So who is doing the shooting, and where in the city are these particular shells landing?" I asked.

"It looks like it is coming from Chiah and Ain al-Rumaneh," said Joseph. The names sounded vaguely familiar from my recent reading, but I was still at the elementary stage of not being able to separate one Arab town from another.

"Have you heard about these famous areas?" he asked. "That is where the civil war officially began."

"Oh, yes, now I place them. Tell me what really happened!"

Joseph began, and others added commentary. "The roots of the civil war go back to the political and economic contradictions of which we have been speaking. By the 1970s the tension had been building between the Phalangists (the largest Maronite militia) and their opposition, which by then included not only the Druze and several Shiite groups, but also several Christian intellectuals and the Palestinians (of whom there are many thousands of Christians).

"Once the Palestinians were driven out of Jordan in the 1970-71 uprising against King Hussein, they shifted their base of operation to Beirut. This tilted the Lebanese political equation significantly, as the Israeli-Palestinian struggle spread to Lebanon. Naturally most Arabs are sympathetic to the Palestinian cause and see it as a just and moral political struggle. In Lebanon, virtually every community, with the exception of the Phalangists, has supported the Palestinians."

"However, in the early 1970s, if not before, Israel began to support the Phalangists, and the Palestinians increased their strikes from Lebanon into northern Israel. The Israelis retaliated brutally, bombing refugee camps and attacking many small villages in southern Lebanon, causing a dislocation of the Shiite population."

"In April 1975, Phalangist militiamen attacked a busload of Palestinians in the district of Ain al-Rumaneh, a Phalangist stronghold and a suburb of Beirut. The Palestinians were from the very poor Chiah district, the next suburb to the west, made up of Shiite and Palestinian refugees. There had been several incidents of kidnappings, snipings, and murders between the two communities. The Phalangists claimed that the Palestinian bus was planning to attack a wedding at a Maronite church in Ain al-Rumaneh. Palestinians deny this and claim it was a massacre. Whoever is to blame, this was the spark that ignited this civil war," Joseph concluded.

"How did the Syrians get involved?" I asked. "I see them everywhere."

"When the conflict intensified, most Palestinian groups stayed out of it," Joseph continued. "There was essentially a coalition called the Lebanese Front, which involved three Maronite militias (the Phalangists, the National Liberal Party, and the Zghorta Liberation Army). They included the three leading Maronite families—the Gemayels, the Chamouns, and the Franjiehs, respectively. On the other hand, the other communities, such as the Druze (the Progressive Socialist Party, led by the Jumblatts), the Syrian Nationalist Party (or PPS, led by Christian Orthodox and Sunni intellectuals), the Lebanese Communists, and the Amal (Shiite, led by Imam Musa Sadr), formed the Lebanese National Movement.

"They are generally called the 'leftists' or Muslims in the West. It is not so. Several Christians are involved in key positions. They are essentially calling for a reform of the Lebanese government, true democracy, and an end to the confessional arrangement that has brought us so many divisions."

"By the spring of 1976, the National Movement was beginning to threaten the Lebanese Forces positions. The Palestinians reluctantly entered the LNM's forces and gave them superiority in the number of fighters. In April 1976, former presidents Pierre Gemayal and Camille

Chamoun, both Maronites, desperately appealed to Syria, the largest military force outside of Israel in the region. Their appeal was essentially an attempt to preserve the status quo.

"The Syrians had at least two motives in entering the war. First, they did not wish to see the popular movements such as the PLO, Amal, or PPS become too strong. It could trigger opposition to Syria's leaders (President Hafez al Assad's Baathist Party) within Syria. But also it could lead to a situation whereby Syria would never regain control of Lebanon. The Baathists wanted to eventually unite the eastern Mediterranean, including Lebanon, Palestine, and Jordan as a "Greater Syria" dominated by the Syrian Baathist Party. Several other Arab regimes, including Iraq and Jordan, opposed this scenario. So it was to these opponents that various LMN, militias turned for arms and economic support."

"The Syrians helped the Lebanese Forces destroy LMN, particularly at the Palestinian refugee camp Tel al Zataar and the mixed Palestinian-Shiite slum, Quarantina, near the port of Beirut. Both areas came under terrible shelling, and their populations were driven from their homes. In the case of Tel al Zataar, it was a Palestinian military stronghold, but there were also twenty to twenty-five thousand refugees living in the camp. The combined forces of the Syrian Army and the Phalangists shelled the camp for fifty-three consecutive days, blockading all medical and food supplies from entering.

"Eventually the camp fell, and there were actual massacres of refugees, including women and children. Some say that up to 18,000 people were killed, mainly Palestinian refugees and fighters. The survivors fled into the camps of Sabra, Shatila, and Bourg al Borajneh. The churches worked with several humanitarian agencies to resettle these poor people. Tel Al Zataar and most of Quarantina were burned and razed to the ground.[6] You can go and see the ruins for yourself."

"Let me take you there tomorrow," said George Bebawi. "It is a terrible but important site to see. Then I will take you to visit some of the refugees who survived and were resettled by the churches not far from where we are sitting."

"I'd like to do that," I responded.

"You need to be careful of the Syrian and Phalangist patrols," cautioned Gabi. "If they catch you and think you are a Western journalist, you will have serious problems."

"Don't worry, I know how to do it," George replied.

We agreed that after the last MECC session on the following day, George and I would hire a taxi and visit the site of what once was Tel al Zataar. I thanked Gabi and his friends for a wonderful evening of fellowship and education.

"Why don't you walk Don back to his hotel?" Gabi asked.

"No, I know the way," I insisted, "and it's only three blocks." I was determined not to put people out any more than I already had. They finally agreed. I said good-bye and headed down one short street, turned right and walked a block, passing the Near East School of Theology on my left. Just as I reached the final block of my journey, I saw two cars screech to a halt in front of a building with a strange flag hanging from its balcony. Suddenly automatic weapons unloaded several rounds of fire into the building. Several hand grenades were lobbed into the offices and a huge fire started.

I ducked into a doorway, scared to death. Then I realized that the doorway did no good because I was facing the gunmen at a distance of less than one hundred feet. I got down on my knees and slowly worked my way up the street, keeping an eye on the gunmen in case they noticed me. Within a minute the car sped off down the street I had just walked, the tires burning rubber. As I was squatting in the doorway, I prayed fervently to God to protect me in this crazy situation. I had never been in combat prior to this and did not welcome the opportunity. It was a frightening situation and completely out of my control. All I could do was surrender myself to God's protection.

I used a momentary lull to run halfway down the block. I was nearly at the Mayflower Hotel when I heard men running out of the office that had been attacked. I could see four gunmen running down the street in the direction of the car. They stayed close to the buildings in case the car returned and they needed to take cover. Then two men headed down the street toward where I was hiding. *Great,* I thought. *What if they think I am with their assailants?* I squatted down in a doorway and made myself as inconspicuous as possible.

Fortunately, they ran right by me, heading up the street. I waited to see if others would follow, but the street was clear. Slowly and cautiously, I slunk from building to building, then dashed at top speed into the hotel. By the time I collapsed on the couch, I was sweating like crazy, a real bundle of nerves.

"What happened?" asked the clerk at the desk. I described what I had just experienced, and he shook his head.

I asked what office it was that they had attacked.

"That's the PPS, and no doubt the Phalangists were involved in the incident, but you never know. I think you should be careful when you are out after dark from now on."

I agreed. I stopped to pray again, thanking God for watching over me.

4

Caught in the Cross Fire!

I saw all the oppressions that are practiced under the sun. Look,
the tears of the oppressed—with no one to comfort them!
Ecclesiastes 4:1

I ran into the Beau Rivage Hotel lobby in West Beirut, ready to apologize to our Palestinian guide because our group was at least twenty minutes late. It was a hot day that Friday, on June 4, 1982. Assam had instructed me to arrive promptly at 2:45 p.m., because we had a 3:00 p.m. appointment with Mahmoud Labadi, PLO spokesman and chief aide to PLO chairman Yasir Arafat. His office was a ten-minute drive from our hotel. Traffic delayed us for at least thirty minutes as we drove from the Maronite seminary and Kasleek University in Jounieh. The checkpoints were particularly long that morning, and I noted that the last Phalangist soldiers near the Green Line were delaying people with detailed searches.

It was like traveling between two planets. The Maronite Christians and Palestinians were light-years apart in terms of history, culture, and politics. In fact, as far as the Palestinians were concerned, we were betraying them by visiting the "heart of the enemy." The Phalangists had slaughtered Palestinians (with Syrian assistance) at Tel al-Zataar, and they continued to be bitter enemies. For the Maronites, the PLO was the epitome of evil. The Maronites blamed them for all of Lebanon's troubles.

That morning I had unfortunately allowed myself to get into an argument with one of the seminary faculty. The priest was claiming that the Maronites were not Arabs, but Phoenicians, a separate and superior race. "The Palestinians have brought all of these troubles to Lebanon. We want them out. Let them go and settle with their brothers in any of twenty-one other Arab countries. Lebanon is for the Lebanese," he claimed.

I tried unsuccessfully to argue the case that Lebanon's problems dated back long before the Palestinians arrived. The Maronites and Druze fought each other in the 1860s. Lebanon's real problems lie in the 1943 Confessional Agreement, which has dealt the poor majority out of the power structure. But my arguments were poorly framed and touched raw nerves in my host. Had I chosen to be more discreet, I would have avoided the topic. At least I stopped myself when tempted to tell him that we needed to leave early to visit the PLO!

We arrived at the Beau Rivage at 3:10 p.m., and I ran into the lobby hoping to see Assam in his familiar position before the television set. At the very moment I set foot in the lobby, an enormous explosion rattled the windows and shook the foundation of the hotel. A series of explosions followed, then the unmistakable roar of a jet airplane sweeping in from the coast. I knew immediately that this was a major bombing raid, and we were near the target.

I ran outside to send our delegation to the bomb shelter in the basement. They were already running full speed toward the elevators. I turned to the hotel concierge, a Lebanese Druze, and asked what was happening: "Get your group into the basement immediately," he replied with a worried look. "This one is very close to us."

Once in the basement I relaxed for a moment, thinking we were safe from flying glass and debris in case the Israelis hit our hotel. Another series of explosions shook the walls and the foundation rumbled as if there were an earthquake. "The Israelis are hitting Fakhani and the Citi Sportive [stadium]" somebody said. *Oh, no,* I thought. *That's where we're supposed to be. I hope Assam and our friends are safe.* I said a prayer for them, then began to pray for our safety.

My friend Dan O'Neill, who founded Mercy Corps in 1978 with his father-in-law, Pat Boone, yelled, "Hey, Don! Come over here and have a look. You can see the F-16s coming in for the kill."

I stepped outside, looked up, and saw three to five jets moving at a phenomenal speed, flying at a very high altitude (fifteen thousand to twenty thousand feet).

Dan said, "They have the latest electronic devices and can program their computers to do pinpoint bombing from twenty thousand feet. The Palestinians' antiaircraft weapons are ancient and can't touch them."

Then I realized, *These guys are using our tax dollars. All of these jets and the bombs are gifts from U.S. taxpayers. Wouldn't it be ironic if one of them hit us?* I didn't like that thought, so my mind moved along. How many innocent Lebanese and Palestinian civilians would die that day, with U.S. bombs causing the carnage? I wondered. Another bombing raid shook our building. This round lasted several minutes.

The more I thought about the situation the more fearful I became. I rarely experience fear, but this was getting too close. My mind was stuck on the idea, *What if one of these U.S.-made bombs goes astray and hits us? I don't want to die yet. I have too much to live for.* I thought of my wife and family back home, and said a fervent prayer, "Oh, God, please make this stop. This is getting out of hand. Protect all of your people and help us escape safely from this rain of death."

It didn't stop. In fact, the bombing seemed to become more intense. For fifteen minutes there was no letup. By this time a large group was sitting on the basement floor in silence, listening to the building rattle from the thunderous attacks. I looked around and noted that, in addition to our eight Americans, there were several European journalists, the hotel staff, and around twenty Palestinian mothers and children who had been attending a meeting at the hotel.

My eye rested on a beautiful young Palestinian mother directly across the hall from me. She was caressing her little girl in her lap, trying to bring comfort during this hellish experience. I wondered how many times they had been through this awful exercise. Perhaps she was a widow, as were the others, and had lost her husband in the civil war. I continued to study her. She was no more than twenty-five years old, perhaps less. But she was completely composed and at peace. I couldn't believe the serenity that radiated from her face.

Then a sense of shame struck me. *Here I am, a Christian clergyman, and my fears are getting the best of me. This is ridiculous. So what if I should die? If I really trusted in the Lord, I would have nothing to fear. I need to get my mind off myself and my fears. I am just like the disciples who were caught in the storm on the Sea of Galilee while Jesus slept* (Luke 8:22-25). I tried to refocus my prayer on God and sought to listen to what the Holy Spirit was saying to me.

At that point I remembered a prayer device that enabled me to focus on God and open myself to God's presence. The vehicle that assisted me was the ancient Middle Eastern Christian practice of praying the Jesus Prayer and synchronizing my breathing, thought, and spirit on the phrase, "Lord Jesus, Son of God, have mercy on me, a sinner."

I breathed slowly, meditating each time on my source of peace: "Lord Jesus, Son of God. . . ." Jesus Christ, the resurrected Lord, knew pain in his crucifixion, and has defeated death and the power of evil forces, even U.S. bombs being dropped by Israeli jets. Then I exhaled, sending fear and evil out of my body, lungs, and mind. "Have mercy on me, a sinner. I am helpless and hopeless without the intervention of grace and resurrection hope in my life. I will let go of all fear and replace its power with the power of God in Jesus Christ."

Suddenly the fear left and a renewed sense of peace and faith came over me. I stayed with the prayer for twenty minutes or more. I opened my eyes and realized that the bombing continued, but with less intensity. Then the raid stopped. Someone in our group said, "Let's go up to the top floor and see if we can get a view of the damage." Five of us ran up to the tenth floor while the others chose to remain in the shelter in case the Israelis returned.

We went out on the balcony and looked through a pair of binoculars at the damage. There were fires everywhere and total chaos at the Citi Sportive. We were told that several thousand Palestinian and Lebanese Shiite refugees lived in the stadium, and several militias used it as a training base and munitions dump. The Israelis knew that and had hit the munitions dump. We could see several fires burning out of control. Firefighters at one end of the stadium were making little progress. We saw ambulances arriving and Red Crescent workers carrying people on stretchers.

"Look, here they come again," one of my colleagues said. He grabbed the binoculars and looked toward the Mediterranean and within a few seconds we could hear the roar of F-16s. The bombs began to hit the stadium. It appeared to be planned in this manner, the second airstrike designed to inflict the maximum number of civilian casualties.

"How demonic," I said. "This is one of the cruelest aspects of this tragic war that I have seen."

We heard later that two journalists and several rescue workers had been killed and many more injured. This all took place on Friday afternoon, June 4, 1982. By the time the second raid had ended, it was well past sundown and the Jewish Sabbath had begun.

That evening the Palestinian Red Crescent Society (the Palestinian branch of the Arab version of the Red Cross), had scheduled a dinner for our group with Dr. Fathi Arafat (Yasir Arafat's brother and Director of the Red Crescent) and his staff. Trying to be sensitive to their grief and the difficult day they must have had in the emergency rooms, I called their information officer, a wonderful woman named Hedla Ayoubi. "No, no! You must come," Hedla said. We discussed the attack and whether this constituted an act of war.

We were then told that Israel was claiming that the PLO had attempted to assassinate one of Israel's diplomats in London the previous day (June 3, 1982). Meanwhile, Scotland Yard had captured the assassin and stated he was from the anti-PLO faction Abu-Nidal. The London PLO official was second on the list of potential victims, right after the Israeli. It appeared that Begin and Sharon were about to use the London incident, which did not involve the PLO, to justify the attack. This incident would create the justification needed for Israel to launch the war against the Palestinians they had been looking for. Thousands of innocent people were going to die, just as the two hundred had died that afternoon.

I learned upon return to the United States that one important aspect of the Israeli attack of June 4 was never discussed. Israel had used U.S. weapons, particularly the most sophisticated aircraft in existence, to mount an offensive against another nation. This action by the Israeli air force constituted irrefutable grounds for the U.S. to cancel all military assistance to Israel. If we had had the financial backing, we could have taken legal action, because a foreign nation had threatened our lives with weapons conceivably purchased with our tax dollars. The basis of the law rested in legislation passed by the United States Congress in 1976 (the Congressional Export Control Act) which made it illegal for a country receiving U.S. military aid to use U.S. weapons in anything but a defensive capacity.

One month after the action I visited Washington, D.C., and met with Elliot Abrams, then with the State Department Middle East Affairs Division. I raised the issue, including personal reports and media footage available from the major U.S. and European networks that gave clear evidence of the destruction and death that rained down from the F-15s and F-16s that day. Abrams categorically rejected any connection between U.S. law and Israel's action and stated he was not interested. Abrams was later convicted of illegal action in the Irangate-Contra arms scandal, but pardoned in the last days of the Bush administration.

On Saturday, June 5, 1982, we went directly to the two Palestinian Red Crescent hospitals in the Sabra and Shatila refugee camps. I'll never forget the face of an elderly man, who stood with several children. He said to us, "Are you Americans?" How could he tell? I wondered.

"Yes, we are," somebody answered.

"I have a message for your president, Mr. Ronald Reagan. Tell him thank you for his gift to the Palestinians: bombs and planes that kill and maim our women and children. Tell him that one of his bombs killed my wife and left my child badly wounded. Why does your government give bombs to Begin, a known murderer and terrorist? Doesn't your government know any better?"

What could I say but, "I am sorry, we are opposed to what our government is doing."

We entered the hospital and visited many victims of the previous day's bombing. The nurses took us to a tiny baby they estimated to be about two months old. Her parents could not be located. The nurse showed us the tiny cast on her broken arm. Then the blanket was pulled back. A portion of the child's buttocks had been blown off in the bombing.

Our next stop was Akka Hospital, the primary medical center for more than one hundred thousand refugees in the three camps. Another bombing raid started just as we pulled into the driveway. Medics rushed us into the hospital basement, which served as the bomb shelter. There we stood with the intensive care patients and others who needed close medical attention. We remained there for over three hours.

Within an hour of our arrival, ambulances began to arrive with the wounded passengers of a United Nations school bus for girls which was attacked on the coastal road. At 11:50 a.m. the bus received a direct hit from Israeli aircraft as it traveled on the road to Sidon. Nineteen girls were killed immediately; the remaining sixteen arrived at the emergency entrance just opposite us.

The first ambulance screeched to a halt and paramedics ran from the ambulance with three stretchers, each carrying a badly mangled girl. They were charred and bloodied. A lump filled my throat and tears filled my eyes. I had never seen human beings this badly torn. I glanced around and saw that two of our group had dropped their heads into their hands and were crying. Two of the physicians with us rushed in to offer assistance.

Another ambulance arrived immediately, and five other stretchers were carried in. The first girl appeared to be badly wounded and missing an arm. A second girl lay limp, with the dusty look of death on her unconscious face. A third was definitely dead, her eyes staring toward the ceiling. Then body bags were carried in from successive cars—nineteen dead teenage girls.

By this time several family members had arrived and were informed of their daughters' condition. One of the girls in the body bags was sixteen-year-old Saidi Sayed. As long as I live I will be haunted by the piercing screams and laments of her eldest sister and mother when they were told of Saidi's death. The elder sister, a beautiful young woman of nineteen or twenty, screamed at the heavens and tried to break through the medics who prevented her from running in to see her sister's body. The more they restrained her the more intensely she struggled. They were firm but gentle with her and held their ground. Then they ushered her to her mother and other family members who sat directly across from us. They hugged the sister, and all cried and rocked in a rhythmic comforting motion.

Then the grief hit her mother. She jumped in the air and wailed in Arabic (a Palestinian friend translated for me), "Saidi, my baby Saidi. Saidi, my baby is gone. Why, O Allah, why is this our fate?" Her hands repeated a clapping movement above her head as she wailed each piercing lament and ululated. Then the elder sister ran to the stairs and tried one more time to break into the room with the nineteen body bags. Again she was restrained. She collapsed with exhaustion on the floor.

Everyone in our group was crying by this time. A clergyman from Seattle was sobbing bitterly. A college professor became sick to his stomach and had to leave. I thought of Jesus' crucifixion and how God descended to the depths of human experience on our behalf. This was a crucifixion experience if I ever witnessed one. Did God hear the cries of these people? I felt anger, grief, and guilt at once.

I reflected on the passage in Matthew 27:46, "And about three o'clock Jesus cried with a loud voice: 'Eli, Eli, lama sabachthani?' that is, 'My God, my God, why have you forsaken me?' " Does God know the grief of these Palestinian people in their suffering? Does it matter whether they are Christians or Muslims? What do Christians have to offer in these situations?

Every one of the deaths that morning was of an innocent young girl. They had their best years ahead. Their bus was clearly marked with enormous letters on the top and sides of the vehicle. It was a senseless exercise in carnage—and for what purpose?

After I reached the United States, a week later, I began to read a small volume by the Catholic mystic Thomas Merton. I was searching for some word from the Lord to help me work through my grief and anger. I felt that no one understood what I had experienced, and it was too difficult for me to reconstruct it. I tried to express my feelings, and people seemed to be either overwhelmed or not very interested. I was filled with anger and wished I could be back with the suffering people. But what good would that do?

In *The New Man*, Merton wrote,

> Hope then is a gift. Like life, it is a gift from God, total, unexpected, incomprehensible, undeserved. It springs out of nothingness, completely free. But to meet it, we have to descend into nothingness. And there we meet hope most perfectly, when we are stripped of our own confidence, our own strength, when we almost no longer exist. "A hope that is seen," says St. Paul, "is no hope." The Christian hope that is "not seen" is the agony of Christ.[1]

Jesus Christ, the Palestinian Jew, calls us into his agony. I am reminded of the "kenosis" (emptying) passage of Phil. 2, which describes our calling in terms of the Incarnation. We his disciples must be completely vulnerable and open to experience the pain of life. The church of Christ is challenged by his life, crucifixion, and resurrection to travel a road of compassionate justice with Palestinian Arab and Jew alike. Is it not to these very situations of nothingness and tragedy that God brings good news? But where are the suffering servants of the gospel today?

5

Where There Is No Vision

Where there is no vision, the people perish. (KJV)
Where there is no prophecy, the people cast off restraint. (NRSV)
Proverbs 29:18

In November 1985, Ray Bakke (then serving as director of the Program for Large Cities for the Lausanne Committee for World Evangelization) and I took a three-week listening tour in the Middle East. Thanks to a small grant from the Mustard Seed Foundation we were able to visit Cyprus and six Middle Eastern countries.

Our purpose was threefold: 1. to discuss with leading religious and political analysts the most urgent problems they faced; 2. to listen to church leaders describe the current state of Christianity in the Middle East; and 3. to discover how Western Christians could more sensitive to the needs of Middle Eastern Christians.

At our first stop in Cyprus, we learned that there were more than thirty separate Western evangelical parachurch agencies operating on the island. Many had fled from Beirut when the Lebanese situation became too dangerous. The most unfortunate aspect of this development was that these evangelical groups had minimal contact with the ancient churches. With two or three exceptions, they generally avoided the indigenous Christian leaders, unless they were having problems with local authorities. Our discussions with Middle East church leaders revealed considerable resentment toward the evangelicals but a keen desire to seek reconciliation. Most evangelicals desired healing in the relationships as well.

We flew from Cyprus to Damascus where an Arab evangelical (in the Middle East, the term *evangelical* denotes a protestant denomination—Presbyterian, Lutheran, Anglican, etc.) pastor drove us to an impressive mountain top vista overlooking this massive city.[1] Damascus is an incredible mixture of ancient and modern culture, architecture, and history. It is the oldest continuously occupied city in the world (Jericho is the oldest city). Only 9 percent of Syrians are Christian, but two ancient churches—the Antiochian Orthodox and the Syrian Orthodox—make their headquarters in Damascus. Damascus is also of historic importance because it was a spiritual center of the early church and later became the capital city for the Caliphate of the Ummayad (Islamic) Empire, beginning in the twelfth century C.E.

The pastor described the extensive campus ministry that he and others are conducting at the University of Damascus, one of the largest universities in the world with more than one hundred thousand students. Quietly, without fanfare, numerous Bible study and prayer groups operate on campus. He works with these groups, but there are few trained leaders and minimal resources to work with. Ray and I concluded that this dear brother should receive in Arabic the outstanding books and Bible studies so readily available to us in English. We thought perhaps some of our friends in campus ministry could become partners with this colleague.

The next morning we spent time in prayer and reflection at the church of Ananias, the early church leader who ministered to apostle Paul immediately after his conversion.

> Now there was a disciple in Damascus named Ananias. The Lord said to him in a vision, "Ananias." He answered, "Here I am, Lord." The Lord said to him, "Get up and go to the street called Straight, and at the house of Judas look for a man of Tarsus named Saul. At this moment he is praying, and he has seen in a vision a man named Ananias come in and lay his hands on him so that he might regain his sight." (Acts 9:10-12)

As we sat in the church, which tradition claims is on the very site where Paul stayed for three days during his loss of sight, I wondered whether such visions can happen again. Can Arabs and Jews, or Western evangelical, Eastern Orthodox, or Catholic Christians overcome their hostilities, historic differences, and the contemporary wall of separation? The Holy Spirit is already at work in this regard, and this may be the decade to listen to the new possibilities the Spirit is opening for us.

We left the church and walked down The Street Called Straight, now a modern version of what Paul visited. We then had an hour with the Antiochian Orthodox patriarch Ignatius IV at his headquarters. Our con-

versation was frank and inspiring. We heard his dream of expanding biblical studies and improving teaching methods for his seminarians, so future priests will be inspired Bible teachers. We raised the possibility that
some large U.S. churches and evangelical agencies which specialize in
adult bible study could be approached to share their expertise. The patriarch beamed with delight and said, "Why not? I welcome the idea."

Then the patriarch leaned forward to say in complete candor, "I am
deeply troubled about the loss of Christians in every Middle Eastern country. Our analysis shows shocking figures. There are several communities
where Christians once were the majority; today virtually none remain. It
is the most urgent situation facing Christians in this region. The 'emptying of Christians' and their emigration to the West is something with
which we need help. It almost feels as if this 'emptying' of Christians from
the Middle East is someone's strategy."

These words were both shocking and challenging. This theme would
become a dominant issue everywhere we traveled.

That afternoon we were asked to be the guests of the U.S. Embassy for
a luncheon reception for the new ambassador. Among the many interesting people in attendance was the Syrian Orthodox patriarch Zakka, the
counterpart to patriarch Ignatius IV.

The Syrian Church is much smaller than the Antiochian Orthodox
Church. As one of the Oriental Orthodox family, the church was founded
by Peter at the city of Antioch. The church still uses the Syriac language.
Patriarch Zakka told us that there are now more communicant members
of his church living in Europe, Australia, and North America than in the
Middle East.

Two days later, Ray and I were meeting with a Jordanian official in the
beautiful city of Amman, discussing Jerusalem. During our meeting the
official's secretary delivered the morning mail to his desk. He receives the
Jerusalem Post on the day of publication (by special arrangement it is sent
over the Allenby Bridge). On the cover was a picture and lead story about
the International Christian Embassy-Jerusalem, a Christian fundamentalist organization which supports Israel uncritically.

"Look at this photograph," said the official. "What do you think this
means to us here, Christians and Muslims alike, who see Western Christian groups claim that Jerusalem and the West Bank belong to Israel because God gave it to them?"

Ray and I said we were both evangelicals and that in circles with
which we were familiar in the United States, most Christians would not
agree with the Christian Embassy's position on Israel and Jerusalem.

He perked up immediately. "The king needs to hear this from you because it would be a great source of encouragement. Would you have time
to meet him if I could arrange it?"

"Of course," we replied, with considerable enthusiasm. We returned
to our hotel, quickly took showers, shined our shoes, and did our best to

look acceptable for a visit to the Royal Palace. The call came in an hour, and a car was sent for us. We strolled into the picturesque Royal Palace, situated on one of the seven hills that constitute Amman. As we were waiting for the appointment, the Minister of the Palace (King Hussein's chief aide), Adnan Abu-Odeh, came in to greet us. Abu-Odeh, like approximately 60 percent of the Jordanians, is a Palestinian. Born in Nablus, he came to Jordan as a refugee in 1948. He was dressed immaculately; I felt some discomfort wearing my slightly stained sportcoat and slacks.

"Do you gentlemen know about a Palestinian priest from the Galilee named Father Chacour?" he asked. "He wrote an excellent book called *Blood Brothers* that moved me very much. I recently purchased three thousand copies and we are in the process of sending one to every political and religious leader in the Middle East."

"Of course, we know him. He is a very dear friend, and we will be staying with him in five days," we replied.

"Do give him my warmest personal greetings and tell him what we are doing with his book," the minister said.

Then it was time to see His Majesty, King Hussein. We walked down a paneled hallway lined with paintings of various scenes in Jordan. The kingdom of Jordan was created as part of the settlement after World War I and the breakup of the Ottoman Empire. Situated on the east bank of the Jordan River, the country was originally called Transjordan. Contrary to some of the mythology created by early Zionists, it was never intended to be a Palestinian state. Jordan's first ruler was King Abdullah, a Hashemite Muslim prince and descendant of Mohammed. The Hashemites are the branch of Mohammed's descendants who lost the political battle to the House of Saud in the Arabian Peninsula. Jordan annexed the West Bank and East Jerusalem in 1948 after Israel was created, and it ruled these Palestinian areas until Israel defeated Jordan in 1967.

King Hussein is a diminutive man, no more than five feet, five inches in height. He came to power as a youth of fourteen when his grandfather, King Abdullah, was assassinated in Jerusalem before Hussein's eyes by disgruntled Palestinians who thought that he had betrayed them. Palestinians have had a rocky relationship with King Hussein, particularly in the early 1970s when, as some analysts claim, certain organizations within the PLO violated their agreements and attempted to overthrow the king. The Jordanian Army dealt with them ruthlessly, killing fifteen to eighteen thousand and expelling most of the leaders to Lebanon. By the late 1980s, relationships had improved but tensions remain to this day.

The king greeted us with a warm handshake and smile. His Cambridge University training gave him a gentle British accent. He was dressed immaculately in a business suit, looking much older than I anticipated, showing the strain of being the longest-ruling Arab politician. He has survived several assassination attempts, coups, war, and the continuous threat of invasion from Israel.

He asked who we were and the purpose of our visit. We referred to the meeting we had in the morning with his official in charge of Palestinian affairs.

"Yes," he noted, "I have been informed about your meeting, and I am very interested in what you have to say. These fundamentalist Christians are gaining considerable attention in Jerusalem, and the Israelis broadcast these images throughout the area. Our people see them in the press or on Israeli television and hear their opinions. It is very disturbing. We do not have any problems between our Christian and Muslim communities in Jordan, but we are concerned that these Christian fundamentalists could stir up unnecessary tensions, even here in Jordan."

We presented our analysis of the International Christian Embassy-Jerusalem and noted that they are a very small organization representing a tiny constituency when compared to the church. Technically, the ICEJ works outside of the local Middle East churches, functioning as a parachurch agency. Many parachurch groups are cooperating with and supporting the local congregations, but the ICEJ presents itself as an alternative to the local Christian churches. Such a situation allows the government of Israel to use them, providing their events with the highest ranking political leadership as speakers, considerable media attention, and possibly financial assistance.

Ray reported testifying before the U.S. House of Representatives' Foreign Affairs Committee in 1984, opposing the Israeli lobby's effort to move the U.S. Embassy from Tel Aviv to Jerusalem. Ray's testimony followed that of Jerry Falwell and the Christian Embassy, both brought to the committee by America Israel Political Affairs Committee (AIPAC), the leading Israeli lobby organization. Falwell claimed in his statement that over 50 million American evangelicals supported his position, which was that Jerusalem and the West Bank belonged exclusively to Israel and the Jewish people.

We heard later that Ray Bakke's testimony, along with significant efforts by all mainline Protestant, Roman Catholic, and Orthodox churches, helped turn the tide concerning this proposed legislation. Had the Israeli lobby and its Christian Zionist colleagues pushed the legislation through Congress, it would have sent a hostile message to the Arab world. Additionally, it would have been a slap in the face to Arab Christians and Muslims alike, who view Jerusalem as a Holy City to all three faiths.

Hussein was interested in our analysis and pleased to know that Western evangelical Christians were a more diverse community than he had understood. Then he added, "But I am very concerned about the Arab churches in Jordan. We need your help in working with the Arab churches in the Middle East. Many Christians are emigrating to the West, and this concerns me deeply. It is my conviction that Christians are the glue that helps hold our societies together. If they all leave and the churches are emptied, I fear for the future in this part of the world."

We were deeply moved by Hussein's remarks. We felt his sincerity and noted the sense of urgency that underscored his message. He offered to do whatever he could to help us with the mission of building understanding between Eastern and Western Christians, especially among the evangelicals. We then discussed the possibility of holding an international conference in Amman to allow Western Christians to experience and meet the people, the culture, and the neighboring faiths (such as Islam) of the Eastern Christians, and to begin to understand this unique part of the world. The king offered to host the event if it became a reality.

That evening we were asked to do a taped interview with Jordan Television, one of the most professional media operations in the Arab world. Ray and I were given thirty minutes to tell our perspectives on the Israeli-Palestinian situation and why we believed that North American Christians could and would play a decisive role in turning U.S. foreign policy toward a more honest and realistic assessment of the Arab world.

The next morning we crossed the Allenby Bridge and caught a taxi to Jerusalem. No sooner had we arrived than we were urged to drop our luggage and catch a cab to the Mount of Olives. The Christian Embassy was beginning its Feast of Tabernacles march through parts of Jerusalem. We greeted an Australian friend of Ray's whom we met by coincidence in the hotel lobby and headed for the Mt. of Olives.

The Feast of Tabernacles procession was an unusual event not adequately described in mere words. There were several thousand participants dressed in white with colorful banners. More than twenty-five countries were represented, with the largest delegations from the United States, South Africa, Holland, and the Scandinavian countries. There were only a handful of black and Oriental participants and no Arabs.

As the parade moved down the Mount of Olives, people danced and sang Christian songs for Israel. The songs praised "the God of Zion," "Jerusalem for the returned Jews," but did not mention the Christian church, let alone Jesus Christ. We felt out of place and were troubled by this Western "import" into Arab East Jerusalem, which was offensive to Arab Christians and Muslims alike. We concluded that the event was a negative witness to the gospel of Jesus Christ.

We returned to the hotel and had coffee with Rev. John McKnight, an Anglican pastor from Melbourne, Australia. John had come on a pastoral mission, sent by his congregation to assist a member in serious political trouble. We found a private corner in the coffee shop, and he began to tell an incredible story.

McKnight ran a Christian coffeehouse as a form of outreach to the unchurched. In the spring of 1986, a young Israeli Jew began attending the coffeehouse sessions and eventually came to Sunday worship services. Within a few weeks he requested private meetings with McKnight. He was searching for a spiritual center and was troubled about the implications of converting to Christianity. A brilliant young man, he was well versed in theology and the Hebrew scriptures, having been raised in an Orthodox Jewish home in Morocco and later in Israel.

During June 1986, McKnight began a sermon series and study on "Following Jesus in Conflict Situations." Through preaching, Bible study, and contemporary resources, he challenged the church to integrate their Christian values with the pressing social and political problems of the day. The church studied apartheid in South Africa, racism in Australia, nuclear disarmament, and peacemaking. Within a few weeks, by then in mid-June, the Israeli came to the pastor and stated that, after a deep struggle, he was led to convert to Christianity.

In a private conversation with McKnight, the new convert revealed that he was Mordechai Vanunu, formerly an employee in Israel's secret nuclear plant at Dimona in the Negev Desert. While working there, he had become increasingly troubled about the nuclear arsenal Israel was secretly developing, much in cooperation with South Africa. Mordechai began to discreetly photograph the entire facility. He told McKnight that he had more than sixty photographs, none of which had ever been shown to anyone. What should he do?

Mordechai had been moved by the example of Jesus Christ and contemporary models of Christian faithfulness in questions related to justice. This was precisely the connection he needed in his soul to accept Christ as Savior. In early August he was baptized and made a public confession of faith. God was working on Mordechai's conscience concerning the Israeli nuclear arsenal and the revealing photographs in his possession. Shortly after his profession of faith, he told McKnight and a support group at the church that he could not sit idly by while Israel was accelerating its nuclear program. As an act of Christian conscience and in the interest of world peace, it was time to reveal these secrets to the world. He fully realized that this revelation could become a matter of life and death for him.

In early September, Vanunu released his story to the *London Sunday Times*.[2] They flew him to London, where he was cross-examined by British experts. They were satisfied he was telling the truth. McKnight stayed in daily communication with Mordechai from the moment he left Australia, to give him encouragement and to be certain about his safety.

On Sunday, October 5, 1986, the *Times* issued a blockbuster story based on Vanunu's photographs, analysis, and drawings of the Dimona facility. The story created an international outcry about Israel's secret nuclear production, which was off limits to U.S. inspection and to the International Atomic Energy Commission.

Suddenly Mordechai Vanunu was missing. McKnight lost contact with him on September 30, at the Mountbatten Hotel in central London where the *Times* was hosting him. It was later learned that the Israeli Mossad (secret service) had lured him to a ship through a liason with an undercover female spy and took him to Israel. When we met John McKnight, none of this information was known. He was only aware that Vanunu had disappeared.

McKnight was holding daily press conferences in various Jerusalem hotels to keep the issue alive. By then it was October 26, and still there was no word about Vanunu. Some feared that Israeli agents had killed him. The official position of Israeli prime minister Shamir was to claim the government had no information. Some press reports referred to his last being seen with a young woman who talked about a yacht in the Mediterranean. Vanunu was single and may have had a weakness during this stressful time that allowed him to be set up for a romantic relationship, a situation Israeli intelligence apparently exploited.[3]

The Israeli government issued an official statement forbidding the press from writing anything about Vanunu in the Hebrew press. Allegedly for the sake of military security, a strict censorship order was given. I recall attending a press conference at Jerusalem's American Colony Hotel and overhearing Israeli journalists complaining vehemently about this order, a matter they took very seriously.

Quickly the Hebrew press discovered a loophole. If stories appeared in the foreign press, they could be reprinted in the Israeli papers. McKnight held another press conference at the American Colony to a standing room only crowd of international reporters. He emphasized that he was on a pastoral mission to ensure the well-being of his parishioner and friend and demanded that the Israeli government reveal Mordechai's whereabouts and his condition. Accounts were picked up around the world and reprinted in the Israeli papers. This process continued for several days until the prime minister was forced to reveal that Israeli agents had indeed kidnapped Vanunu and that he was being held in solitary confinement.

McKnight's pastoral perseverance and the excellent work of the Israeli press corps had forced the hand of the government. While Vanunu was not freed, Israel was accountable to the public concerning the health and security of its prisoner. Following a long and complicated trial, Vanunu was convicted of the highest form of treason and sentenced to life imprisonment. However, Mordechai Vanunu was a pioneer and a prophet, for he raised the issue of Israel's dangerous nuclear arsenal at a time when no one discussed it and few knew about it.

He remains in solitary confinement to this day, abandoned by all except a lawyer and one brother who can visit him once a month. He depends on his Christian faith as the source of hope and inspiration in his complete solitude. To my knowledge Vanunu has received little support from the peace movement (Israeli or international) and even less from Christians.

We took an evening flight to Cairo and viewed the vast expanse of the Sinai desert below us. The next morning our Coptic Evangelical and Coptic Orthodox hosts took us to the Zebalin, the "garbage people." We drove down a long, bumpy road that led into miles of garbage, where thousands of people live on top of the smoldering refuse. They are the poorest of Cairo's poor, and approximately 90 percent are Christians.

In Egypt, where a million souls are added to the population every seven to eight months, and where 60 percent are below the age of fifteen, the cycle of population explosion and grinding poverty is devastating. Many of the rural poor have fled to Cairo, a city that urbanologists say might manage a population of 5 million. Today its population is over 15 million and rising at such an alarming rate that experts anticipate 19 million souls in Cairo by the year 2000.

The church is present with the Zebalin in deeply meaningful ways. We visited two clinics where they teach basic health care and birth control, and share the gospel through teaching reading and writing skills in addition to the love they give. Trained Christian social workers go into the tiny homes in the midst of the garbage. The flies, dust, and stench are more than the average Westerner can manage. After an hour in one of the garbage cities, I felt as if every pore was clogged with germs and disease.

Yet these are the people of God, and Christ is shared in direct ministry to human needs. I could do nothing but marvel at what the committed teams of workers were doing day after day. The ministries are wholistic and well integrated, while stressing relief and development, caring for family structures, health, literacy, hygiene, as well as worship and Bible study. Surely this is a fulfillment of Jesus' call to bring good news to the poor.

On the following day we were privileged to have ninety minutes with Pope Shenouda of the Coptic Orthodox Church. He is the spiritual leader of approximately seven million Coptic Orthodox Christians in Egypt and an additional million in diaspora. Pope Shenouda is considered the 118th successor to St. Mark, who brought the Christian faith to Egypt after Pentecost.

I first met the pope in 1979, when he toured the United States and spent significant time in major cities where Copts live. He is an energetic and jovial person with a wealth of spiritual experience. He spent twelve years as a hermit, living a life of asceticism and silence in the Western Desert. This tradition goes back to St. Antony and others, who in the third century C.E. began the tradition of monasticism. The Copts took this tradition to Europe, and their models served as the basis for Roman Catholic and many Eastern Orthodox monastic orders.

The pope was in a wonderful mood, and although we were scheduled to have just twenty minutes with him, the meeting continued for ninety minutes. One of his chief bishops might well have been upset over the length of our session but was most gracious in waiting. The pope began with several religious and political jokes. When we mentioned our concern about the Palestinians, he remarked that he was a close personal friend of PLO chairman Yasir Arafat, and that they had been classmates at Cairo University.

When we shifted the discussion to recent developments in the Coptic

Church, he became even more energized. He described a church that has undergone continuous renewal during the past three decades. Monasticism, nearly dead in the early 1950s, is now flourishing to the extent that the Copts have added new structures to many of the desert monasteries in order to house new monks. The monks are primarily professional people, businessmen, doctors, professors, journalists, former government employees. They have grown tired of the pace of city life and are seeking spiritual wholeness. The rigorous but peaceful life of prayer is bringing renewal to the church. Most of the Coptic Orthodox leaders come from the monasteries.

In addition, as Copts emigrate in large numbers due to the economic crisis and relatively high rate of education, they are taking their faith with them. There are now major Coptic communities on every continent. The Coptic church is exploding throughout Africa, where the Egyptian leaders can travel quickly and easily. Bible study and youth ministry are on the rise. Many churches report midweek lay academies that are training from 750- to 1000 people for ministry and Bible study each week.

But the situation is far from peaceful. The rise of militant Islamic fundamentalism keeps the churches in tension and living on the edge of persecution. In 1992-93, a wave of violence against the Copts left more than seventy dead and hundreds wounded. Several churches were firebombed. Christian villages in upper (southern) Egypt lived in absolute terror. The next decade will be a critical one for the Copts in Egypt; they will need to reconcile with their Muslim sisters and brothers and at the same time provide the spiritual and economic resources to keep large numbers of Christians from emigrating.

We left for the United States with a sense of gratitude for the experience we had shared for three weeks. We had witnessed firsthand that our Arab Christian sisters and brothers are signs of renewal and hope for the church. We had also noted the difficult, often threatening, conditions under which they live.

But more importantly, we left the region with a commitment to act as soon as possible to prayerfully and sensitively respond to the many cries for help we heard from every leader and layperson. After praying and thinking through our limited powers and options, we felt that God was calling us to reach out to our North American evangelical sisters and brothers. Both Ray and I came from evangelical roots and have numerous contacts in these quarters. No organizations were advocating the concerns we shared for the Arab churches, the Arab peoples in general, and a just peace for the Israeli-Palestinian conflict. These three issues seemed to be the consistent message we heard throughout the Eastern Mediterranean. Was it possible that evangelicals could be encouraged to build bridges of prayer, fellowship, and support for Middle East Christians and peoples?

About one year later (October 1986), helped by the hospitality of John

Stott, prolific evangelical author and former rector of All Soul's Church in London, Evangelicals for Middle East Understanding (EMEU) was born. We had ten U.S. evangelical leaders representing major groups of churches join us, as well as leading British evangelicals and Anglicans responsible for Missions in the Middle East (Church Mission Society of the Anglican Church). Gabi Habib came representing the Middle East Council of Churches. Fr. Chacour came from the Galilee. Two Coptic Christians, one Orthodox and the other evangelical, came from Cairo.

We spent three days in prayer, Bible studies (led by the British evangelical author Colin Chapman), and discussion. On the last day we felt God's hand leading us to establish a new evangelical initiative we called Evangelicals for Middle East Understanding. Our primary responsibility would be to bring the message of Arab Christians and their deepest concerns to North American evangelicals.

We had no budget, no staff, and no office. We would begin *de novo* as an evangelical response to the pleas of our sisters and brothers in the Middle East. We left with the hope and prayer that God would bless the vision we had for North American evangelicals to one day be reconciled with their Arab Christian sisters and brothers.

6

The Land of Palestine: Holy and Cursed

I will bless you, and make your name great,
so that you will be a blessing.
Genesis 12:2

The land of Palestine, also known in ancient times as Canaan, today includes the nation Israel and the occupied West Bank, East Jerusalem, and the Gaza Strip.[1] Located on the western edge of the continent of Asia and the eastern extremity of the Mediterranean Sea, the land area is bordered by Lebanon and Syria on the north, Jordan on the east, and Egypt (Sinai Peninsula) and the Gulf of Aqaba on the south. The total land area is 10,162 square miles (26,323 square kilometers), roughly the size of the state of Maryland.

This beautiful and diversified area contains wonderful beaches along the Mediterranean as well as mountains refreshed by moderate temperatures and ocean breezes which sometimes see snow during the abbreviated winter months. The lowest point on earth—the Dead Sea—is found here and is surrounded by desert and wilderness areas. In the coastal regions, vegetables are grown throughout the year, as well as oranges, bananas, figs, lemons and many tropical flowers. Produce is sold primarily in Europe, and the land has always been capable of feeding its own peoples.

No other land area has provoked as many conflicts nor historically been oppressed by as many foreign occupiers as the "holy" land. In addition to its political and geographical centrality, which led to a literal parade of colonizers, the land of Palestine has been charged with religious importance. It was the cradle of monotheism and is recognized as holy by three great faiths—Judaism, Christianity, and Islam. Many of the holy sites in the religious heritage of these faiths are found in such cities as Jerusalem, Bethlehem, Hebron, Jericho, Nazareth, and in the Dead Sea area.

According to historians and biblical archaeologists, this land[2] has been occupied continuously since the earliest moments of human life on the planet, with Jericho the oldest known city. A local historian, Prof. Albert Aghazarian of Bierzeit University (who grew up in the Old City of Jerusalem) has both firsthand experience and scholarly knowledge of the history of this land and is a specialist on Jerusalem. In mid-August 1991, Albert stood near his home in the Armenian Quarter of the Old City of Jerusalem and spoke to one of our tour groups.

> When Abraham and Sarah arrived in Canaan sometime during the second millennium B.C., they found a number of Semitic tribes who had been living here for thousands of years. Because we lie at the crossroads of western Asia and Africa, we were blessed and cursed at the same time. Trade brought many goods and cultures to us, but they also brought foreign occupation, from which we still suffer. The Pharaohs from the First and Second Dynasties conquered Canaan around 2800 B.C.E., for example, and set up a primitive colonial rule. Around 1700 B.C.E., the Hyksos invaded from Syria and seized much of the land. Quite possibly Abraham arrived during this period from what is today Iraq, as did many immigrants from the north and east.
>
> In 1480 B.C.E., another Egyptian invasion returned the Pharaohs to Canaan. In approximately 1400, Jacob's family settled in Egypt thanks to Joseph, whose story we read in Genesis 37-50. Then the Hittites arrived from the north and, Philistines settled on the coast, coming quite possibly from the Greek Islands in the Aegean. Around 1290, Pharaoh Ramses I defeated the Hyksos. Moses and the Hebrew tribes fled in 1225 from Pharaoh Ramses II, arriving in Palestine in approximately 1184.
>
> When Joshua brought the Hebrew people over the Jordan River, (Josh. 4), they found small city fiefdoms, many of which they conquered (Jericho, Ai, Gilgal, etc.). But the book of Joshua (16:10; 17:12-13) itself tells us that Canaanites and Philistines remained in certain areas. A small Jewish state emerged under Saul around 1050 B.C.E., and expanded under David in 1011, reaching its zenith under King Solomon.
>
> In this form it lasted only about fifty years, dividing into Northern and Southern Kingdoms. Both were weak and under constant attack. The Northern Kingdom fell in 722 to the Assyrians, and Judah (Southern Kingdom) fell to Babylon in 587-586. Palestine remained under their control until Alexander the Great conquered it in 330.
>
> Another Jewish state emerged briefly under the Maccabees in 165, lasting until the Roman general Pompey took control in 63 C.E. and set up a Roman puppet named Herod. Rome remained in control until the Byzantine Empire replaced it in 395 C.E. During this time, while Byzantium was ruthlessly in charge, most here were Christians, with a tiny Jewish community in the Galilee, and a handful left in Jerusalem.

In 638 the followers of Mohammed arrived from Arabia and peacefully took Jerusalem, with all the local people welcoming them with open arms after their negative experience with the Greeks of Byzantium. Thus began Arab culture, language, and civilization. Christians and Jews remained as protected "People of the Book."

As you see, many, many foreign people have settled and intermarried here. We native Palestinians, Christians, and Muslims, are a mixture of Semitic tribes and peoples. The same with Jews, whose roots are here, and not in Europe or North Africa. I am a living example, for I am half Armenian and half Palestinian Arab. Nobody here can honestly claim to be of a pure race. We are Semites. Nobody can win the historical argument as to who might have prior claims to the land. It is far too complicated a history.

To come now and say, as do fundamentalist Jews or Christians, that God gave this land to the Jews only, is to ignore history and create a myth not grounded in reality.

A few days later we visited the new Israeli settlement of Eleazar, south of Bethlehem on the road to Hebron. It is a relatively new colony of approximately fifty houses built between 1979 and the late 1980s. The spokesman, a middle-aged businessman named Robert from Brooklyn, New York, told his story.

I came here because, as I discovered my Jewish identity, I realized that it was important for me to be here, on the front lines, as we reclaimed the land that was rightly given to us by God. I can open my Hebrew Bible and see that God gave us Jericho, Bethel, Shechem, and this land on which we stand today. I have a clear record of the places and even which tribes God gave the land to in the book of Joshua.

We are living in a time of redeeming the land. We are retaking what is ours to begin with. If possible we would like to purchase the land and do this legally, according to Jewish law. Just a few years ago there were no Jews out here in Judea and Samaria, but now we are in the Age of Redemption.

I should think that in fifteen or twenty years, when you come back, there will be few Arabs here and we will be in total control.

Today these two views clash over this central issue of who owns and controls the land. Palestinians claim they have been here continuously since the ancient Semitic Canaanite tribes and derive their heritage from them. The Jews claim that, since Abraham, God gave them this land as an inheritance for the Jewish people. Both have strong cases, deep personal feelings, determination, and convincing religious and historical arguments to justify their particular case for the land.

In the Semitic mind and experience, land means more than it does to the Westerner. An ancient Arabic saying has the Palestinian farmer claiming, "My blood is in the land." He is not only referring to his toil and sweat necessary to make a living, but his family's blood for unbroken generations dating back perhaps 1000 to 1500 years. Jews from the Orient, and some from Europe, have similar perceptions. The familial and communal ties to the land are today supercharged with political and religious content.

The question of who owns the land, to whom was it given, and how one decides a just and legal resolution of the Jewish and Palestinian claims to the land continues to resurface at the highest levels of the international political agenda. In the following section of this chapter, I will present three voices of experience, rather than a strict political or theological analysis, to raise several of the issues that might encourage Western evangelicals to consider old questions in a different way.

The Land Question

When I first became involved in the Israeli-Palestinian conflict, I was confused and felt guilty whenever I was critical of modern Zionism and Israel's policies. Having been sympathetic to Israel all of my life, I was unaware of the complex nature of this conflict. Nor did I recognize the option of being simultaneously pro-Israel and pro-Palestinian. I had always taken sides in this conflict rather than studying, praying, and searching for what God was saying about the essential peace and security of both peoples. Because both Jews and Palestinians are Semites, the task is to oppose all anti-Semitism and find a prohumanity position that will affirm both peoples.

Coming from a pro-Israel evangelical orientation, it was necessary for me to rethink my biblical understanding of the "holy" land and the Jewish people. The land question is at the center of the conflict and at the heart of biblical discussion of the issue. The solutions for Christians, as for all concerned people, are not as simple as we in North America often think.

The first Christian leader to help me with this question was Fr. Paul Tarazi, a brilliant Palestinian Orthodox theologian and biblical scholar. Born in Jerusalem and raised in Lebanon, he followed his father's dream that he become a surgeon. However, during his last year of residency, he sensed a strong call to the Christian ministry. He left medical school and entered seminary the next year, concentrating on Old Testament and New Testament studies. Today Tarazi is a leading Eastern Orthodox theologian, dividing his ambitious schedule between the pastorate and teaching at St. Vladimir's Orthodox Seminary in New York.

I first heard Father Paul lecture on the theology of the land in late 1977. He pointed out that the foundational biblical issue concerning the "holy" land was that God owned the land and gave the covenant as a gift of grace to Abraham (Gen. 12:1ff., 17:4-8) and his descendants. In all biblical covenants (*berith* in Hebrew), God is the initiator and the human partners are to be accountable to God in a variety of ways. In the Abrahamic covenant, the recipients are told they are blessed so the nations will be blessed. Fr. Paul added that it is the nation that is emphasized, for "the families of the earth" shall be blessed by Abraham.

The people of ancient Israel were rescued by God from slavery in Egypt. In the covenant at Sinai, they assumed the obligation to live in a faithful relationship under the Law (Torah). Moses mediated between God and the Israelites and during the wilderness wanderings served as God's voice calling the people to obedience and witness.

Within this biblical context, the land (Hebrew *eretz*) is not an end to itself but an instrument or means by which the people fulfill their high calling. The Israelites were in effect God's tenant farmers or caretakers. The land is a derivative of the covenant and not the goal. Whenever land becomes a people's primary focus, they are guilty of idolatry. The recipients of the covenant must recall that the primary reality for them is to be faithful to Yahweh and to the terms of the covenant.

Several important points are to be made concerning the land in this biblical perspective. First, as stated above, land is a gift of grace from Yahweh. The recipients are obedient servants who are caretakers or stewards of the gift. Whenever the land is discussed, it is clearly within the sense of Yahweh offering the land to Israel, not as an outright gift, but as a conditional loan.

Second, Genesis 13:15 is often translated as "everlasting possession" in relation to the land. This translation is incorrect in three aspects.

a. The land is never an exclusive possession of the human owner. It is offered by Yahweh to Abraham and his descendants as ("families of the earth"—Gen. 12:3) a place to live in return for services rendered. Abraham and Sarah never owned any land in Canaan aside from the burial cave at Macpelah near Hebron (Gen. 23:4-20). Abraham offered to pay Ephon the Hittite the full real estate price, but Ephon preferred to give it at no cost.

b. The term *everlasting* has often been misinterpreted as perpetual occupation of the land. The remainder of Scripture, whether one studies from the Hebrew Bible alone or includes the New Testament, gives another perspective. The restatement of the covenant in Deuteronomy 27—30 is among the passages that provide clear conditions for faithfulness to the covenant, with the Israelites losing the land as a consequence of disobedience. If they fail to practice justice (Isa. 34:10), if they abuse the sojourner or worship idols (Deut. 4:25-26), Scripture teaches that they will lose the land, but not the relationship with Yahweh. Indeed, the people of ancient Israel did lose the land as Isaiah, Jeremiah, and other prophets predicted, falling to the Assyrians in 721 B.C. and to Babylon in 587-586 B.C. However, Yahweh was with them even in their captivity.

c. Futurist premillennialist Christians and others project to some future date the fulfillment of the texts promising Israel's return to the land. This will come about following the realization of certain signs (rebuilding the Third Temple, the battle of Armageddon, etc.). Whereas the apocalyptic and millennarian forms of Christianity and Judaism date back to the intertestament period, futurist premillennialism enters rather late in Christian history (eighteenth century). Moreover, it shifts the terms of the covenant obligations away from Yahweh's original terms of obedience to supernatural signs.

In Deuteronomy 4:25-26 we read,

> When you have had children and children's children, and become compla-
> cent in the land, if you act corruptly by making an idol in the form of any-
> thing, thus doing what is evil in the sight of the Lord your God, and provoking
> him to anger, I call heaven and earth to witness against you today that you
> will soon utterly perish from the land that you are crossing the Jordan to occu-
> py; you will not live long on it, but will be utterly destroyed.

But Christian and Jewish Zionists tend to reverse the Deuteronomic
order in their theology. They elevate the role of the land above that of the
covenant relationship and Yahweh himself. Thus does the land issue become one of idolatry, particularly in most forms of the contemporary Zionist movement and its Christian fundamentalist counterpart. The fervor
over attaining and expanding the land eclipses any relationship to Yahweh, the Torah, and humane treatment of the sojourner. Further, Israel
loses its fundamental calling, of being a blessing to all "the families of the
earht" (Gen. 12:2-3).

It should be noted that the vast majority of Jews in Israel are secular.
The political leadership, like the ideological principals of Israel's major
political parties, the Labor and Likud coalitions, is a form of secular Zionism. Religious language and symbolism are used primarily by secular
Jews to achieve political goals, although a smaller minority are driven by
religious motivations.

It is this influential Zionist fundamentalist religious movement that
has been a significant pressure group on the Likud coalition, especially
concerning the issue of settlements. A leading spokesperson, Hanan
Porath, offers insight into how fundamentalist religious Zionism elevates
the land issue above everything else.

> The value of the land of Israel exceeds that of peace. . . . We are not com-
> manded, at the outset, to make war upon and destroy the non-Jews living in
> the land . . . but if the peoples who control the land at present do not accept
> the presence of the people of Israel and their sovereignty over the land of Is-
> rael, then . . . we are commanded to conquer the land by war, even at a high
> price.[3]

Thus it appears from a strict biblical argument, that is, one that ac-
cepts the essential faithfulness of the texts as God-inspired, that neither
the Jews nor the Palestinians can claim ownership of the land by divine
right. Instead, the land is to be shared, and the "caretakers" will be judged
by Yahweh as to how they treat the other parties.

Obedience to the Covenant

A second experience with an Arab Christian helped me see a familiar biblical text in new light. In May 1979, several organizations combined to
convene one of the first Christian conferences in the United States to dis-

cuss the Palestine question. Among the Christian organizations sponsoring the event were *Sojourners* magazine, the Presbytery of Chicago, and Pax Christi, the Catholic peace organization. Several Christian leaders assembled to deliver lectures on various aspects of land, people, human rights, and peace.

Among the guests was the official representative of the Palestine Liberation Organization at the United Nations, Zughdi Terzi, an Orthodox Christian layperson. The U.S. State Department allowed him to attend the conference on condition that he not address the assembly. He was, however, allowed to answer questions.

During one of the evening worship services, there was time allotted for people to express "joys and concerns." Wes Michaelson, then a *Sojourners* editor, stood and addressed a question to Terzi.

We are honored to have a Christian Palestinian leader in our midst, but at the same time, I regret that we are prevented by our government from hearing from you. I would like to ask you to simply tell us from a biblical perspective, how should we be thinking as Christians about the plight of your people?

We asked Mr. Terzi to come forward and speak from the pulpit. A hush fell over the congregation as this grandfatherly figure came to the front and opened his Bible.

Thank you for this wonderful question. I cannot tell you what this gathering means to me, a Palestinian Christian from Jerusalem, and now forbidden to return to see my mother, sisters and brothers, or our home. The passage that comes to mind is the story of Naboth's vineyard in 1 Kings 21. You may recall how King Ahab coveted the beautiful vineyard of a peasant named Naboth. Ahab returned home one evening and complained to Jezebel, who said, "Aren't you the king?" She then arranged to have the peasant framed and murdered. Ahab took the land, and then was confronted by the prophet Elijah. The prophet would not allow the king to steal the land, despite his power.

Terzi went on to tell how the Palestinians face the same situation in the "holy" land today. The state of Israel behaves toward Palestinians much like Ahab and Jezebel. He added, "Are you aware that we have lost over 400 villages, razed to the ground, since 1948? Did you know that Jewish settlers can confiscate land and build their own colonies on land that legally belongs to Palestinians?" Most of us were unaware of these issues and sat in some form of disbelief or shock.

Then he paused and looked directly at us:

I stand before you in Naboth's place today, as do thousands of my countrymen. Where are the Elijahs today? Where are the voices of the powerless? As I read the Prophets and the Gospels, this is the responsibility of the church. Have Christians in the West abandoned us? Did not Jesus come to seek and save the lost? I recall his first sermon in Nazareth: "The Spirit of the Lord is upon me, because he has anointed me to preach good news to the poor. . . to set at liberty those who are oppressed." Is this not your role to-day?

Silence fell over the congregation as Terzi returned to his pew. Could it be that one whom most Americans would dismiss as a terrorist was a prophet? The PLO official, who was the cause of former United Nations representative Andrew Young's dismissal from office for simply meeting with him, spoke "the truth in love" (and justice) to us.

The issue of the covenant is central to a biblical understanding of the land and its people. There are four key elements to the Hebrew under-standing of covenant. First, God is always *the initiator* in a biblical cove-nant. It is Yahweh who called Abraham and Sarah from Ur of the Chaldees and later reached out to Moses and the entire Israelite community. In the Genesis 12:23 passage we see that God chose the Israelites from the fam-ilies of the earth, not because they were more deserving, but simply out of God's graciousness.

This leads us to the second key element in the covenant relation-ship—*grace*, or unmerited favor. This bespeaks of God's very character, for God loves Israel and the Jewish people with an unconditional love (*hesed* in Hebrew), a love that often tests God when Israel becomes un-faithful and turns its back on God (Book of Hosea). But God's grace and unconditional love remain steady even today.

The third element is the response of *faith* and the condition of faith-fulness or obedience expected of the recipient. The covenant is essential-ly a relationship of faith and faithfulness, whereby the recipient Israel is given "the blessing" by God as a gift, but with the condition that Israel be faithful. This does not mean that God's unconditional love is jeopardized, but that certain elements of the relationship are granted with the under-standing that they can be temporarily lost if Israel is unfaithful.

Finally, there are certain instruments by which the covenant is lived out or experienced. The instruments are gifts or *sacred trusts* granted by the Creator God to the recipient, such as "chosenness" or God's favor; the land; and God's promise to make their name great (see Gen. 12:1-3; 17:1-4). These elements or instruments are not ends to themselves but means through which the people can more effectively serve God and live a full life.

For example, the land is clearly given in Genesis 12:1-3 as a blessing through which Israel will be a blessing to the families and peoples of the earth. The land is a means to serve God and reflect God's salvation for the world.

Israel's Calling

Who is the true Israel? Who are the people of God? Does one discern the answer through ethnicity or inheritance? Is it through some outward sign, such as ritual or circumcision? Does the Old Testament conclude with this issue unanswered?

One biblical account that begins to answer this question is the familiar story of Jonah. The parable-like book of Jonah can be portrayed as a four-act drama. Act One opens with Jonah receiving the call from God: "Go at once to Nineveh, that great city, and cry out against it; for their wickedness has come up before me" (1:2).

Nineveh was located in the north of modern Iraq and was the capital of the Assyrian Empire that overran Israel in 721 B.C.E. The call to Jonah may be compared to a contemporary Israeli receiving word that he or she is to do missionary work in Baghdad.

Jonah heard the call and left immediately for Jaffa (the port city near modern Tel Aviv), which was in the opposite direction. In fact, the prophet boarded a boat bound for a destination in the western Mediterranean. But a mighty storm convulsed the sea and threatened to destroy the ship. The sailors were superstitious people and decided that someone on the ship had brought them bad luck (1:7). They cast lots and the lot fell on Jonah. After Jonah admitted what he had done, the sailors threw him overboard to save the ship. "So they picked Jonah up and threw him into the sea; and the sea ceased from its raging" (1:15). Act One ends with Jonah being swallowed by a large fish.

The curtain rises on Act Two with the prophet in the belly of the fish. The entire act deals with Jonah's song of thanksgiving for being rescued from certain death by the great fish. Then at the close of the chapter, Jonah seems to come to his senses, saying, "What I have vowed I will pay" (2:9). He cried for deliverance and the fish spewed the prophet out on dry land.

Act Three opens with Jonah receiving the call once more to preach in Nineveh. He set out and quickly came to the gates of the great city. The metropolis was so large it took him three days to walk across it. After Jonah traveled a full day, he ended up in the center of Nineveh, where he began to preach, "Forty days more, and Nineveh shall be overthrown" (3:4).

The people heard the message and repented. Everyone from the king to the lowly peasant (and the cattle) put on sackcloth and ashes. The king had proclaimed a fast throughout the land. They called on Yahweh and repented of their wicked ways (3:8-9). When God saw how they responded to the threat of destruction, God "changed his mind" and spared the city. Act Three ends with this change of heart among the Ninevites, despite the reluctance of Jonah.

The final act opens with Jonah fuming around the stage in great anger. He was terribly upset because God changed his mind about destroying Nineveh, Israel's enemy. "What about our future security? These Gentiles are outside the privileges due to the Jews. How does this square with our calling?" Jonah was so upset that he asked God to take his life, saying, "It is better for me to die than to live." Probably he felt unable to return to his hometown and face his role in the conversion of the enemy.

Jonah left the city and sat down in a small hut to see if God would still destroy Nineveh. The sun became unbearable, but God made a large bush to grow over Jonah's head for shade. Alas, it died the next day and a hot desert wind came from the east. Again the sun was unbearable and Jonah became faint, asking a second time for God to take his life.

At this point God addressed Jonah, who is a symbol for all of Israel (and the church).

> Why are you so preoccupied with yourself and your privileges? Are you more interested in the non-essential issues and miss the point of why God called you in the first place? You were called to be God's agent of love and reconciliation to all the nations, not your own people alone. You have become more interested in yourself. Your God is too small. God is doing a new thing in the world, and you need to catch up with it. Only when you are faithful to your original calling of being a blessing to the nations (Gen. 12:3) will you truly be the people of God. (rephrasing of Jon. 4:9-11 by author)

It is clear from these passages that the covenant blessing was not given to Israel alone. There was no favoritism with God. As the great prophet Jeremiah taught, prior to and during the exile, the true covenant people were those whose hearts were changed and truly who lived the faith.

> "The days are surely coming," says the Lord, "when I will make a new covenant with the house of Israel and the house of Judah. It will not be like the covenant that I made with their ancestors when I took them by the hand to bring them out of the land of Egypt—a covenant that they broke, though I was their husband, says the Lord. But this is the covenant that I will make with the house of Israel after those days," says the Lord: "I will put my law within them, and I will write it on their hearts; and I will be their God, and they shall be my people." (Jer. 31:31-33)

This understanding of the people of God as transformed beings— identified not by outward rituals, ethnic pride, nor legal codes but by faithfulness to the covenant-keeping God—are indeed the true covenant people. The universal scope of God's love and justice became more clear by the time of the Babylonian exile (586-531 B.C.). This more mature understanding, which is more universal and inclusive, is taken further by the message brought by the Palestinian Jew from Galilee, Jesus of Nazareth.

7

Jesus and Armageddon

*I*t is not for you to know the times or periods
that the Father has set by his own authority.
Acts 1:7

In October 1991, our tour group included evangelical pastors, mission executives, and laity. At first we sat in stunned silence as we listened to Jan Willem van der Hoeven, spokesperson for the International Christian Embassy-Jerusalem, tell us why we should support Israel in the same manner he did.

> When a Christian sees the cross, he sees forgiveness; but when a Jew sees the cross, he shudders because of what Christians, including Nazis, have done to him. I have no choice as a Christian but to stand behind the Jewish people, because I believe they are right. God gave them this land as the Bible tells us, and God promised not only to bless Israel, but to bless even the Arabs through Israel.[1]

One of our group members, a young Christian lawyer from California, opened his Bible to the book of Amos. He stood and read the following:

> Fallen, no more to rise, is maiden Israel; forsaken on her land, with no one to raise her up. . . They hate the one who reproves in the gate, and they abhor

the one who speaks the truth. Therefore because you trample on the poor and take from them levies of grain, you have built houses of hewn stone, but you shall not live in them; you have planted pleasant vineyards, but you shall not drink their wine. For I know how many are your transgressions, and how great are your sins—you who afflict the righteous, who take a bribe, and push aside the needy in the gate. . . . I hate, I despise your festivals, and I take no delight in your solemn assemblies. Even though you offer me your burnt offerings and grain offerings, I will not accept them; and the offerings of well-being of your fatted animals I will not look upon.

Take away from me the noise of your songs; I will not listen to the melody of your harps. But let justice roll down like waters, and righteousness like an everflowing stream." (Amos 5:2, 10-12, 21-24)

John, the lawyer, closed the Bible and said,

This present nation Israel stands before the judgment seat of God. Israel is a sinful nation. Her human rights record in Jerusalem, the West Bank, and Gaza Strip is shameful. Many Christians are suffering under this occupation. Israel may be seeking physical and military security through nationalism, but she is not seeking the heart of the Lord. How can you remain silent, as the prophet Amos warns us all, and not tell Israel that it is sinning?

Jan Willem became red in the face and began to pace back and forth in front of our group. The inflection of his voice became higher and higher as he responded,

This may have been the word of God at that time, but it is not for our time. After 2000 years of suffering and losing their land, God has brought them back. God has determined after all of Israel's suffering, as we see in Ezekiel 37, to bring Israel out of ashes. Out of the Holocaust itself under Hitler, the Jews felt, "Our hopes are lost" or "Our nation is destroyed."

This is how they felt after the Holocaust. But from the valley of bones and ashes, God produced Israel. We Christians must comfort and support her—this is how I see it.

We were shocked at what we had just heard: "This may have been the word of God for that time, but it is not for our time." One of my dear friends, Darrel Meyers of Los Angeles, a pastor who has been involved in Middle East education since 1968, became deeply disturbed over Jan Willem's use of Scripture and insensitivity to the poor who were all around him. Others in our group were very direct with their questions, which in turn put Jan Willem on the defensive. People felt that he was not addressing the biblical issues and that he continued to invoke the Holocaust and Christian guilt to deflect attention away from what God's Word seemed to be saying. Eventually he began shouting and an argument ensued. One of his staff came over to apologize, and we left the embassy, having reached a complete stalemate. It was not a pleasant scene, and neither party behaved in an exemplary Christian manner. However, the issues were unmistakable.

These diametrically opposed positions held by Christians raise a series of questions, most of which cannot be answered here due to space limitations. I would, however, like to concentrate on certain critical issues that the above discussion avoided and examine three questions that bring New Testament issues to the forefront.

The first is the *question of land*. How does the New Testament treat the question of land in relation to Israel and the people of God? Second is the *question of Israel the nation versus the church as the people of God*. Who are the true people of God in the New Testament? Is Israel replaced by the Christian church? Third is the *question of eschatology* or the future. Do Jesus and Paul reject predictive prophecy? Or do they imply that several prophecies—such as the rebuilding of the temple, Israel's return to the land, the rapture, and the final Battle of Armageddon—are yet to be fulfilled?

The Question of Land

Land was fundamental to the Israelite's [2] self-understanding from the time of Abraham forward. There has always been a strong territorial dimension to Judaism, as many Jewish authors and Christian theologians have confirmed. As a Christian I can affirm the centrality of land in the Jewish experience, but with certain biblically based conditions. A biblically based understanding of land must be approached within the faith context of the Abrahamic and Sinaitic covenants, lest it be secularized and politicized in an adversarial manner inconsistent with the entirety of the biblical message.

Those who interpret the land promises literally must also take the Law literally. Israel cannot have land and oppress the poor, according to the Bible.

As we discussed in the previous chapter, a faith perspective concerning land affirms God as the initiator of the covenant. Land is an instrument that enables the covenant people to fulfill conditions of obedience, which include just treatment of all inhabitants (Lev. 25:23). Land, however, is not necessary for faith, nor is it a priority over the obedience to Yahweh required in the covenant relationship.

We recall the exile experience, as the prophets Jeremiah and Ezekiel interpret it. Following the Assyrian conquest in 721 B.C.E., the weakened Southern Kingdom of Judah was all that was left to Israel, causing new religious and political definition. The Jews of Judah were forced by the exile in Babylon (587-586 B.C.E.) to search for new personal and corporate systems by which to sustain worship and hope. Many came to recognize that God gave them "new wineskins" of faith and worship in the synagogue and the invitation to a covenant faith written "on their hearts" (Jer. 31:31-34).

Psalm 137:4 asks painfully, "How could we sing the Lord's song in a foreign land?" No doubt many had given up on God when the temple was destroyed and they were carried into Babylon. Others came to recognize that God had met their needs in a profound manner, through spiritual resources that had actually been there all along if they only had had eyes of faith to see them. They built new communities with old friends. They did not forget the covenant but discovered through it new possibilities for faithfulness. They had not been abandoned. God's suffering love and covenant-keeping faithfulness (*ḥesed*—Hosea 6:6ff.) turned a potentially disastrous experience into a blessing for those who by faith turned to Yahweh. They were among the faithful remnant who eventually returned to their beloved homeland.

Christian Zionists (and many liberal Zionist Christian theologians such as Franklin Littell, Roy and Alice Eckart, and Paul VanBuren) take a different starting point when developing their biblical basis for Israel and the land. Our subject here is the evangelical and fundamentalist tradition, represented by the International Christian Embassy-Jerusalem.

In the Christian Embassy publication, *Christian Zionism and Its Biblical Basis*, Malcolm Hedding writes,

> For Christian Zionists, then, the restoration of the State of Israel to her ancient soil is evidence that there is hope and redemption for this world. To support Israel (Gen. 12:3), comfort her (Isa. 40:1-2) and pray for her peace (Ps. 122:6, Isa. 66:6-7) is to work in harmony with God.[3]

"Restoration" of the Jews to the land—without taking into account the historical processes through which God refined the faith of the people, nor citing the spiritual and moral requirements raised by such prophets as Jeremiah—becomes the starting point for the Christian Zionists. Their failure to take seriously biblical history and such essential biblical themes as justice and covenant faithfulness leads them to conclusions based on limited portions of the biblical record. Lacking a complete biblical foundation, they fall into the trap of granting to the Jewish people an unconditional divine land grant, which is utterly contrary to the biblical accounts.

In an effort to anchor the Christian Zionist theology in the New Testament, Hedding points to Romans 9—11 and Luke 21:23-24. He moves to the New Testament, however, only after the "restoration of the Jews" theme is established as the presupposition for his argument. The New Testament texts are secondary and supply proof-texts.

A central biblical issue to be considered here is the relationship between the Old and New Testaments. Most evangelical Christians follow one of three models in this regard. The Christian Zionists, as seen above, believe that the Christian church will be replaced by the nation-state Israel in the last days, and God will restore Israel as the primary instrument of God's blessing for the world. This interpretation is also known as the "restoration of the Jews model." Some Christian Zionists adopt this position from a dispensational theology, while others come to it as a result of other interpretations of Scripture.

A second model is represented by Martin Luther and some reformed Protestant and Eastern Orthodox theologies. This is the two-covenant model, wherein the church replaces Israel as the fulfillment of the covenant. Israel loses its role as God's instrument of salvation and blessing. The Law is replaced by faith, and the believer comes to redemption *sola fide* (by faith alone) and *sola gratia* (by grace alone). The problem with this approach is that it does not account for Romans 9—11, where Paul states that God never abandons the Israel of faith.

The third model is that of John Calvin and some Roman Catholic theologies. This model allows for a continuity between the testaments and an ultimate role for Israel. By no means do Calvin or others taking the "continuity" position, as it is called, allow for a modern political nation or for land ownership questions to enter the discussion. They simply state that God uses the church and in a mysterious way will keep the blessing upon the faithful Jews.

Most Western evangelicals have not followed Calvin or Luther in these matters but have adopted some form of the Christian Zionist model. The contemporary political issues turn, it seems to me, on the biblical understanding of land and nation. If one adopts an ethnocentric or exclusively Zionist understanding of land and nation, they may miss the wider blessings of God that the prophets and Jesus saw. Some evangelicals are beginning to rethink their approach to this question. A leading Anglican evangelical and charismatic author and pastor, Michael Harper, created controversy in British evangelical circles when he wrote in early 1988, "The New Testament never includes the land as one of the promises to the people of God. Even if it did, it would be impossible to sustain the argument that it was exclusively for the Jews." [4]

During the New Testament period, the land, temple, Jerusalem, and future promises were given spiritual or allegorical interpretations. Jesus repeatedly practiced this principle. In his meeting with the Samaritan woman (John 4), Jesus extended the covenant to the Samaritan people, seen as hated heretics by mainstream Judaism. When the woman raised questions about worship of God and faith, Jesus responded, "Woman, believe me the hour is coming when you will worship the Father neither on this mountain nor in Jerusalem" (John 4:21).

In other words, specific hallowed territory, on ethnocentric nationalism and sacred buildings are not necessities for covenant faithfulness. Jesus never elevated land above faith. Further, the Samaritan woman expected the messianic promises to be fulfilled in the future, for she says, "I know that Messiah is coming (who is called Christ). "When he comes, he will proclaim all things to us" (John 4:25). Jesus rejects the futurist approach to faith as he responds, "I am he, the one who is speaking to you" (v. 26).

It is also striking that Jesus extended his ministry to Phoenician territory (southern Lebanon) and the Decapolis ("Ten Cities" including modern Jaresh and Amman, Jordan) thereby reaching out to the Gentiles. His ministry certainly knew no ethnic nor territorial boundaries. In Mark 7:24-30 he brought healing and a message of good news to a Gentile, the Syrophoenician woman in Tyre (Lebanon), affirming her as part of the household of faith. Jesus repeatedly deemphasized land, territorial, gender, and ethnic limitations during his ministry. The good news proclaimed by Jesus was that these boundaries were a thing of the past. God's redemption offered a new realm to all who believed.

The first great Christian martyr, Stephen, made a similar case in his defense before the Jerusalem high priest.

> God had him [Abraham] move from there to this country in which you are now living. He did not give him any of it as a heritage, not even a foot's length, but promised to give it to him as his possession and to his descendants after him, even though he had not child. And God spoke in these terms, that his descendants would be resident aliens in a country belonging to others, who would enslave them and mistreat them during four hundred years. (Acts 7:4-6)

Stephen went out of his way to demonstrate that Abraham was from "outside the land," that he owned no land, and yet was "the Father" of a people later called Israelites. Stephen then made the same case with such Jewish heroes of faith as Moses (who sojourned in Midian, outside the "holy" land). It was in Moses' experience of standing on "holy ground" somewhere in Egypt that he found faith in Yahweh (Acts 7:30-34). Moses' epiphany experience with the living God took place outside the boundaries of what most Jews and Christians consider the "holy" land.

Or consider Joseph, who was faithful after being transported into Egypt and ultimately saved his people. By citing these examples, Stephen was challenging both the territorial and the nationalistic dimensions of Jewish faith: "You stiff-necked people, uncircumcised in heart and ears, you are forever opposing the Holy Spirit, just as your ancestors used to do. Which of the prophets did your ancestors not persecute?" (Acts 7:51-52).

They took up stones and killed him, and "the witnesses laid their garments at the feet of a young man named Saul" (v. 58), a Jew from Tarsus (modern Turkey).

Stephen's testimony had a lasting influence on Saul, who was not only an accomplice in Stephen's murder but a witness to the courageous manner in which he died. After his conversion and a three-year training period, Paul later became the great "Apostle to the Gentiles." He experienced the new covenant in a direct revelation from Jesus Christ, which opened the possibility of a covenant relationship to every person, regardless of ethnicity. Paul's initial mentors in the faith were Gentiles, and no doubt he came to understand the implications of Jesus' gospel for everyone during this formative period.

In his Galatians debate with the Judaizers (those who would have Christians maintain the Torah and rituals of Judaism), Paul used spiritual arguments against circumcision and other rituals (Gal. 3). The temple became the body of Christ or the seat of faith in the individual believer (1 Cor. 12:12-31). Faith issues did not focus on land, place, race, law, or ritual. Being a Jew, Paul claimed, provided no advantages unless you were righteous through faith alone (Rom. 5:1-2).

However, let us be clear that the Jews are neither replaced nor rejected. There is a special status preserved for the Jews in God's plan of salvation, as Paul argues in Romans 9—11. But even in this section of Romans, where Paul argues the case for the Jews, there is no mention of land as a benefit.

The very chapters cited by Christian Zionists as biblical justification for an exclusive Jewish claim to Palestine do not in fact justify the claim. Those who insist on modern Israel's presence in the land as an article of faith miss the central message of the New Testament.

Having stated the above position on the land question, I must add two provisions. First, in response to the Holocaust, Christians must have a special sensitivity to the Jews' need for security and place. This provision need not, however, necessitate a Jewish state or national rights exercised at the expense of another population. The security of the Jewish people is a fundamental right that must be guaranteed by the family of nations—but not at the cost of another people's suffering. Moreover, Jews as a people and the State of Israel must, like other nations, be accountable to international law.

Today several Jewish thinkers are challenging their people concerning these issues. They argue convincingly that the security of Jews and the Jewish state itself will not last long unless they are built on justice toward Israel's Arab neighbors and a right relationship with God. *Israel's Fateful Hour*, by Yehosophat Harkabi (former head of military intelligence in Israel) argues from a secular and pragmatic approach that Israel must leave the occupied territories and make peace with her neighbors. The writings of Marc Ellis, an American Jewish theologian, have challenged the assumptions of "Holocaust theology" and many of the presuppositions of modern U.S. and Israeli political Zionism.[5]

A second issue is raised by the great Dutch Reformed Evangelical theologian, Hendricus Berkhof.

> In God's land promise to Israel, we see that he is a geo-political God who is concerned with righteousness upon the whole earth, with a peaceful living together of all nations. God's ways with Israel are the ways with a nation, a people, a community—not primarily or mainly with individuals. . . . The Spirit has two irons in the fire: His work in the individual and his work in human history. God remains faithful in history from generation to generation.[6]

Thus Berkhof utilizes Romans 11:29 ("for the gifts and calling of God are irrevocable") as one of his biblical references for this argument. He states that somehow in God's mysterious wisdom, God is not finished with the Jews and the land may play a role in the future. Nowhere, however, does Berkhof state that the standards of the old covenant (grace and Torah) are superseded. Quite to the contrary, the Jews have been called to be even more faithful and are held up as a living illustration. Berkhof also notes that "all nations" will be the beneficiaries of God's peace on earth.

Berkhof states in clear terms that this particularistic form of nationalism found in secular and many forms of religious Zionism are inconsistent with what he calls "Biblical Zionism."

> If Zionism wants to continue in the line of the Old Testament preaching about the land, it must not only be aware of this particular kind of land possession, but also act upon it. It must know that this land was allotted to Israel by mere grace. And it must know that Israel's inhabitation had to be an example, a model, an inspiration, a blessing to the surrounding peoples and eventually to the whole of mankind. For that reason biblical Zionism can never be a nationalistic movement of the same kind as other such movements. It has to know the origin of Israel's relation to this land: the blessing of the whole earth.[7]

Modern political Zionism, while supporting an exclusive Jewish state that relegates its Palestinian Arab citizens to second-class status and holds 2 million Palestinians in the occupied territories under a brutal military occupation, is not in moral conformity to the above guidelines. Modern secular Israel, the dream of the Zionist and Christian Zionist movements, seems a far cry from the biblical conditions necessary to live in the land of Canaan. Faithful Christians and Jews must challenge Israel to practice basic justice and not lend unqualified support to whatever form of military aggression Israel adopts in the name of national security.

Who Is the True Israel: The Nation or the Church?

ICEJ spokesman Jan Willem van der Hoeven, and most Christian Zionists, see the modern state of Israel as the fulfillment of biblical prophecy. According to their theology, biblical references which applied to ancient Israel are literally applied to the Zionist state called Israel.

Christian Zionists (of the evangelical or fundamentalist persuasions) use classical Christian dispensational arguments to elevate the modern Israeli state above the church as God's primary instrument in these "latter days." The argument claims that God will restore Israel to her "ancient soil as evidence that there is hope and redemption for this world."[8]

The Christian Embassy's leaders and others believe that we have entered the historical period when God will begin to withdraw his blessing from the Gentile world and "restore the kingdom to Israel" (Acts 1:6). Ironically, van der Hoeven uses this text from Acts to lay the foundation for his argument—but fails to see the categorical rejection of this theology by Jesus himself in the next verse: "It is not for you to know the times or periods that the Father has set by his own authority" (Acts 1:7—a text I will examine more closely at the end of this chapter).

Van der Hoeven also uses Luke 21:24 ("Jerusalem will be trampled on by the Gentiles, until the times of the Gentiles are fulfilled") and Romans 11:25-26 as additional texts to buttress his dispensational argument. This theology includes the rebuilding of a third temple (on the site of the Dome of the Rock in Jerusalem), the rise of the Antichrist (possibly through the European Economic Community), Israel becoming a major military power, and an eventual Battle of Armageddon (in the plain of Megiddo in northern Israel). According to van der Hoeven, the birth of Israel "signals the return of the Messiah and the fulfillment of all the prophecies."

So who are the true people of God? According to the Christian Zionists, the answer is Israel, the Jewish state. The role of Christians is merely to comfort and support Israel, who will usher in the messianic age. The church will be removed from history through the rapture and not play a role in the "latter days."

Evangelical leader John R. W. Stott, rector emeritus of All Soul's Church in London and member of the Lausanne Executive Committee for World Evangelization, cautions Christians to look more carefully at Scripture when interpreting Israel. He reminds us that there are four Israels—but only three are mentioned in the Bible. The first Israel was the second son of Isaac, also known as Jacob. The second Israel was the chosen people of the Old Testament. The third Israel becomes the messianic community of the New Testament, now including Gentiles. The fourth Israel is the secular Jewish state established in 1948.

Stott turns to Romans 9 and asks,

> Who, according to the New Testament perspective, is Israel today? And what answer we are going to see from the Bible is this extraordinary event—that the true Israel today is neither Jews nor Israelis, but believers in the Messiah, even if they are Gentiles. . . . The physical descent from Abraham, Isaac, and Jacob is not regarded as being sufficient to be a true member of the covenant. Of course, the people thought it was. They interpreted election as favoritism, but the prophets kept insisting to them that their choice by God to be the covenant people of God would not guarantee them immunity from the judgment of God.[9]

Stott develops his theological argument from the prophet Amos, John the Baptist, the Gospels, and Romans 9—11. He cites Amos 3:2, "You only have I known of all the families of the earth: therefore I will punish you for all your iniquities."

Stott adds, "The prophet tends more and more to draw a distinction between Israel as a whole as a defenseless nation and the Israelites' faithful remnant within the nation." In other words, the true people of God must be determined more by covenant faithfulness than by national or ethnic identity.

John the Baptist, whom Stott rightly calls "the last Old Testament prophet," preached the same concept and added a new twist. John taught that there is not only a remnant within Israel. God will also go outside of Israel to the Gentiles to find faithful people. "I tell you, God is able from these stones to raise up children to Abraham" (Luke 3:8). The stones were the Gentiles, to be included in the new vision for the people of God taught by Jesus.

Jesus' own genealogy, as recorded in Matthew 1, makes the case clearly. Raymond Brown, brilliant New Testament scholar, argues convincingly in *Birth of the Messiah* that, of the five women who appear in the genealogy, two were Gentiles—and Tamar had an incestuous relationship with her brother, Judah. Rahab the harlot, a Gentile Canaanite from Jericho, is included in the messianic line because her faithful action helped God's work in history. Bathsheba, an adulteress with King David, is included. Ruth, a Moabite/Jordanian (Gentile) appears as well. Finally comes Mary, mother of Jesus—teenage mother of a boy who was illegitimate in the eyes of her peers.

Brown demonstrates that these unique women of faith, half-Gentiles and (according to Jewish law) half sex-offenders, set the tone for the "new age" the Messiah Jesus inaugurated. The new people of God are those called by faith to turn toward God and join the kingdom, demonstrating by their very lives God's remarkable grace. Dr. Brown writes,

> It is the combination of the scandalous or irregular union and of divine intervention through the women that explains best Matthew's choice in the genealogy. . . .
> It was to Matthew's interest that the four Old Testament women were also Gentiles or associated with Gentiles (Uriah's wife). This did not foreshadow the role of Mary, but it did foreshadow the role of the Messiah who was to bring Gentiles into God's plan of salvation—people who, though not Jews, were like Jesus in their descent from Abraham.[10]

Through the divine inspiration of the Holy Spirit, Jesus proclaimed this message of divine grace and inclusiveness, and by his lineage he was a living example that God's salvation reached out to all people, regardless of their ethnicity. He repeatedly stunned his disciples, other followers, and especially the Jewish authorities because he preached that the Gentiles would be brought in as equal partners of the covenant. This new kingdom would be built, not on ritual and blood lineage, but on faith and repentance.

Near the end of his ministry, Jesus seemed to direct his message toward the authorities to force a confrontation and perhaps a change of heart. Note, for example, the parable of the vineyard, where the householder sent tenants to care for the vines. The tenants beat the messengers and eventually kill the son of the householder. Jesus adds, "The stone that the builders rejected has become the cornerstone" (Matt. 21:42). This is a hint of the Gospel going out to the Gentiles. In case the listeners miss his subtle message, Jesus gets to the point: "Therefore I tell you, the kingdom of God will be taken away from you and given to a people that produces the fruits of the kingdom" (Matt. 21:43).

"A people" is none other than the Gentiles, "the sign of Jonah" of whom Jesus spoke earlier. The Jewish authorities, including the chief priests and scribes, were enraged. They tried to arrest him on the spot but he slipped away.

The Palm Sunday processional should be seen not as a beautiful ritual of the Messiah riding into Jerusalem on a humble donkey, but as a public demonstration of the newness of the kingdom of God, which rejects all nationalism and ethnic pride in the Jewish people. The donkey was an expression of royal humility, in opposition to the military nationalism that confused the coming Messiah with a military deliverer who would restore Jewish pride and establish their sovereignty on the land. Jesus was striving to transcend the ethnic and nationalistic trappings of Judaism and direct the people of God toward faithful living based on unconditional trust in Yahweh.

The cleansing of the temple offered a similar message. It was a parable in action. Jesus was not merely judging those who bought and sold pigeons and sacrificial animals. Too much biblical interpretation domesticates Jesus in this regard. The cleansing of the temple is a messianic action declaring the liberation of the very center of the Jewish faith. The priestly leadership had for generations aligned themselves with the rich, the corrupt, and the occupying power. They had sacrificed their faithfulness for power and control of the people. Jesus' actions called people to think and act in the opposite manner. Jesus intended to reclaim the temple for the faithful and declare the true meaning of the heart of Judaism, "My house shall be called a house of prayer; but you are making it a den of robbers" (Matt 21:13). Here he quotes from a familiar text in the Hebrew scriptures to reclaim the temple.

Again, covenant faithfulness was the thrust of Jesus' message. The true people of God are those who believe and act out of kingdom principles. One's ethnicity, rituals, land, nationalism, and institutions are irrelevant.

Stott notes that Paul, a Pharisee, developed the same message. Romans 9, a passage used by the Christian Zionists, becomes a key text for Stott's argument. Paul stated in verse 6, "Not all Israelites truly belong to Israel." He later added, "Even us whom he has called, not from the Jews only but also from the Gentiles" (v. 24). Those who follow Jesus, whether Gentiles or Jews, are the "circumcision" (or people of God), as he stated in Philippians 3:2. Physical descent and blood lineage had nothing to do with faith and membership in the new kingdom.

As Paul argued in Romans 4, the seed of Abraham was extended by God's grace to all people of faith.

For the promise that he would inherit the world did not come to Abraham or to his descendants through the law but through the righteousness of faith. . . . For this reason it depends on faith, in order that the promise may rest on grace and be guaranteed to all his descendants, not only to the adherents of the law but also to those who share the faith of Abraham (for he is the father of us all, as it is written, 'I have made you the father of many nations') (Rom. 4:13, 16-18).

Paul gave new meaning to the fatherhood of Abraham and those who inherited the blessings promised in Genesis 12, 15, and 17. This is not to argue a replacement theology. God ultimately has a role for the Jews (Rom. 11), but it will undoubtedly be one consistent with biblical history (i.e. *ḥesed*—steadfast love and faithfulness), not necessarily a nation state.

The condition for belonging to the people of God, the covenant, is one consistent message from Genesis to Revelation. The faithful people of God are those who through the gifts of God's grace and faithful living (discipleship) inherit salvation and eternal life. Land, ethnicity, and limitations on the covenant to Jews alone are now extended to include Gentiles and Jews through faith. There is no place here for God's rejection of the Gentile world or for a dispensational theology which elevates the Jewish state above the church in the last days. The New Testament seems to be stating exactly the opposite in this regard. The church, including Jews and Gentiles, is now grafted in as a full partner in the new kingdom. Paul argued the case again in Galatians, where he concluded in chapter 3, "The one who is righteous will live by faith" (v. 11). Abraham is a model of faith to all who believe. He is not the exclusive domain of the Jews nor of Zionist nationalism.

It is little wonder that Galatians 3:11 has spoken through the centuries to people such as St. Augustine and Martin Luther, inspiring their spiritual conversion. The message demands retelling and amplification in the strongest terms, particularly for those who would revert back to a pseudo-Christian form of legalism or dispensational eschatology.

Stott concludes his remarkable sermon by asking, "What about the Promised Land?" How does his discussion of Israel relate to dispensational theology and those who would give the land to the Jewish state? Stott says he does not see the Zionist argument in Scripture. He notes that we are free as Christians to disagree on these matters—but must be clear about what the Bible says and the political implications of Zionism.

In a private conversation with Stott in February 1987, I asked directly about his personal position on Zionism and Christian Zionism. He paused and looked me in the eye, saying, "I have recently come to the conclusion that political Zionism and Christian Zionism are biblically anathema to Christian faith."

At the end of the sermon, Stott makes the case in gentler terms.

1. The Old Testament promises about the Jews' return to the land are [accompanied] by promises of the Jews' return to the Lord. It is hard to see how the secular, unbelieving state of Israel can possibly be a fulfillment of those prophecies.

2. The Old Testament promises about the land are nowhere repeated in the New Testament. The prophecy of Romans 11 is a prophecy that many, many Jews will turn to Christ, but the land is not mentioned nor is Israel mentioned as a political entity.

3. The Old Testament promises according to the apostles are fulfilled in Christ and in the international community of Christ. The New Testament authors apply the promise of Abraham's seed to Jesus Christ. And they apply to Jesus Christ the promise of the land and all the land which is inherited, the land flowing with milk and honey, because it is in him that our hunger is satisfied and our thirst quenched. A return to Jewish nationalism would seem incompatible with this New Testament perspective of the international community of Jesus.[11]

To summarize, the New Testament deemphasizes the role of land and concentrates on the faithful community, who through Jesus Christ are brought into the kingdom of God. The faithful remnant concept of Isaiah is continued and elevated in the New Testament. The premillennial dispensationalist doctrine, which creates two separate tracks for God's faithful people and the chosen people, creates serious problems. The biblical record appears to elevate the role of the church, whereas the dispensationalists remove the church from history.

In their zeal to support Israel, the Christian Zionists contradict the message of Jesus and the New Testament concerning mission and the believing community. The theological switch, which places modern Israel above the church as God's instrument in the latter days, misses the essential teachings of Jesus, the early Christian writers, and the Reformation theologians.

This theological diversion was prominent in the teachings of John Nelson Darby, viewed by many as the father of futurist premillennialism (see chapter 8). Darby stated this clearly in his lecture, "The Hope of the Church of God."

> Israel is the theater upon which God has displayed all his character . . . It is in this people, by the ways of God revealed to them, that the character of Jehovah is fully revealed, that the nations will know Jehovah, and that we shall ourselves learn to know him.[12]

Israel replaces the church in dispensational theology. The Darby system and that of those who follow in his footsteps, repeats the Judaizing heresy Paul fought in Galatians.

Many dispensationalists believe their theology is consistent with the ancient church and Scripture. It is not. In the New Testament there is no elevation of Israel, either as a people, nation, or land, above the church and the faithful remnant.

Israel and Eschatology

The basic hermeneutical method of Christian Zionism (and other forms of dispensationalism) is the projection into the future of several Old Testament and New Testament promises. This is another major flaw in Christian Zionist doctrine. Consider, for example, Malcolm Hedding's defense of Christian Zionism.

> The biblical teaching, however, that requires a Christian Zionist position is also found in the New Testament. Firstly, Jesus himself spoke of the scattering and latter-day regathering of the Jewish people (Luke 21:23-24). Indeed, he placed their second regathering in an eschatological setting (Luke 21:28). Thus Christian Zionists simply seek to give voice to that which Jesus himself has already said, namely; that the modern day restoration of the state of Israel is not a political accident, or merely the result of a secular political Zionist plot but rather the fulfillment of God's own word.[13]

What the Christian Zionists fail to note is the fact that these New Testament texts say nothing about the restoration of Israel or Jerusalem to the land. Rather, the texts point to the destruction of Jerusalem, which occurred under the Romans in 66-70 C.E., later culminating in the Bar Cochba revolt and massacre at Massada (132-135 C.E.). These texts were already fulfilled. Moreover, to develop a theology of the future on the basis of three or four selected texts, often out of their context, misses the point of the biblical message of salvation. There is no future realm called the "Time of the Gentiles." Nor is this topic discussed anywhere else in Scripture. If it were a central doctrine, it would certainly be discussed elsewhere.

Jesus himself was aware of this form of misinterpretation because it was popular in his own time. This highly speculative interpretative method, called Apocalypticism, had been in vogue since the dark days of the Maccabean Revolt (167-164 B.C.E.). It may have been the primary hermeneutical tool of the Qumran community of Dead Sea scrolls fame. Among the extra-biblical works found at the Qumran Library were eschatological texts that referred to a future restoration of the Jewish people in the "holy" land. The topic often came up in Jesus' ministry, and at least two disciples—Simon the Zealot and Judas Iscariot—seem to have subscribed to a form of this theology.

According to the biblical account, just prior to his ascension into heaven (Acts 1:6-9), Jesus met his disciples for the last time. They were well aware that this would be their final meeting with Jesus in person, and no doubt they had several vital questions about their responsibilities. I have often thought of placing myself in their shoes and wondered what I would ask Jeus. In a nutshell, the entire Christian mission and ministry of Christ was about to be turned over to this ragtag group. Suddenly two disciples ask, "Lord, is this the time when you will restore the kingdom to Israel?" (v. 6).

It was as if these disciples were saying, "Well, Lord, we were truly impressed by the miracles you performed while we labored with you. We were inspired as well by your great teachings. Then the resurrection was truly fantastic. But now, will you do the 'big one?' Will you restore the kingdom to Israel now and drive the Romans from our land?"

I think the Lord needed to employ every bit of his sense of humor at this point. I can see him saying, half in jest, and half seriously, "I don't believe it! Where have you people been for the past three years? You've missed the point of everything!"

Then Jesus became very harsh with the disciples. The text states, "It is not for you to know the times or periods that the Father has set by his own authority" (v. 7). This is a clear word from the Lord to the futurist dispensationalists and apocalypticists. God does not ask us to use the Bible as a timetable to predict historical events. Instead, we are encouraged to trust in God as the sovereign Lord over all history and to live the gospel of the kingdom today and every day.

Jesus gave clear directives to the disciples in the very next verse, "But you shall receive power when the Holy Spirit has come upon you; and you will be my witnesses in Jerusalem, in all Judea and Samaria and to the ends of the earth." This event took place on the eve of Pentecost, the birthday of the Christian church. Here Jesus was telling the disciples not to place their trust in nor devote their energy to endtime prophecy or the militant Zionist ideology of the Zealots.

Instead, the disciples are told they will "receive power when the Holy Spirit has come upon" them at Pentecost. This is a clear imperative statement to work in the church under the power of the Holy Spirit, trusting in God's power alone.

And when the disciples, at Pentecost and today, receive the power of the Holy Spirit, Jesus states that we will become his witnesses. The Greek word for "witnesses" is derived from the root word *martyrion* or martyr. The implication is that once Jesus' disciples receive the power of the Holy Spirit, they will be faithful in proclaiming Christ's love, even unto death.

The Acts 1:6-8 passage has its antecedent in Luke 24, the story of two disciples walking to Emmaus, fearing for their lives as they fled Jerusalem after the crucifixion. A stranger joined them, and they discussed Scripture as they walked. Then they stopped to break bread together, a reminder of the Lord's Supper. It was at the table, in this sacramental experience, that "their eyes were opened." Then they knew that Jesus was alive, and he "vanished out of their sight" (v. 31).

The two disciples were revitalized in their faith and their ministry was empowered by the Spirit of the resurrected Christ. This chapter is parallel to the ascension passage of Acts 1, where again Jesus challenged disciples whose vision for the kingdom was limited by faulty hermeneutics and limited faith. The ministry of proclaiming the kingdom *now*, not later, was left in their hands as empowered by the Holy Spirit in the church.

Another remarkable aspect of the Emmaus story is the total change of direction it represents for the disciples. They had been running from Jerusalem, perhaps anticipating additional crucifixions and persecution from the Roman and Jewish authorities. Immediately after the eucharistictic faith experience (a mini-Pentecost preview), the disciples turn back to Jerusalem. They find the eleven and tell them, "The Lord has risen indeed."

As they were talking, Jesus appeared to them (Luke 24:36-49). Again he "opened their minds" and expounded upon the Scriptures (v. 45). Then he commanded them to preach "repentance and forgiveness of sins . . . in his name to all nations [Gentiles and Jews] beginning from Jerusalem" (v. 47).

The city of crucifixion now becomes the city of resurrection faith and the hub from which the message of salvation goes forth to Gentile and Jew alike. This is the true ministry of the church. Again Jesus followed with the same mandate: "You are witnesses of these things. And see, I am sending upon you what my Father promised; so stay here in the city until you have been clothed with power from on high" (vv. 48-49).

Translated for us today, Jesus' command for mission are the same: "Go to the Jerusalems, the urban centers, the places of population density and strife. Proclaim the kingdom of God to all people, not for the elect or restricted to those of your own race and class." The kingdom has begun with the first coming of Jesus Christ. His followers, the church, are called to proclaim and live its power now (not later) as a gift of the Holy Spirit.

There is no sense in awaiting a future fulfillment of biblical promises, a form of interpretation that Jesus counseled against. The only things we are told to anticipate are the receiving of the Holy Spirit and Jesus' promised return, the timing and manner of which are unknown to us. Our task is to be faithful witnesses now, living in the kingdom of God which has already come and contrives to break through to the suffering, the lost, the victims of injustice and darkness. This joyful task can only be fulfilled through the community of believers, the church, as they are granted the grace and power of the Holy Spirit.

8

Backing into the Future: Britain and Zion

*T*his generation is an evil generation; it asks for a sign, but no sign
will be given to it except the sign of Jonah.
Luke 11:29

The library at the British Museum in London is a remarkable place in which to conduct research. It contains many historical treasures of Western civilization and priceless literary works. Thanks to a wonderful friend and former Member of Parliament, I was able to obtain an entrance card, giving me access to special literary collections not open to the public.

I entered the library with an extensive bibliography and requested three documents dating back to the late 1500 to mid-1600 C.E. era. In ten minutes a young woman delivered three ancient texts to my table. I carefully removed the old rope that held one volume together and looked at the title page. I realized I was holding one of the oldest monographs on Christian Zionism in the English language. *Apocalypsis Apocalypseos,* a pamphlet of less than fifty pages, was written by Thomas Brightman in the year 1585. To my knowledge, *Apocalypsis* is the first Christian publication in English that calls for the creation of a Jewish state in Palestine in order to fulfill biblical prophecy.

Historian Barbara Tuchman's outstanding work *Bible and Sword* has explored the curious history of England's fascination with the Jews, citing

a body of literature that dates back to the fourth century C.E. A more critical volume, *Non-Jewish Zionism*, by Regina Sharif, analyzes much of the
same material from the standpoint of the literature's pro-Zionist bias.
Read in tandem, the two volumes offer the two sides of debate on this
body of material.

It should be noted here that interpreting certain biblical texts with an
anticipation of future fulfillment is an approach dating back to the book
of Daniel and perhaps to the influence of Persian religions. Our purpose
in this chapter is to concentrate on one particular school of this style and
examine its western development in England and the United States.[1]

Tuchman cites *The Epistle of Gildas*, written in the sixth century C.E.,
as the first attempt to interpret British history through the framework of
Israel's history, using such biblical texts as Joshua's conquest of the
Canaanites (Joshua 1-12). One hundred years later, The Venerable Bede's
(673-735 C.E.) *Ecclesiastical History*, which many scholars feel may be the
first major literary work in the English language, followed similar themes
of interpretation.[2]

Brightman, a priest in the Church of England, added the novel idea
that all Christians (and all of England) had a moral responsibility to support a state for the Jews in Palestine. Brightman believed that the restoration of the Jews in Palestine was necessary if Britain was to be blessed by
God when history entered its latter days and the prophetic texts of Scripture were fulfilled.

Brightman's argument was grounded in a particular interpretation of
apocalyptic passages from such prophetic texts as Daniel 7—12, Ezekiel
38—39, and the book of Revelation. The futurist premillennial dispensationalist method of biblical interpretation was generally unknown
in established Christian circles of this era. This interpretative system,
which views prophetic texts as pointing toward a future fulfillment, came
into prominence in the nineteenth century.

When Brightman proposed that the Jews be reconstituted as a nation
and "return to their land" in order that they not "strive any longer as
strangers and inmates with foreign nations," [3] he drew a curious and often hostile reaction. In fact, he was forced to take his views underground
and developed a secret following.

As I read through these pages in their original Elizabethan English, I
experienced a sense of timelessness. I felt that aside from the archaic language and style, I could be reading a volume written by Hal Lindsey, Pat
Robertson, or Jerry Falwell. Many of the theological ideas were the same
themes used by twentieth-century evangelical Christians.

From his underground fellowship, Brightman planted the seeds of a
doctrine that would bear fruit in a generation. In this sense, he should be
seen as the British forerunner of Christian Zionism, a type of John the
Baptist in this field. He assimilated various Christian teachings concerning Israel and the endtimes while developing a theology based on Jewish

restoration in Palestine. While there may have been others before him, Brightman is the first futurist premillennial dispensationalist whose writings are available to us today.

One of Brightman's followers was a member of the British Parliament and also the preeminent legal expert of his time. Sir Henry Finch served in a role comparable to that of the present attorney general of the United States. In 1621 his views on Christian Zionism were published in the controversial pamphlet *The World's Great Restauration [sic] or Calling of the Jews and (with them) all the Nations of the Earth, to the Faith of Christ.*

I untied another shabby cloth ribbon and started to read Finch's remarkable volume, feeling a deep sense of privilege in that few have had the opportunity to read this work during the previous three centuries. A quarter of the way through the pamphlet I read this following paragraph:

> "Where Israel, Judah, Zion and Jerusalem are named, the Holy Ghost meant not the spiritual Israel, or the Church of God collected of the Gentiles or of Jews and Gentiles both—but Israel properly descended out of Jacob's loynes . . . these and such like are not allegories, setting forth on terrene similitudes or deliverance through Christ but meant literally and really the Jews." [4]

In my estimation, this is the most important paragraph in Finch's pamphlet. It states the basic hermeneutical principle of Christian Zionism more clearly than did Brightman. Finch synthesized the literal interpretation of key prophetic Scriptures with a premillennial dispensationalist eschatology. Prior to this time, these texts were interpreted either in an allegorical or symbolic manner. Therefore, Finch did not interpret the Israel of the Bible in terms of the church or the faithful remnant—but literally as modern Jews to whom God would grant future fulfillment in a nation-state. Finch's hermeneutics would not become popular until the British evangelical movement refined them two hundred years later.

Additionally, Finch's writings had considerable political implications. One must remember that Finch had access to the highest echelons of power in England. Once his volume appeared, it stimulated broad debate and his reputation gave it a significant hearing. More important were the political and demographic ramifications of Finch's ideas, such as the following statement: "[The Jews] shall repair to their own country—shall inhabit all the parts of the land as before, [they] shall live in safety, and shall continue in it forever." [5]

One might have asked, "Who will insure that the Jews will return?" At that time there were few Jews in Palestine, perhaps less than 2 percent of the population. What of the Palestinian Arab majority? Was there no concern for the well-being of the indigenous Christian community there?

Finch was arrested shortly after his pamphlet was issued, he was tried for treason, and eventually released after he disavowed any passages that might have been construed as antagonistic toward King James. Ironically, the antimonarchy movement, which later led to the Cromwell Revolution, used similar language, although they did not adopt a futurist eschatology calling for Jews to return to the "holy" land. Instead, the anti-monarchists saw themselves fulfilling the role of the chosen people, and they proceeded to act on their convictions following the beheading of King Charles II in 1646.

The brief success of Cromwell's experiment gave credence to various Christian Zionist themes for a brief period, as the writings of Milton, Dryden, and others attest. However, the failure of Cromwell's Revolution forced the Christian Zionist views underground again, due to the political changes brought by the restored monarchy. Christian Zionist themes were not to be revived for another one hundred years.

The revival came at the end of the eighteenth century as people anticipated the next millennium. It is not accidental that Christian Zionism and millennial thinking has become popular in decades prior to the turn of a century, as was the case in the 1590s, 1690s, 1790s, 1890s (as we shall observe later in this chapter), and is the case during the late 1970s-1990s.

The revival during the 1790-1800 period was a direct result of the turmoil Europeans felt in the wake of the French and American revolutions coupled with the approach of a new century. The British, like Europeans on the continent, began to feel that their world was falling apart. People turned away from new secular philosophy and political answers and embraced a more fundamentalist form of Christian teachings that included a revived form of prophetic interpretations of the Bible. In this troubled and uncertain climate, Christian Zionism began to take root.

One of the first organizations to emerge from the new trend was the London Society for Promoting Christianity Among the Jews (LSPCJ). Their journal, *The Jewish Expositor*, was read by many influential British academics, clergy, and intellectuals. One of the British literary figures who subscribed to the journal was the brilliant but eccentric writer Samuel Taylor Coleridge. He became a serious supporter of the LSPCJ and appears to have subscribed to many of the Christian Zionists' beliefs.

Undoubtedly the most influential figure in the development of Christian Zionism was John Nelson Darby, originally a minister in the Church of England. I had often heard his name mentioned as the founder of the Plymouth Brethren movement but knew little about him. A quick background check and a perusal of several volumes of his collected writings revealed that Darby was a deeply spiritual, compassionate, and talented Christian leader.

Born during the year 1800, when the West seemed to be falling apart, he was a product of his times, revolting against authoritarian church structures and turning to more literalistic interpretations of the Bible to provide answers for an uncertain future. Darby believed the state churches of England and Ireland were hopelessly corrupt. As an alternative, Darby chose to establish a house church movement. These smaller fellowships provided the intimacy and purity he felt was necessary for believers to remain faithful to the Lord during the final days of history.

The Plymouth Brethren focused on Bible prophecy and predicted increased corruption of the "worldly" churches and the nations in the latter days. They built a large and significant movement in Europe and North America by calling upon true believers to leave the corrupted churches and stand against the evils of the day. The evil forces would be personified in a world leader called the Antichrist.

By the time Darby died in 1885, there were over 1500 Plymouth Brethren fellowships worldwide. As early as the mid-1830s, Darby personally established Brethren fellowships in Germany, Switzerland, France, and throughout the British Isles. They later spread to Africa, the United States and Canada, the West Indies, and eventually reached as far as Australia and New Zealand. During his lifetime, Darby wrote more hymns than the Wesleys, traveled further on missionary journeys than the Apostle Paul, and was a Greek and Hebrew scholar. His writings filled forty volumes.[6]

Darby was both charming and charismatic. He was fond of children and went out of his way to develop positive relationships with them. One of my favorite stories about him took place during one of his seven missionary journeys to the United States. On a Sunday afternoon following worship services, Darby decided to dine with a humble family from one of the Plymouth Brethren fellowships. He generally avoided hotels and fancy restaurants, choosing instead to stay with poorer families.

When Darby and the family sat down to eat, he asked the boy why he was so sad on such a delightful occasion. The lad blurted out that his parents had cooked his pet rabbit. Refusing to eat another bite, Darby excused himself and left the table with the young boy. They walked to a nearby pond. Darby produced several toy ducks from his pocket and entertained his new friend for the entire afternoon. The two returned much later, the little lad beaming with joy.

If Brightman was the father of Christian Zionism, then Darby was its greatest apostle and missionary, the apostle Paul of the movement. Darby spread its teachings to every continent and was a persuasive speaker, capable of inspiring large or small audiences to adopt his perspective.

Following 1862, Darby's primary arena of influence shifted to North America, where he eventually completed seven missionary journeys. In more than twenty years of travel to the United States and Canada, he became personally acquainted with the emerging leaders of the new Bible and Prophecy Conference movement, which set the tone for the evangelical and fundamentalist movements in North America between 1875 and 1920. Darby had direct contact with and considerable influence on such evangelical leaders as the Presbyterian James Brooks of Philadelphia; Dwight L. Moody of Chicago; the early evangelical author, William E. Blackstone; C. I. Scofield of Scofield Bible fame; and many others.

Two aspects of Darby's theology merit special comment, inasmuch as they represent a significant departure from historic Christian doctrine. Darby's unique contribution rested not only in his futurist premillennial dispensationalism. As we have seen, these views were known throughout the British Isles at least since the Elizabethan era. Darby's practical role came in his linking futurist dispensational theology with two unique aspects of ecclesiology (doctrine of the church).

First, he taught that the church would have a limited role, what he called a mere "parenthesis," during the latter days. In an essay titled "The Present Dispensation," Darby wrote,

> The Church has sought to settle itself here; but it has no place on the earth. . . . [Though] making a most constructive parenthesis, it forms no part of the regular order of God's earthly plans, but is merely an interruption of them to give a fuller character and meaning to them (the Jews).[7]

Thus did Darby reduce the body of Christ from its central role in the New Testament as the locus of the Holy Spirit and collective expression of Christ's ministry on earth, to a nebulous parenthesis status. Replacing the church in Darby's scheme was the nation Israel.

Second, Darby introduced a new doctrine called the "pre-tribulation rapture." Through this theological maneuver he removed "born again" Christians from history at a time of considerable warfare called "the Great Tribulation." According to Darby, the nation Israel will become the primary instrument to carry out God's will. This novel twist becomes a central doctrine in Darby's dispensational eschatology and a foundation for contemporary Christian Zionism.

Like many of today's televangelists and political Christian Zionists, Darby believed that, following the rapture, a final battle will take place at the end of history. Jesus' second coming will occur in two stages. First, Darby interpreted 1 Thessalonians 4:14ff. in literal and futurist terms, believing that all Christian believers will literally vanish to meet Christ in the clouds at an appointed time. The tribulation, or reign of terror, will end seven years later when Jesus returns to establish his millennial kingdom in Jerusalem.

Some contemporary dispensationalists debate whether Christ will return at the midpoint of the seven year tribulation. Hence they are mid-tribulationists. Pre-tribulationists see Jesus returning prior to the tribulation and post-tribulationists believe Christians will go through the suffering and then Jesus will return. Nevertheless, this double second-coming doctrine is another departure from historic Christianity.

In Darby's own day, his chief assistant, B. W. Newton, saw the error of these teachings and confronted him. Newton believed Darby's thinking had departed from historic Christianity concerning the pre-tribulation rapture and the dual second-coming doctrine. For Newton, the teachings were heretical; he warned the Brethren to beware of this false gospel. The original Plymouth fellowship split as Newton and several followers departed.

Darby's new teachings remained strong in England and were largely adopted by the emerging evangelical movement. The great British philanthropist and architect of Britain's child labor reform, Lord Shaftesbury, was convinced of Darby's teachings. Known as the "Evangelical of Evangelicals," Shaftesbury became the champion of the poor and a leader of the influential Clapham Sect. This small fellowship consisted of important evangelical Christians who were also statesmen and philanthropists. The Clapham Sect in the generation that preceded Shaftesbury included William Wilberforce, credited with abolishing slavery in England.

A lesser known aspect of Shaftesbury's faith and life was his passionate devotion to Christian Zionism. In 1839 Shaftesbury published a thirty-page essay in the distinguished British journal *Quarterly Review*, entitled "State and Restauration of the Jews." The article began with a review of the suffering of the Jews, God's chosen people, and the claim that a new age was dawning for the Jews. Shaftesbury pointed out that "the Jews must be encouraged to return [to Palestine] in yet greater numbers and become once more the husbandman of Judea and Galilee."

Shaftesbury then submitted two pragmatic, political suggestions for Britain: (1) that Britain play the critical political role in allowing Jews to return to power and presence in ancient Palestine; (2) that the Church of England establish a bishopric and cathedral in Jerusalem.

Shaftesbury cited both spiritual and political motivations for England's role in implementing Jewish restoration to Palestine. He noted that Britain would be cooperating with the very plan of God and fulfill biblical prophecy should the nation choose to pursue this course. God would surely bless England, as promised in Genesis 12:3, "I will bless those who bless you." Demonstrating keen political insight, Shaftesbury saw three distinct advantages for England in this plan: (1) England would outpace France in the colonial competition to control the Near East; (2) England would be insured a direct land passage to India, the "jewel" of the British Empire; (3) vast commercial markets would be opened for British economic interests.

It was not a mere coincidence that these political goals matched those of the British Foreign Office concerning the Near East. Through the Clapham Sect and his shrewd political networking, Shaftesbury had gained access to the latest thinking within the Foreign Office. His next step was to take out a paid advertisement in the *London Times* on November 4, 1840, to give public visibility to his vision. The advertisement stated in part,

RESTORATION OF THE JEWS: A memorandum has been addressed to the Protestant monarchs of Europe on the subject of the restoration of the Jewish people to the land of Palestine. The document in question, dictated by a peculiar conjunction of affairs in the East, and other striking 'signs of the times,' reverts to the original covenant which secures that land to the descendants of Abraham.[8]

One cannot overstate the influence of Lord Shaftesbury on the British political elite, church leaders, and the average Christian layperson. His efforts and religious-political thought may have set the tone for England's colonial approach to the Near East and in particular to the "holy" land during the next one hundred years. He singlehandedly translated the theological positions of Brightman, Henry Finch, and John Nelson Darby into a political strategy. His high political connections, matched by his uncanny instincts, combined to advance the Christian Zionist vision.

Lord Shaftesbury, like Moses, did not see his hopes for the Promised Land come to fruition during his lifetime. However, his careful and extensive work with British parliamentarians insured that others would become the Joshuas and Calebs carrying the mantle on his behalf. Lord Shaftesbury's dream of placing an Anglican bishopric and cathedral in Jerusalem was realized during his lifetime, with the establishment of St. George's Anglican Cathedral in 1843. Interestingly, the first Anglican bishop was a former rabbi, Michael Alexander. The one hundred fiftieth anniversary of his consecration was commemorated in 1993 by the present bishop, a Palestinian, Samir Kafity.

Through his writings, public speaking, and lobbying efforts, Lord Shaftesbury did more than anyone before him to translate Christian Zionist themes into a political initiative. In addition to influencing British colonial perceptions of the Near East, Shaftesbury also predisposed the next generation of British Conservative politicians favorably toward the World Zionist movement, which led eventually to British support of the Jewish state.

A final (albeit unknown) contribution of Shaftesbury, was his formulation of a form of the phrase that became the slogan of the Zionist movement: "A land of no people for a people with no land." Zionist leaders Israel Zangwell and Theodor Herzl are credited with this slogan, but it is likely that they borrowed it from Lord Shaftesbury, who first cast the idea somewhat differently a generation before them: "A country without a nation for a nation without a country." He advanced the theme during the 1840s, more than fifty years before the Zionist movement held its first Congress.[9]

The vision of Lord Shaftesbury found an immediate advocate in F. Laurence Oliphant (1829-88), a highly influential member of Parliament in his day and a committed evangelical Christian. Oliphant had advocated in Parliament that the British should undertake to revitalize the Ottoman Empire through various means at its disposal, including the settlement of a large number of Jews in Palestine. He made several visits to Palestine to study the feasibility of the project and became convinced that it was a worthwhile idea.

In 1880, Oliphant published *The Land of Gilead*, a book in which he argued in favor of the Zionists' themes. He then called on the British Parliament to support the settlement of Jews from Russia and Eastern Europe in Palestine. How ironic it is that, exactly one hundred years later, the United States pursued similar policies in cooperation with Israeli political authorities. This took place as hundreds of thousands of Jews from the former Soviet Union were moved into West Bank settlements, with an intensive concentration in East Jerusalem. Oliphant addressed the fate of the Palestinians by simply recommending that they be placed on reservations, like the Native Americans or as seen in the Bantustan concept, later used in South Africa.[10]

While Oliphant had a deep evangelical Christian Zionist orientation and advocated a political solution for the Jews based on his particular theology, he did not focus his energy as efficiently as did Shaftesbury. Oliphant was a political and religious maverick, and his colleagues were aware of this. Had he possessed the strategic abilities and consistency of Shaftesbury, history might have seen the Zionist ideas bear fruit much earlier.

By the time the World Zionist Congress met in Basle, Switzerland, in 1897, the way had been prepared for high level British politicians to support the Zionist program. The final steps of Zionist political lobbying of the British began with Theodor Herzl, the father of political Zionism, who died at the young age of forty. His efforts were followed by those of Chaim Weitzmann, a professor of chemistry at the University of Manchester in England. By 1905, Weitzmann began to meet with the leading member of the Conservative Party, Lord Arthur James Balfour.

Having been raised in an evangelical home, Balfour was predisposed to the Zionist positions solely on the basis of his limited understanding of the Bible. He subscribed to a simple, layperson's version of the premillennial dispensational theology. Predisposed as he was to Zionism, Balfour met Chaim Weitzmann in London on January 9, 1906. Balfour stated in a letter to his wife, written the evening of that day, that he saw "no political difficulty about obtaining Palestine, only economic ones." [11]

Weitzmann led the Zionist subgroup in lobbying for Palestine as the future Jewish homeland—in opposition to other Zionists who were campaigning for Uganda, Rhodesia, Argentina, or perhaps a section of Utah or Arizona in the United States.

According to Balfour's niece, Blanche Dugdale, the conversation with Weitzmann on that day convinced Balfour that the Jewish homeland could be established only in Palestine. Shortly before his death, Balfour told his niece, "It was from that talk with Weitzmann that I saw that the Jewish form of patriotism was unique. Their love of their country refused to be satisfied by the Uganda scheme. It was Weizmann's absolute refusal even to look at it that impressed me." [12] This meeting between the two men blossomed into the famous declaration eleven years later.

On November 2, 1917, Lord Balfour, then foreign secretary for the government of England, wrote the following memorandum to the prominent British Jew Lord Rothschild:

His Majesty's Government views with favour the establishment in Palestine of a national home for the Jewish people, and will use their best endeavors to facilitate the achievement of this object, it being clearly understood that nothing shall be done which may prejudice the civil and religious rights of the existing non-Jewish communities in Palestine, or the rights and political status enjoyed by Jews in any other country.[13]

This single declaration gave the Zionist movement its first political legitimacy in history and created a platform for its leaders to accelerate colonization of Palestine (a matter we will discuss in chapter 12). In many ways, Balfour's classic colonialist declaration was the undoing of the Palestinian people.

Ironically, when the declaration was issued, over 90 percent of the population in Palestine was Palestinian Arab, including 18 to 20 percent Christians. Apparently this was of little importance to both the British and the Jewish Zionists, who were intent on achieving their own agenda. The British then provided the international and regional guarantees for the Zionist movement to accelerate the settlement of Jews in Palestine. The Zionist strategy had won the day.

Lord Balfour's attitudes toward Arabs are a matter of public record. Of equal significance are his attitudes toward Jews in general. As a member of Parliament, Balfour opposed various legislative attempts to allow Jews to settle in England while they were undergoing pogroms in eastern Europe. Balfour apparently preferred to enforce a settlement several thousand miles away rather than allow Jews to become his neighbors in London.

The same views that Balfour, Oliphant, and Shaftesbury had articulated were held by none other than the new prime minister of England during World War I, David Lloyd-George. Lloyd-George's Christian Zionism was even more ardent than Balfour's version. He had been raised in Wales by a maternal uncle, Richard George, lay preacher in a millenarian Baptist church. Uncle Richard insured that young David would have a solid evangelical upbringing and educational foundation by enrolling him in a strict evangelical school atmosphere. Lloyd-George later described his education: "I was brought up in a school where there was taught far more about the history of the Jews than the history of my own land." [14]

One of Lloyd-George's critical biographers, Christopher Sykes, was aware that his own father had signed the secret Sykes-Picot Agreement which undermined the future independence of many Arabs. An eminent British journalist, Sykes wrote that prior to the Paris Peace Accords (1919),[15] advisers attempted to brief the prime minister concerning the central issues with which he would need to be conversant. After interviewing the advisers, Sykes concluded that Lloyd-George was unable to grasp the issues in the Palestine settlement, largely because he could not move beyond the Christian Zionist worldview of his youth. When briefed repeatedly on the contemporary geography of Palestine, Lloyd-George insisted on reciting from his memory of childhood Sunday school lessons the biblical cities and lands of Bible times, some of which no longer existed.

Thus the two most influential political leaders in England during World War I were committed Christian Zionists. Their childhood training in evangelical churches or schools had predisposed them to adopt the program of the new World Zionist Movement. Moreover, these views remained with them throughout their political lives and facilitated the British colonial predisposition toward Zionist interests and the disenfranchisement of the Palestinian people following World War I.

9

Inside the Christian Embassy

I saw no temple in the city, for its temple is the Lord God the
Almighty and the Lamb. . . . The nations will walk by its light,
and the kings of the earth will bring their glory into it.
Revelation 21:22, 24

It was February 1988, at the height of the Intifada (the Palestinian uprising, with the literal translation being "the shaking off"). Kathy Bergen,
then Mennonite staff in Jerusalem, and I decided to visit the International
Christian Embassy-Jerusalem (ICEJ) in their West Jerusalem headquarters. The organization had been very active in the early to mid-1980s but
was relatively silent at the moment. A colleague told us they were planning a major event for the spring of 1988 that would involve Western
evangelical Christians in the celebration of Israel's fortieth birthday.

The trip from Kathy's office in East Jerusalem to the busy shopping
district and embassy section of West Jerusalem is only a mile, but the
physical, cultural, religious, and political contrasts are immense. Israel
proper, including West Jerusalem, has a Western flavor that reminds one
of Western Europe or the United States. Arab East Jerusalem, the West
Bank, and Gaza Strip are distinctively Arab and belong in every way to the
East. By early 1988, the Intifada had served to deepen the separation between the two societies.

Palestinians were greatly empowered during this period as they employed a variety of resistance strategies against the Israeli occupation, then entering its twenty-first year in the Occupied Territories and fortieth year in the Galilee. Businesses closed promptly at noon in Jerusalem, a great personal sacrifice for the shopkeepers. Palestinian youth confronted the Israeli military with a boldness that left the army thoroughly confused. Palestinians everywhere were energized by this slight taste of freedom and self-determination, which was to last more than three years.

Brenner Street, where the embassy was located, was in a well-to-do section of older homes in West Jerusalem, just four blocks from the prime minister's house. The recent history of the Christian Embassy is traceable to the summer of 1980, when several nations removed their embassies from Jerusalem in response to passage by the Israeli Knesset (Parliament) of the Jerusalem Bill which declared Jerusalem its eternal capital. Thirteen embassies moved to Tel Aviv, stating that Israel had violated international law by this decision, and they would not grant legitimacy to such an illegal action. When Chile moved to Tel Aviv, Israel turned the building on Brenner Street over to the International Christian Embassy.

As we stood outside the building, I recalled that the structure was once the home of the Said family, whose son is the well-known Palestinian-American scholar and author, Edward Said, of Columbia University. In 1948, the Saids evacuated their home during the battle for Jerusalem and settled for several months in Cairo. When they returned, the famous Jewish philosopher Martin Buber had been given their fully furnished home; he refused to leave. It seems that even this great man of peace and understanding had a blind spot when it came to the Palestinians.[1]

We entered the beautiful stone home and received a warm welcome from the receptionist. She encouraged us to watch a video of the First Christian Zionist congress, organized by the ICEJ in Basel, Switzerland, in 1985. The Congress was held in the same hall where Theodor Herzl had launched the Zionist movement in 1897. I found the video revealing and could not miss the extent to which the ICEJ provides a contemporary Christian adoption and advocacy of the more militant Likud brand of political Zionism.

I returned to the receptionist and asked about the Second Christian Zionist Congress, scheduled for April 1988. She encouraged me to attend and added, "We are hoping for between 5000 and 7000 participants in April but are finding that people are reluctant to come. The trouble those Arabs are causing is giving Israel a bad image in the media. But we have staff in at least twenty-five countries who are recruiting and we should do well."

I asked whether the director or spokesman was available for a brief meeting. She responded, "The spokesman is out of the country, but Mr. Luckhoff, our director, is here. Let me see if he is free." Within two minutes I was taken to his spacious office.

Johann Luckoff is a warm, bespectacled man in his midfifties. His heavy South African accent rolled off his tongue as he said, "Welcome to the Christian Embassy. What brings you to Jerusalem?"

I described my interest in the Arab-Israeli conflict and research on Christian Zionism, not wanting to say much about my relationship to the Middle East Council of Churches.

Luckoff picked up on my comment about Christian Zionism and asked, "Tell me about your work on Christian Zionism and how you are approaching the subject."

I described the historical research I had been conducting and referred to the documents I had read in the British Museum on Christian Zionism, some dating back to 1585.

"This is remarkable!" Luckoff said, leaning forward in his chair. "Please, tell me more."

I went on to discuss my reading of Thomas Brightman, Henry Finch, Henry Drummond, Lord Shaftesbury, and the others leading up to Lord Balfour himself.

He replied, "This is fascinating. Would you be willing to deliver a paper or lecture at our upcoming conference?"

The offer presented me with an interesting predicament. I had not expected this question. I was appreciative of the invitation but clearly could not accept it. To be listed on the program of the ICEJ would undermine my credibility in the Arab countries and destroy whatever trust I had established with Palestinians and other Arab Christians. We parted cordially and I left the room in disbelief.

Two months later our family returned to Jerusalem, arriving on the day the Second Christian Zionist Congress began. On April 10, my wife and I walked through the doors of the Christian Zionist Congress with several friends.

To my surprise, within two minutes, Luckoff spotted me at the registration table. "Oh, Reverend Wagner," he exclaimed, "welcome back. Have you reconsidered the possibility of doing a presentation? I have discussed your work with our board, and we all would like to have you address our Congress. Is there any possibility?"

Again, I needed to say, "No, I am honored, but I just won't be able to do it."

Luckoff was hurried and responded, "I need to go in a minute to meet Prime Minister Shamir, but I have one other request. Would you be willing to serve on our drafting committee that will write the conference declaration? This would be a good opportunity for us to get to know each other."

I thought it over for a minute, because it would give me the opportunity to understand these Christians on the other end of the political and theological spectrum. But in good conscience I could not do it. "I'm sorry, but unfortunately I have a number of meetings throughout the week, and it would not be right for me to do this," I said.

"I understand," Luckoff said graciously. An aide tugged on his coat, saying, "The prime minister is arriving in one minute. We must go." Luckoff excused himself and wished me an enjoyable stay.

As we entered the convention hall, we were confronted immediately with a barrage of images and an energized Western atmosphere. There was loud electronic music, singing, and about seventy-five dancers raising their arms in well-choreographed praise to Israel. Large banners greeted us with slogans such as "I will make my home in Zion." The songs were contemporary and all had Christian Zionist themes. The elaborate scene left me feeling uncomfortable.

Our group took seats in the middle of the hall; I stood to analyze the crowd while the dancers and chorus went into another song of praise for Israel. I was stunned to note that the audience was dramatically smaller than anticipated. Walking up and down the aisles as the singers and dancers went into a second number, I counted just under 750 people, trying to err on the high side (not counting the chorus and dancers on the stage). The overwhelming majority were white, elderly, and sat under banners indicating they were from Europe or the United States, plus a large delegation from South Africa. There were a handful of Africans and Asians but—to my knowledge—no Arabs.

Luckoff walked to the microphone to open the program. He mentioned the great speakers and events scheduled throughout the week, then introduced Yitzhak Shamir, prime minister of Israel. A diminutive man, Shamir has the overall appearance of a mean teddy bear. The audience stood and gave him a thunderous ovation as we sat silently.

Shamir's speech was devoid of spiritual content and seemed insensitive to a Christian audience. The Christian Zionists, however, absolutely loved him, even when he chided Christians about their lack of loyalty to Jews. Shamir's remarks concentrated on the Palestinian Intifada, which he characterized as a "force of evil" that was "endeavoring to undermine the stability of the country and safety of its citizens." He added,

> What is happening in Judea and Samaria and Gaza is a continuation of the Arabs' war against the Jewish people. We have not returned to 'Eretz Israel' to be frightened by rocks and stones and firebombs. Here we are and here we will stay forever.[2]

Immediately, the crowd was on its feet cheering, applauding, and yelling, "Praise the Lord," with hands waving above heads. I was fascinated by the scene: a militant secular Zionist politician, still wanted by the British as a terrorist until his election in 1983, receiving the affirmation a great Christian evangelist might be accorded at a revival. Shamir concluded his speech in fifteen to eighteen minutes, then left the stage, praising the ICEJ as "true friends of Israel."

History of the ICEJ

The International Christian Embassy-Jerusalem (ICEJ) opened its doors at 10 Brenner Street in West Jerusalem on September 20, 1980. The grand opening occurred ten days later in a ceremony at which Jerusalem's popular mayor, Teddy Kollek, praised the ICEJ for standing with Israel.

The visibility and international role of the ICEJ developed quickly as the Likud Party, a more militant Zionist group which viewed the West Bank, East Jerusalem, and the Gaza Strip as part of Israel, came to power under Prime Minister Menachem Begin. Likud found Christian Zionist organizations politically useful in gaining western evangelical Christian support for Israel's policies. Likud was also smart enough to know that the evangelical and fundamentalist communities represented Israel's largest potential block of political and economic support in the West.

By the mid-1980s, the ICEJ could boast of having "branch offices or representatives in thirty-eight countries throughout North and South America, Europe, Australia, Africa, and the Far East." [3] Its international network is significantly smaller today, but the ICEJ remains active in Jerusalem and many countries around the world. ICEJ representatives or offices can still be found in Washington, D.C.; Johannesburg, South Africa; the Netherlands; Finland; and Switzerland. Volunteers in fundamentalist and charismatic churches around the globe advocate ICEJ religious and political programming and seek to convey the ICEJ message wherever possible.

In Jerusalem the ICEJ staff varies in size from twenty-five to forty people, depending on the current level of activity and funding. Each fall, during their popular Feast of Tabernacles Week, the paid ICEJ staff number forty or more plus many volunteers. The *Jerusalem Post* has reported that the monthly budget of ICEJ is in the range of $80,000 (just under $1,000,000 annually), but I was unable to gain from ICEJ staff access to data that would confirm this number. [4] The ICEJ sources of income are veiled in secrecy.

The ICEJ Belief System

1. A Futurist Dispensationalist Eschatology

The leaders who established ICEJ in late 1979-1980 were from Western Christian fundamentalist and charismatic backgrounds. Virtually all of these leaders subscribed to the futurist premillennial dispensationalist eschatology and continue to be in general agreement with classic futurist dispensationalist teachings (as described in chapter 8). At the heart of their beliefs is the doctrine that the restoration of the Jews to Israel is a fulfillment of biblical prophecy. The existence of the modern state of Israel is viewed as being that fulfillment.

The current ICEJ director, Johann Luckoff, writes in the ICEJ publication, *A Christian Response to Jerusalem*, "The return to Zion from exile a second time (Isa.11:11) is a living testimony to God's faithfulness and his enduring covenant with the Jewish people." [5]

ICEJ's promotional literature for the Second Christian Zionist Leadership Congress (1988), states that "biblical Christian Zionism includes the following basic tenets: Belief that the restoration of the modern State of Israel is no political accident, but rather a visible fulfillment of God's word and promise" (Isa. 11:10-12; Jer. 31:10-20).[6]

The same themes that guided Thomas Brightman and Henry Finch, and those popularized by John Nelson Darby and the Scofield Bible, are at the heart of the ICEJ today.

2. The Holy Land

A second major plank in the ICEJ-Christian Zionist belief system holds that God gave the "holy" land to the Jewish people "as an everlasting possession." The plank states that "Israel is the rightful homeland of the Jewish people, being promised and bequeathed by God to Abraham as an everlasting possession and inheritance" (Gen. 17:7-8).[7]

Having defined the territory of the "holy" land as "the rightful homeland of the Jewish people," the ICEJ takes a political position on this controversial subject that is consistent with the Likud Party's. They go on to support the Likud Party on similar issues related to land, settlements, and peace negotiations with the Arabs. This position has been stated repeatedly in ICEJ literature. The "Declaration of the First International Christian Zionist Leadership Conference," (Aug. 27-29, 1985), clarified this position in Resolution 4, titled "All Nations Should Recognize Judea and Samaria as Belonging to Israel." The declaration said, "The Congress declares that Judea and Samaria (inaccurately termed 'the West Bank') are, and by biblical right as well as international law and practice ought to be, a part of Israel." [8]

This claim by ICEJ, like that of Israel's Likud Party in Israel, is erroneous on three counts. First, Israel is the only government in the world that takes this position. International consensus, on the other hand, states that the Israeli-occupied West Bank, East Jerusalem, and Gaza Strip come under the authority of the Fourth Geneva Conventions of 1949, as territories occupied as a result of war.

Second, the ICEJ's and Israel's use of the so-called biblical names for the territories attempts to invoke a divine argument, which essentially turns God into a cosmic real estate agent who favors one party in the conflict, the Jews. As we have seen (chapters 6 and 7), this view is inconsistent with the Hebrew Scriptures and is clearly at variance with the teachings of Jesus.

Third, the position of the entire world, aside from Israel and its Christian Zionist supporters, is that Israel should withdraw from the occupied territories in accordance with international law and United Nations resolutions 242 and 338, preferably through an international peace conference (U.N. General Assembly Resolution 38-58C). Most major church bodies in the United States and Canada, plus most European churches, take the same position. Attempts to resolve the conflict outside of the international conference and a legitimate international forum such as the United Nations will result in partial solutions, such as the Sept. 13, 1993, Middle East accords, but they do not address the basic issues in the Palestine question.

3. ICEJ's Eschatology

The ICEJ takes the standard futurist premillennial dispensationalist approach to Israel and eschatology, but with several contemporary political implications. Its view of the future is typically pessimistic. Conditions in the world will deteriorate according to their unique understanding of the Scriptures. The role of the true Christian becomes one of perpetual support for the modern State of Israel, which the Christian Zionists see as a criterion of faithfulness to God.

The ICEJ foresees all of life degenerating as history moves toward the final battle of Armageddon. In this ultimate battle, Israel will be challenged by the Antichrist and a coalition of nations.

> Nations will increasingly shut Israel out of their councils until they finally find themselves coming up against her at Armageddon (Zech. 14:2-3). Disaster will surely strike every nation that turns against Zion (Isa. 60:12). . . . Repeatedly the Bible states that the betrayal of Israel will be a major reason for the wrath of God being heaped upon the nations in the latter days.[9]

At times the ICEJ will speculate as to the identity of these nations. In a speech I attended at the Second Christian Zionist Congress in Jerusalem, ICEJ International Spokesman Jan van der Hoeven stated that he believes we have entered the time of the decline of Gentile nations and their power, but the Antichrist is alive today in Europe and likely to arise within the European Economic Community during the 1990s.[10]

Van der Hoeven also saw the massive settlement of Soviet Jews in the occupied territories during the early 1990s within this eschatological context:

> Now is the time to act and speak in behalf of Soviet Jewry. Jeremiah prophesied (Jer. 14:14-15) that the greatest exodus of all will come from the north and other lands; it will be of such magnitude that memories of the deliverance from Egypt will be eclipsed. It is my belief that the spiritual restoration of Israel prophesied by Ezekiel for the latter days cannot happen until this promise is fulfilled.[11]

4. Christians, Israel, and the "Holy" Land

Christians have a biblically mandated responsibility, according to the ICEJ, to "comfort and support the modern Jewish state." Their promotional brochure, *Prepare Ye the Way of the Lord*, states their position: "Did you know that God has his own plan and purpose for the land and people of Israel, and that we as Christians, as children of Abraham by faith, can have an integral part in this?" [12]

ICEJ interprets this "plan" of God as one of "comforting Israel" through a variety of activities. At this point the ICEJ has consistently compromised the essential evangelical mandate of Christian mission and evangelism. This decision represents a clear departure from the evangelical Christian doctrine, yet they continue to claim the label "evangelical."

Not only does the ICEJ compromise on the issue of mission as evangelistic outreach, but it subverts and diminishes the mission of the church to that of public servitude to a modern political State of Israel. Clearly, there are significant benefits to the ICEJ in doing so, including access to Israel's top political leaders, direct and indirect economic payoffs, significant media visibility and, perhaps most important, diplomatic status as an embassy. But to call these activities Christian is out of the question.

One additional point must be made in connection with the evangelistic outreach issue. On Christmas Day 1977, the Israeli Knesset passed a law making it illegal for anyone in Israel to proselytize or convert Jews from their Jewish beliefs. Then on February 2, 1993, a vote by the government of Israel to expel certain Messianic Jews from Israel sent a shockwave through evangelical Christians.

Despite the official ICEJ position on evangelism and its obvious compromise with the policies of Israeli authorities, the embassy remains under constant attack from various political leaders within Israel. The Israeli chairperson of the International Conference on Halacha and Jewish Women attacked the ICEJ in an extensive article. Featured prominently in the *Jerusalem Post*, which then reflected the positions of the Israeli government, the article warned Zionist leaders to "be aware of the price we are paying for this ever hard to come by commodity: well-wishers of Israel."

The author then stated a blunt critique of the embassy for its support of the Voice of Hope radio station in south Lebanon "that has been blatantly missionary in its broadcasts since its inception." [13]

The Voice of Hope was formerly owned by Christian fundamentalist entrepreneur George Otis, Sr., a supporter of renegade Lebanese army major Saad Haddad, whom Israel assisted with a militia and financial support in the Israeli-controlled sector of south Lebanon. The Voice of Hope station broadcasts to northern Israel and Lebanon frequent messages from Haddad, American Christian country-and-western music, and fundamentalist Christian radio programs. The ICEJ took over the major operations in the mid-1980s. The Pat Robertson-operated Middle East Television of the Christian Broadcasting Network is a separate operation. One sees, however, the tension within Zionism caused by Christian Zionists.

In October 1986, I had opportunity to discuss this tension with Daniel Rossing, then director of Israeli Religious Affairs. I was direct with my question: "How can you in the government continue to support a movement that believes Jews must ultimately be converted to Christianity or face a cosmic holocaust at the battle of Armageddon?"

His response was instructive: "We need support from wherever we can find it, but we keep these people on a very short leash."

5. The Restoration of the Jews in Israel

The ICEJ claims that it has a mandate to proclaim its message of political Christian Zionism to the international community. Thus does the ICEJ hope to rally support that will encourage Christians to take the position that the Jews must be restored to and in control of Palestine:

> The embassy believes that God wants us to stimulate, encourage, and inspire Christians amongst the many nations concerning their role and task in the restoration of Israel. The Bible says that the destiny of nations, Christians, and even that of the church is linked to the way in which these groups respond to this restoration.[14]

Again, the basic theology revealed here is consistent with classic futurist premillennial dispensationalist teachings that elevate Israel above the church. In this case, the ICEJ position has considerable theological and political importance. If the church is deemphasized and a modern secular/ethnic government assumes total authority, the Christian message is clearly undermined. The gospel of Jesus Christ becomes secondary. The task of doing justice and proclaiming salvation in Jesus Christ is lost. The future survival of all nations, their prosperity and destiny, are made conditional on the degree to which they support the political state of Israel.

ICEJ's program makes it clear that the support will involve economic, political, educational, and prayer support of Israel and its policies. The ICEJ has thereby surrendered the central doctrines of Christianity for a nationalist political ideology—Zionism—whose very morality is inconsistent with biblical teachings.

Examination of the essential doctrines and practices of the ICEJ suggests that it should be declared a heretical cult which contradicts the doctrines and ethics of historic Christianity. In some ways the ICEJ is an anachronistic return to the Judaizing tendency the early church rejected at the first ecumenical council, recorded in Acts 15.

Again, in the promotional pamphlet *Prepare Ye the Way*, the ICEJ raises the question, "Is standing with Israel a political act?" The answer seems to be contradictory as stated in the pamphlet: "[The Christian support of Israel] is not primarily political but a part of the warfare to help protect the Lord's people and to help preserve them for that time when the Lord will fulfill his promises" (Ezek. 37; Zech. 12; Joel 3).[15]

But the very next paragraph goes on to state, "To stand with Israel politically and practically, therefore, has ultimate spiritual implications even if Israel has to go through agonizing birth pangs to arrive at God's destiny for her." [16] Thus it seems that this work is called "not primarily political" in one clause—but is clearly political in the next sentence.

Goals of the ICEJ

The embassy claims to represent "millions of Christians who love and honor the Jewish people." Beyond the above summarized belief system, the ICEJ states the following goals:

> To show concern for the Jewish people, and especially for the reborn State of Israel, by being a focus of comfort according to Isaiah 40:1, 'Comfort, comfort my people, says your God.'
> To remind and encourage Christians to pray for Jerusalem and the land of Israel.
> To be a center where Christians from all over the world can learn what is taking place in the land and be rightly related to the nation.
> To stimulate Christian leaders, churches, and organizations to become effective influences in their countries on behalf of the Jewish people.
> To begin or assist projects in Israel, including economic ventures, for the well-being of all who live here irrespective of race, ethnic background, or religion.
> To be a reconciling influence between Arabs and Jews. [17]

From my perspective, the ICEJ has been very effective in fulfilling goals one through four in a manner consistent with their stated theology. Goal three is to "be rightly related" to Israel, which according to the ICEJ is to avoid criticism of Israel and to endorse the policies of the Likud government. Goal five, however, gives the impression that economic benefits shall be granted to recipients "irrespective of race, ethnic background, or religion." Here the ICEJ's stated theology and practice are inconsistent. ICEJ has by its words and actions pursued a policy hostile toward Arabs, both Christian and Muslim. I will confine my remarks to only two aspects of the discussion.

The ICEJ has been a divisive rather than a reconciling factor in the Middle East, particularly between Arab and Jew in the "holy" land. ICEJ's literature and presentations by its leaders convey of hostility toward Islam and the Arab governments. A 1987 newsletter elaborated on five methods by which supporters can "come against the spirit of Islam." [18]

Repeated statements against the Palestinians' national aspirations for freedom and a state of the organization's anti-Palestinian policies have been made. Add to this the close relationship between ICEJ and the Likud political elite, and one understands why the Palestinians view them with suspicion, not as a force of reconciliation.

Goal five in the ICEJ strategy states that they will be engaged in services regardless of race, etc. However, in the "holy" land, Palestinian Christian churches and Muslim organizations will not accept grants or donations from the ICEJ.

The Palestinians who are most critical of the ICEJ come from the Christian churches of Jerusalem and the West Bank. They have warned their people to maintain a policy of non-cooperation with the ICEJ, particularly if offered financial grants. I am personally aware of three Palestinian Christian churches or organizations, all in desperate financial straits, which have refused ICEJ grants. Palestinian Christians oppose the political Christian Zionist theology which, when taken to its logical conclusion, negates Palestinian claims to their land, livelihood, beliefs, and very presence in the land.

Palestinian Christians have consistently distanced themselves from the ICEJ. The widely circulated April 1988 statement by the Middle East Council of Churches and Heads of Churches in Jerusalem dissociated Middle Eastern Christians from the ICEJ and Christian Zionism. The statement categorically rejected the ICEJ as "a Western intrusion" having no authority to speak for the Arab Christian community. The statement challenged Western Christians to engage the Christian Zionists in their Western countries of origin, and thereby help the Palestinian Christians in their struggle to survive in the land of Jesus.[19]

A second case against the ICEJ's self-declared goals comes from within the embassy itself. In 1985, as five hundred ICEJ supporters flocked to Jerusalem for the annual Feast of Tabernacles, news broke that there was a serious rift within the organization. The *Jerusalem Post* account of October 12, 1985, referred to three key issues in the dispute. First, the British branch of ICEJ (others were involved as well) protested the manner by which the director (Luckoff) and spokesman (van der Hoeven) were controlling the organization to meet their personal agenda. The news article referred to an anonymous former ICEJ member who opposed the "authoritarian style of leadership" imposed by the two leaders.

Second, Luckoff and van der Hoeven were accused of being too closely identified with Israel's Likud Party. They felt that one could barely differentiate between the ICEJ programs and the strategy and the key emphases of Likud, except that the ICEJ sought to add biblical justifications. The former ICEJ members felt the Christian aspects of the ICEJ were diminished in the process.

Third, many of the former members, the British branch in particular, desired more reconciling programs between Arabs and Jews. Some members, like colonel Orde Dobbie, had approached Palestinian Christians to begin the long process of reconciliation. Their initiatives, however, were blocked by Luckoff and van der Hoeven. The most outspoken critic was Dobbie himself, who made these views known in the press and to Palestinian Christians in the fall of 1985.

Dobbie had been a long time supporter of Christian Zionist causes and was the cousin of the famous colonel Orde Wingate, an internationally known British army officer in charge of training Zionist fighters during the 1930s in Palestine. Among his proteges was the future Israeli defense minister and military hero Moshe Dayan. Wingate's commitment to political Zionism was based on his Christian Zionism.

In the wake of the resignations at the Christian Embassy in 1985, Rev. Audeh Rantisi (see chapter 11) told the Palestinian daily *Al-Fajr* in Jerusalem that the primary reason for nine staff resignations was the blatantly political nature of the leadership's actions. He cited a decision by the ICEJ to finance a settlement on the West Bank as a violation of international law and as an offense to the Palestinian victims. Rantisi added, "Christians have no embassy. Our message is that of reconciliation between ourselves and our sisters and brothers and with God. All efforts not geared for these principles will ultimately fail." [20]

I personally observed this settlement under construction in October 1992. ICEJ literature promoting the settlement and fundraising material are available from the ICEJ headquarters.

However, the continued favor the ICEJ receives from the highest echelons of the Israeli government give it a favored status in the country. The late former prime minister of Israel Menachem Begin stated at a Feast of Tabernacles celebration that "your decision to establish your embassy in Jerusalem at a time when we were being abandoned because of our faith was an act of courage and a symbol of the closeness between us." [21]

Chief Rabbi Shlomo Goren (now retired), also close to Likud, had little positive to say about other Christian organizations. However, he had this praise to give the ICEJ: "Your sympathy, solidarity, and belief in the future of Israel, this to us is tremendous. Your presence here will always remain a golden page in the book of heaven. May the Lord bless you out of Zion." [22]

And Prime Minister Yitzhak Shamir added, "The Christian Embassy in Jerusalem and your pilgrimage to this city carry a message which cannot be overlooked or discounted by governments and statesmen in all five continents."[23]

Whether this favored status will continue with a Labor government in power by the late 1990s remains to be seen.

Political Activities of the ICEJ

In addition to such major projects as the Feast of Tabernacles and periodic conventions, there are certain ICEJ programs that merit a brief discussion. First, the ICEJ has been engaged in direct political lobbying activities in cooperation with the government of Israel. While the United States has been the primary focus for these activities, they are evident elsewhere.

Speaking at the April 1988 Christian Zionist Congress was a Swiss government official and member of the parliament, elected in the canton of Bern on a Christian Zionist platform. He urged participants to form a political party in their own countries in cooperation with ICEJ and to campaign vigorously in their home countries for PLO offices to be removed.

There are numerous incidents of ICEJ lobbying in the United States. Here are two examples. On February 23, 1984, the ICEJ sent Richard A. Hellman to Washington, D.C., to testify before the U.S. Senate Committee on Foreign Relations, arguing that the U.S. government should move its embassy from Tel Aviv to Jerusalem. In the course of his testimony, Hellman claimed that the ICEJ was a "spiritual rather than political" organization.

The Israeli lobby AIPAC organized the pro-Israel testimony and included Rev. Jerry Falwell of the Moral Majority. Speaking in opposition as an evangelical Christian was Dr. Ray Bakke, of the Lausanne Committee for World Evangelization and at that time also with World Vision International. Bakke opposed the proposed move, noting that this would violate international law and send the wrong message to Christians (and Muslims and concerned Jews), that the United States did not care about legality nor about the suffering of Palestinians. The bill was tabled.

In February 1991, at the National Prayer Breakfast for Israel, right-wing political activist Ed McAteer announced the founding of Christian Israel Public Affairs Committee (CIPAC), modeled after the powerful Israeli lobby AIPAC. Its board of directors included AIPAC director Tom Dine and Herbert Zweibon, president of Americans for a Safe Israel, another powerful pro-Israel lobby organization. Both groups have for fifteen years espoused a Likud political ideology.

The goals of CIPAC matched those of AIPAC but added the Christian dispensational rationale. Its director, Richard Hellman, former aide of U.S. senator Howard Baker, has been a long-term ICEJ supporter. The major emphasis of CIPAC became supporting $10 billion in U.S. loan guarantees for Israel toward the settlement of Soviet Jews in Israel and the West Bank.

During the fall of 1991 and winter-spring of 1992, CIPAC, like AIPAC, found significant opposition to their lobbying for the loan guarantees from the Bush administration. The administration linked the loan guarantees to the illegal construction of settlements in the occupied territories, which it decried as an "obstacle to peace in the Middle East." ICEJ spokesman Jan Willem van der Hoeven told the *Jerusalem Post* that the "religious Christian community finds the Bush administration's policy on the loan guarantees totally unacceptable." He estimated that eighty percent of America's 40 million Bible Belt Christians would support the guarantees.[24]

Second, in addition to the political lobbying, the ICEJ was busy during this period helping with the recruitment and settlement of Soviet Jews in Israel. The ICEJ raised several million dollars in 1990-1992 to fly more than thirty-five planeloads of Soviet Jews to Israel and then to assist in their settlement. During the October 1991 Feast of Tabernacles festivities, representatives from twelve countries presented checks to Prime Minister Shamir to finance the settlements. Shamir told them that the arrival of Soviet and Ethiopian Jews confirms that we are "living in a period of the fulfillment of prophecy and miracles." [25] Many of the Soviet Jews were settled in the West Bank including East Jerusalem, which violated international law and U.S. policy.

The third political activity involved the ICEJ in direct support connection with the U.S.-sponsored Contras in Central America during the mid-to-late 1980s. When the ICEJ proudly established an "embassy" in Honduras and in Guatemala, they worked closely with the government of Israel in bringing funds into the countries. ICEJ was granted diplomatic status in both countries and allowed to bring goods and funds into the country without inspection by customs agents.

In September 1988, the investigative journal *Israeli Foreign Affairs* noted that the ICEJ "ambassador to Honduras," Marta Rodriguez, told journalist Deborah Preusch that ICEJ had brought in vehicles and other items for the Contras. Other fundamentalist Christian groups that cooperate with ICEJ, include Gospel Crusade of Bradenton, Florida, whose head, Gerald Derstine, is a founding member of ICEJ. [26]

This project, in close cooperation with the Israeli government and its embassies in Guatemala and Honduras, operated in total violation of United States law and policy.

A Christian Response to ICEJ: Seven Theses

Having lived and worked with churches in Cyprus and Jerusalem, I have come to love and respect the Christian commitments, people, and struggle to be faithful to Christian principles of the shrinking Palestinian church. The International Christian Embassy-Jerusalem is neither from the indigenous Christian community nor connected to the body of Christ in these lands. In fact, the ICEJ programs are working toward the ultimate demise of the local Christian community at a time when it is under duress.

Scripture calls Christians to be "wise as serpents and harmless as doves." We are to evaluate the choices we make in our ministries and their consequences in relationship to the message and ministry of Jesus Christ. If Christ's message and ministry was to proclaim "good news to the captives, to set at liberty the oppressed," today's churches must be about this kingdom business. If we are to proclaim God's love and salvation to all persons, then Christians cannot choose to support one race or government to the exclusion of another. The ICEJ has made repeated decisions to take the side of the powerful, of the oppressor, of the Zionist political elites in direct opposition to all Palestinians, including the churches. Therefore, its message and ministry must be rejected according to the following biblically-based critique.

1. **The ICEJ allows the gospel and lordship of Jesus Christ to become subservient to the modern political ideology of Zionism.**

"You cannot serve two masters," says Jesus in the Sermon on the Mount. The Christian Embassy has compromised the gospel in every instance when issues of Christian mission, human rights, justice for the oppressed, and racism have confronted it. Both the Old Testament Law and the Hebrew Prophets make it clear (as we demonstrated in chapter 6), that the Jewish people themselves are under a divine moral obligation to treat the poor and sojourner with dignity and justice. By encouraging theft of the land from Palestinians, by denying their suffering, and by affirming the Israeli government's military occupation, the ICEJ has undermined the work of Christ and the church.

2. **The International Christian Embassy is guilty of the sin of idolatry by worshiping state power in Israel and benefiting from its praises.** In practice and in theory, the form of Christian Zionism practiced by the Christian Embassy inverts the power of Christian faith and the church while it elevates the Zionist state and its policies. Throughout Scripture, there are more condemnations of idolatry in its various forms than of any other sin. Idolatry need not set up a literal golden calf nor bow at the feet of an alternative god. Rather, it evolves out of the seductive replacement of God with various benefits of power—in this case, Israeli state power.

The ICEJ has elevated the ideology of Zionism and the government of Israel to such a lofty altar that it actually worships at its feet. Songs of praise literally sanctify Zionism, both as an ideology and as a government. The ICEJ enables Christian pilgrims to be manipulated by biblically-sanctioned sermons and programmatic efforts that further the suffering of the Palestinian community. It demonizes Palestinians and conditions the public for the ultimate demise of the Palestinians. It refuses to hear the word of the Lord when he calls for reform, for justice, for true repentance and change. Christians must reject the ICEJ and its programs in order to avoid the sin of idolatry and maintain faithfulness to Jesus Christ, the only Lord.

3. **The ICEJ obscures the call to reconciliation in the Christian gospel, especially as it applies to Palestinians and Israelis.** By perpetuating the myth of Jewish state superiority and by taking the side of the Zionists in the Arab-Israeli conflict, the ICEJ alienates the Arab and protects the Zionists with shallow words of "comfort." Whereas Jesus and the New Testament call upon Christians to break down "the dividing wall, . . . the hostility" between Jews and Gentiles (Eph. 2:14-22) and speak the truth of God to power, the ICEJ continues to reestablish the walls of separation. Biblically-based reconciliation cannot occur when there is a gross imbalance of power and one party is repeatedly trampled down by the other. Ephesians 2 claims that the reconciling work of Christ creates "one new

humanity in place of the two" by destroying the old divisions. The Apostle Paul specifically mentions Jews and Gentiles as the benefactors of Christ's reconciling activity.

Paul speaks about this activity as an ongoing ministry of the Christian church, that begins now, not in a future eschatological age. We must labor now for the goal so that we are "no longer strangers and sojourners," as we were in the old arrangement under the law. We must confront this archaic and sinful arrangement by which Zionism, both Christian and Jewish, seeks to negate the Palestinian people to advance its political agenda.

4. The ICEJ reduces the gospel to material and partisan political dimensions while it ignores the ultimate principles of the Christian message and its immediate kingdom implications.

The ICEJ has sanctified Israel's theft of Palestinian land (now approximately 70 percent of the West Bank and 45 percent of the Gaza Strip by Israel's own admission). It has participated in this so-called biblically-justified land grab but has missed biblical injunctions against such political maneuvers (see chapters 6 and 7). In so doing, it has misled Christians and Jews who have made financial contributions that ultimately undermine justice.

In addition, its collaboration with Israel in the illegal settlement of Soviet Jews on Palestinian lands has violated international law and biblical norms of responsible living. Reducing God to a cosmic real estate agent who will allow one people to suffer and be removed from their cities and farms is clearly inconsistent with the whole message of Scripture. By projecting the modern Zionist state as an eschatological fulfillment of the biblical Israel, the ICEJ reduces eternal truths to material terms. This truncated gospel of reductionism is inconsistent with the message of Jesus and the task of the church.

5. The ICEJ has become a heretical cult by reducing the Christian church to a mere "parenthesis" and by rejecting the local Christian community. By rejecting the local Palestinian churches in Israel and occupied Palestine (and the Arab world in general), and by theologically reducing the church worldwide to a "parenthesis," the ICEJ is teaching and practicing a heretical doctrine. By teaching the doctrine of the pretribulation rapture of the church, combined with the political identification of the modern Zionist State of Israel as the fulfillment of biblical prophecy, the ICEJ contradicts historical Christian and biblical teaching concerning the church of Christ.

God has not created two separate tracks of history to fulfill the divine plan of salvation, as the ICEJ and futurist premillennial dispensationalists teach. There is but one movement of history, and the church of Christ has been chosen as a vehicle that God uses to proclaim salvation and the kingdom of God. Christ came proclaiming that the kingdom begins now in the very ministry and teaching of Jesus. The church continues as the vehicle of God, imperfect as it is, living the mission of Jesus.

There is no evidence in Jesus' teachings that Israel will be reconstituted as a state to serve as God's primary vehicle in the latter days. Jesus in fact rejects this teaching in Acts 1:6-8. Not only does Jesus reject the futurist pro-Zionist state scenario, but he challenges true disciples with the task of taking the gospel into the entire world, including Jerusalem and the most difficult places. This mission has not changed, despite the revision of Christianity by the ICEJ and other Christian Zionist advocates.

6. **The ICEJ represents anti-mission activity in the Middle East, in relation to both Islam and Judaism.** The Christian Embassy operates in direct opposition to Christian mission in three ways. First, by undermining the very existence, continuing presence, and future of the indigenous Arab churches of the Middle East, it is working toward the demise of the local churches. The ICEJ makes no contribution in spiritual or practical support to the local Arab Christian communities, who are undergoing a severe period of trial and loss.

Because the ICEJ has sided with Israeli political injustice from the Palestinian community as a whole, the local churches are forced into a situation of survival and accelerated emigration, to the extent that many fear it will barely exist after the year 2000 unless drastic changes occur. The local Arab churches are the strongest potential agents of mission in the Arab world, and they have the best opportunities to bear witness to Christ's message of love. The actions and stated goals of the ICEJ are in direct opposition to the survival of the Palestinian church.

Second, the ICEJ has alienated itself toward Islam, both in the public eye and in its ideology and practice. Muslims know very well where groups like ICEJ stand on critical issues such as their endorsement of Zionism and its negation of Palestinian rights. Already Muslims reject the ICEJ and are as hostile toward it as the ICEJ is toward them. The ICEJ will not be welcomed into the homes or institutions of local Muslims and will not have future ministries in predominantly Muslim areas.

Additionally, the considerable publicity generated by the ICEJ in the Middle East has caused many Muslims to become confused and more deeply alienated from Christianity. Most Muslims do not differentiate one Christian denomination or movement from the other. When the average Muslim sees ICEJ spokesmen on television or reads about them in the press, they react defensively and often with hatred. Christian love cannot grow and build bridges in this charged climate. The Islamic revival of the 1990s makes it crucial for Christians to build bridges of trust toward Muslim leaders, lest the fundamentalists of the various Muslim movements attack and reject indigenous Arab Christianity because they view it as a Western intrusion.

Inasmuch as the ICEJ sees its role as bringing "comfort and praise to

Israel and its leaders," by default it does not engage in Christian mission and evangelization. In practice and in doctrine, the ICEJ undermines the Palestinian church's continuity in the "holy" land and contradicts its witness of love and service.

7. **The ICEJ does not take Jesus Christ as its alpha and omega but focuses on Zionism in theory and practice.** Thus the ICEJ is a pseudo-Christian movement that attempts to baptize a modern political ideology with some Scripture and revisionist Christian dispensational theology. In fact, the ICEJ goes well beyond classical premillennial dispensationalism in its claims that modern Israel fulfills Scripture and that its actions are beyond reproach.

Christians need to be agents of prophetic critique and of eventual healing and salvation of this misguided movement. Western Christian evangelical organizations, theologians, and churches have a special responsibility in that their members lend primary economic and theological support for the enterprise. Western evangelicals are encouraged to build close relationships with Middle East churches in order to obtain accurate information and encourage the Arab Christians, lest they feel abandoned and forgotten by the church universal in their struggle for survival.

10

Another Man from Galilee

He loves righteousness and justice; the earth is full of the steadfast
love of the Lord. . . . Truly the eye of the Lord is on those who fear
him, on those who hope in his steadfast love, to deliver their
soul from death and to keep them alive in famine.

Psalm 33:5

We asked several people about the road to Ibillin, a small Palestinian
village we had planned to visit. By this time my wife and I, on our
honeymoon, had been riding for about forty-five minutes from Nazareth
on the old Arab bus. We were the only Western passengers, and the Palestinians were very curious about this obviously American couple traveling
with backpacks. I asked the bus driver to leave us at the road to Ibillin, according to the directions I was given. "Over there," said one of the passengers, pointing to a one-lane road on the right.

The bus driver stopped and we jumped off, waving good-bye to the
passengers. There were no signs to indicate how far down the road we
would need to walk. After walking about 200 yards, I told Drew I was going to hitch a ride with the vehicle that was coming toward us. I put out
my thumb and they stopped. "Ibillin?" I asked.

"Yes, yes," one of the young passengers said in English. "Abuna Elias
Chacour?" I inquired, once we had climbed into the truck.

"In Ibillin," he said, as we flashed confirming smiles to each other.

After driving six or seven miles, we entered a small town set in the midst of the Galilean hills. We drove up and down several narrow streets and eventually the truck pulled over.

"Abuna Chacour here," our friends said with big smiles.

We thanked them and walked through a gate. By now we were being followed by an entourage of about thirty children who were trying out a few words of English: "Hello. How are you? What is your name? Where are you from?" they asked. When one of them heard "Chicago," he responded with the customary "rat-a-tat-tat, shoot-em up, Al Capone."

We responded jokingly and asked for Father Chacour. They directed us toward a staircase and pointed to a door.

We walked up and a young Palestinian woman named Marina greeted us, "Welcome! You must be Don and Drew." I had called from Tiberias to be certain the well-traveled priest would be home that evening.

"Yes, we have come to talk for a few minutes with Abuna Chacour."

"He is expecting you and will be free in fifteen minutes or so. Could I get you something to drink?"

Marina, a gentle young Palestinian from Bethlehem, was an assistant to Chacour. She had completed her undergraduate work at Bethlehem University and had done postgraduate studies at the Sorbonne in Paris. During her teenage years, she felt the call to a life of prayer and entered a cloistered nunnery in Jerusalem but left for a more active life. For the time being, she was helping Chacour coordinate the youth camps which ministered to 3000-4000 children from various Galilean villages.

The door opened and out walked a short, dark man who radiated warmth, "Welcome to the Galilee! I am Father Chacour." He wore a clerical collar with a gray shirt and had a long beard that gave him the aura of an Old Testament prophet. His bright eyes and energetic presence made me feel he was a very self-assured leader.

"I bring you greetings from Bruce Rigdon, our mutual friend in Chicago," I said, seeking to establish common ground.

"Oh, how is Bruce? Tell him he must come back soon to see the progress we are making here. Next year we will begin building an elementary school for the children you see here. They must know our history as Palestinians, and learn the importance of Christianity which began in these hills with Jesus."

Drew and I had heard a great deal about this visionary priest and were looking forward to spending an hour with him. He took us out on his rooftop patio and pointed toward Haifa and Mount Carmel in the west (where Elijah defeated the priests of Baal in 1 Kings 18); to Acre in the northwest, where Napoleon was defeated; toward the hills of Lebanon just twenty miles to the north; and the Galilean mountains to the east. "We Palestinians have been here from the beginning, and the Christians here are all descendants of those who never left Palestine since our compatriot Jesus Christ lived here," he said.

We sat down as a beautiful sunset ushered in the dusk of a warm July evening. We sipped Arabic coffee and I began the conversation, "Tell us your story. I have heard about your village, Biram, and what happened there in 1948. We would like to hear more about Biram but also about what you are doing in Ibillin."

Chacour sat back in his chair with a pensive look. "It's a long story but I know you must return to Jerusalem tonight. You Americans are always rushing things. You should come and stay with us at least three days if you want to learn who we are," he added pointedly, but with a smile. Now more comfortable having issued that challenge, he launched into the story.

"We had always lived peacefully with the Jews in these small villages near the Lebanese border, Biram and Ikrit. We had everything we needed in terms of our daily needs. We were a deeply spiritual people, and I imagine you know that these were Christian villages who identified closely with the man from Galilee.

"One evening my father sat down with my sister, my three brothers and me, and said, 'We will have special guests staying with us in the coming weeks. They are Jews who have suffered greatly under an evil man in Germany named Hitler. He has slaughtered millions of their countrymen and they are fleeing for safety. We must help them. We will offer our hospitality, so I want you boys to sleep on the roof the few days they are here. Please do everything to make them feel at home.'

"As children we were always excited to sleep on the roof during the summer. It was not only cooler, but we had many games we played together. These were idyllic times. Soon the Jews came to our villages and I was shocked to see that they all carried guns. Nobody used a gun in our area, except to chase the wolves away from our sheep and goat herds.

"One day my oldest brother, Rudah, brought home a rifle. My father became the angriest I have ever seen him. He told Rudah to take the gun out of the house and never use one again. Rudah protested, claiming that he had heard there was fighting nearby [the 1948 war had begun], and we might need to defend ourselves.

" 'No, we do not use violence to defend ourselves, ever,' said Father. 'We have nothing to fear from the Jews. We share the same Father, Abraham, and we worship the same God. We are blood brothers and have lived together for generations. We must never forget that.'

"I might add that our villages had been hiding Jews for two years or more, as they were smuggled over the borders from Europe to Lebanon. We kept them in our villages at considerable risk and as a sign of our good will toward these poor immigrants.

"Finally the Jewish guests arrived at our home. My father had planned a wonderful roast lamb dinner for the new guests, and Mother had cooked for two days. It was the biggest feast of the year for us. As we ate, I noticed that the Jews were very cold and distant. They did not give me a good feeling, and they ate as if there were no tomorrow."

"Two weeks after the first soldiers arrived in Biram, we had a visit from an Israeli army officer. By now it was mid-November 1948. The officer told my father that due to security problems along the Lebanese border they would need to ask us to leave our homes temporarily. We would be able to return within a few weeks when the hostilities ended.

"I remember walking out one morning when we had planned to leave, and the entire village was doing the same thing. I did not know that they were evacuating the entire village. This was the first of many shocks I would endure. At first we stayed in the olive orchards and caves on our farm land, near the village. We had brought only a few blankets and clothing for two weeks because we expected to return very soon."

"One day a small group of our men went back to the village to see if it was time to return home. The evenings were beginning to be very cold, and we knew that winter and the rainy season were a few weeks away. They entered the village and one man stopped at his house. He was shocked to see that his furniture had been ransacked and the home was in terrible condition. Others then checked their homes and discovered the same situation. They looked for a commanding officer, demanding an explanation.

"They were asked, 'What are you doing? Get out of here.'

" 'Where is the commanding officer?' the villagers asked.

" 'He has gone and we are in charge.'

"One of the soldiers cocked his gun and pointed it at the men. 'Get out, *now.*'

"The men returned to their families in the hills with the sad news. They felt used and humiliated. And now their land and homes were gone. Then we began the long march to Gish, a village approximately five miles away through the Galilean hills. Gish was to become our home. What we did not know at the time was that almost all the residents of Gish had been expelled in a similar way and driven into Lebanon, where they became refugees. Now we too were refugees in our own land."

"That year over 770,000 Palestinians were forcibly expelled from their homes and driven out of the country. These are figures from the United Nations, not from me. This number does not include people like my family, who became refugees inside our country."

"The villages of Ikrit and Biram protested their tragic loss of land and went through several appeals to the High Court of Justice. This took years of waiting and hoping. During these years we started life over, from scratch. More shocking news reached us one day that the Israeli government had seized our farmlands and given them to a new kibbutz for Jews only. This was extremely painful for Father but also for all of us. We loved our fig trees and the olive orchards. Our farmlands were like a part of the family, and we cared for them as if they were human beings."

"Then Father heard that the kibbutzim were hiring several men to come and dress the fig trees. Immediately my father and three oldest brothers applied for the job and were hired.

"This greatly disappointed my mother, who felt we had more dignity than to stoop to this unjust arrangement. 'How can you work for somebody who has stolen our land?' she cried. 'This is so wrong, Michael, I beg you not to do it.'

"But Father was determined. 'If we care for our trees and land, we know that we will do the best job,' he said.

"So every day Father, Mother, and my brothers left the house early in the morning to travel the long distance to our beloved Biram, where they could see our house but not visit it, and work our land but not own it."

"In late 1952 the High Court decided that we would be allowed to return to our homes. It was officially decreed that we were citizens with certain rights within Israel. By December 1 we planned to return to Biram on Christmas Day."

" 'What an incredible Christmas gift,' we said to each other. 'At last we can return to our beloved homes and have the peaceful life we knew before 1948.' The Christmas Eve worship service became a celebration as everyone anticipated the joy of returning home on the next day."

"We awakened early, put on heavy sweaters and coats, and began the five-mile walk to our beautiful Biram. The long journey seemed to go quickly because we sang Christmas hymns and were filled with joy as we traveled.

"We finally reached the hill overlooking Biram and a sickening feeling overwhelmed us. We stopped dead in our tracks and looked down on our beloved village. What we saw turned our joy to tears and grieved us no end. We witnessed the Israeli Army with tanks and grenades blowing things up. Every house was demolished before our eyes. They even shelled the church, and one of its walls collapsed. Miraculously, the old bell tower did not fall and remained like a tiny sign of hope overlooking our crumbled homes.

"Our spirits plummeted. 'Why, O God, do you allow this to happen? What have we ever done to deserve this fate?'

"So on Christmas Day, the village of Biram was destroyed, all of it. The poor families stood, numbed by the horror of this spectacle. You can not imagine the pain that we felt, the anger, the hopelessness as we turned and made the long journey back to Gish."

An Israeli law professor, Amnon Rubenstein, dean of the law faculty at Tel Aviv University, wrote the following about the incident, in the leading Israeli paper *Ha'aretz*.

> There is no doubt that their expulsion was committed without authorization, without confirmation of the commander in chief, without the confirmation of the government, and without legal basis. The whole thing was done according to the disputed tradition of establishing facts (on the ground), a tradition which reached its epitome in the illegal blowing up of a whole Arab village.[1]

Chacour was a young boy, twelve years old, when his village was destroyed. I was struck by the man's commitment to be a reconciler and the way he was going about that mission. He was not giving up the grievance that had brought his family so much suffering. But he had turned the vindictiveness over to God. As a result, Chacour was filled with a new, creative spirit of love for his people. He had decided to concentrate his energies on the youth, building a new generation of aware citizens.

"The Israeli Jews will never have security until they learn to respect us as true brothers and sisters and begin to cooperate," he said. "So long as there is a Palestinian suffering and treated as a third-class citizen by Israel, then no one will live in peace and harmony. But let Israelis learn and treat Palestinians with dignity and we will be their brothers."

Many have wondered why Israel targeted two Christian villages for demolition and refused to allow them to resettle. There were neighboring Muslim and Druze villages in the Galilee that were thankfully spared. But why the Christian community? There are no easy answers. Some have speculated that there has always been a strong anti-Christian bias in certain quarters of Zionism, dating back to the suffering the Jews experienced in Europe. This is a theory of vengeance, as Jews attempted to pay back their history of suffering.

Still others indicate that it may have been a case of retaliation against the Catholic White Fathers in Jerusalem. Jesuit Middle East scholar Joseph Ryan alludes to this theory in his study of Ikrit and Biram. He notes the discontent felt in high Israeli circles over the strongly critical statements of Thomas J. McMahon, the first president of the Pontifical Mission in Palestine and national secretary of the Catholic Near East Welfare Association. McMahon wrote to the United Nations secretary general Trygve Lie in March 1949. He called for the UN to force Israel to grant the right of return to Palestinian refugees and full repatriation in their homes. He also urged that international status be granted to Jerusalem, Bethlehem, and Nazareth to protect the holy sites of the three religions. Ryan notes that previous letters from McMahon had requested that the secretary general "make an inquiry regarding criminal acts against Christian persons and places."[2] The vengeance theories are speculative and may never be confirmed unless Israeli military records are opened to the public or officials confess to such motives.

Another possible motive is that the villages lay in a security zone on the Lebanese border. Still, the destruction of the villages in the name of security is illegal and unjustified.

As I reflected on the Biram story, it seemed to me that the central issues had to do with the old Zionist strategy of removing non-Jews from Palestine. The basic strategy of the Zionist movement throughout the land of Palestine from the beginning was to take the land, inch by inch, wherever and whenever possible. It was purely a question of seizing land from a defenseless population at a time when nobody would oppose them. The centrality of the land seizure issue was borne out by the follow-ing events.

In 1965 the residents of Biram proposed a compromise solution to the Israeli authorities. They offered to remain in the new villages in which they had settled for an indefinite period, up to the conclusion of a peace treaty between Lebanon and Israel. In the meantime, the status quo would continue. Israel had given the villages' farmland to two kibbutzim; the kibbutzim were benefiting from the arrangement. The villagers would not even claim the farms after the treaty, only the homes which remained demolished and had not been reconstructed. Further, the residents would stop protest activity and drop their case against the government, which was by now drawing significant attention.

The Israeli newspaper *Ha'aretz* endorsed this position in an April 1965 editorial. Other Israelis came to support it as a fair settlement. The government rejected the proposal.

In the mid-1970s villagers proposed to the Israeli authorities that they reconstruct the churches in each village at their own expense. They were granted permission. Hoping that the government position was softening, the residents brought forward the previous proposal to return only to their homes. The case was debated long in the cabinet, with army chief of staff Eleazar and defense minister Moshe Dayan opposing it. Four were in favor, finding no security issues at risk. By the end of the debate, Dayan convinced the others that this case would set a precedent for other de-stroyed villages (of which there are over 400) to make the same appeal. The appeal was rejected.

Other strategies have been used by Israel to weaken Christians com-munities and to secure inexpensively large tracts of Christian property. In 1952, an Anglican priest was approached by the Jewish Agency (created by the Zionist Movement to handle the purchase of land for a future Jew-ish state) and offered money if he would sell church property and con-vince the parishioners to leave. Each family would be compensated at a rate below the full value of their home but they would be given full trans-portation to Brazil, where there would be assistance in resettling. Father Saba, the Anglican priest in Lydda, rejected the offer outright.

Canon Shehadeh, currently the pastor of an Anglican church in Haifa, personally told me of a similar strategy that worked for the Zionist agen-cies in Haifa. "After the Israeli army and terrorist organizations forced over 75 percent of the Palestinians to flee the city in 1948, the Jewish Agency approached the sizable Armenian Christian community with the offer to sell their homes and move them to Europe. Gradually the strategy has worked. What once was a large and thriving Armenian community in Haifa today has only three families." [3]

I have returned to Ibillin every year since that initial visit in the sum-mer of 1979. What continues to amaze me is the steadfast commitment of Father Chacour to help his deprived people, the Palestinians, and to simultaneously work for reconciliation based on Jesus' message in the Sermon on the Mount. I am amazed because it would be natural for a young boy who suffered such pain and injustice at the hands of Israeli Jews to turn to vengeance and bitterness. Instead, Christ's message of reconciliation and justice has filled every day of his life.

I recall the personal visit I made to Ibillin during the winter of 1982. We shared a delightful evening together and the next morning I woke early, but Chacour had left. I looked across the valley and there he was, with another parishioner, pouring concrete and doing physical labor. They were pouring the foundation for Prophet Elias School, which would be completed in time for enrollment in the fall of 1982.

But the school was to bring more difficulties from the Israeli authorities. Despite his applications and meeting all requirements, they would not grant the school a permit. In addition, they would not give him an electrical hookup. Over five hundred children were enrolled for school. "What will I do?" asked Chacour.

He opened the school without the permit and told the Israeli officials exactly what he was doing. "Not only will you disappoint our children and our villages throughout the Galilee, but I will notify every church that is helping us build this school. You will hear, not only from church officials, but from their governments in Switzerland, Germany, France, England, Holland, the United States, and Canada."

Not only did the school receive the permit, but it has flourished. The elementary school soon expanded to include a high school, which had the same struggle for a permit. It too has excelled. By June 1994, the little Palestinian school that the Israeli government threatened to destroy became the second ranked high school in all Israel.

In 1991, Chacour began construction on a college near the Prophet Elias School. Again, the government refused a permit. Construction began anyway, amidst threats by the government to demolish the new building. I visited the site in October, 1991 and found several college classes meeting secretly in the basement while construction continued above them. At the same time, Chacour had made contact with U.S. secretary of state James Baker and his wife, Susan. Susan Baker visited Ibillin and was inspired by the ministry of Father Chacour. She read *Blood Brothers* and *We Belong to the Land*, passing them on to her husband, who also read them.

When Baker visited Prime Minister Itzhak Shamir in November 1992, just prior the Madrid opening of the Middle East Peace Conference, it is reported that his final request to Shamir was to grant the permit to Chacour's college. Observers stated that Shamir, wanting to be rid of the troublesome priest, agreed. Before Baker left the meeting, he handed Shamir a copy of *Blood Brothers*, urging him to read it. We have no reason to believe Shamir read the book, but two weeks later the Prophet Elias College had its official recognition from the government of Israel.

11

Victims of the Victims

*A*nd I thought the dead, who have already died, more fortunate than
the living. . . . but better than both is the one who has not yet been,
and has not seen the evil deeds that are done under the sun.

Ecclesiastes 4:2

O n a humid Friday afternoon, May 14, 1948, at precisely 4:00 p.m.,
more than 200 leaders of the Zionist movement gathered in a small room
for the most important meeting of their lives. They had been dreaming
and working for decades to see this meeting take place. Now the hour of
destiny had arrived. They were the survivors of Hitler's death camps, having lost family and friends at such terrible places as Auschwitz, Dachau,
and Bergen-Belsen. Still others had come to Palestine, often at great risk,
from Russia, Poland, Hungary, and other parts of Europe. A few were from
Arab countries and were far more oriental in their language, customs, and
worldview than their white European comrades, who dominated the
meeting.

Despite their diversity, they stood united on two vital issues—an unswerving commitment to the Zionist movement and the hope of completing their dream of establishing a Jewish state on Palestinian soil. As
they gathered under a portrait of Theodor Herzl, father of the Zionist
movement, the small room in Tel Aviv's Dizengoff Museum was charged
with emotion, anticipating the historic event about to unfold.

Their designated spokesman, David Ben-Gurion, rose and pounded
his gavel on the table, calling the meeting to order. His long white hair

and deliberate style projected a dual image of the famous Jewish atomic scientist, Albert Einstein, or one of the ancient Hebrew prophets, such as Elijah or Jeremiah.

Ben-Gurion's story was typical of those who stood together on May 14. Born as David Green in Plonsk, Poland, in 1886, he became active in the Zionist movement at the age of seventeen. He joined a Jewish self-defense cell in Poland, moving to Russia during the 1903 pogroms. In 1906 he arrived in Palestine to work as a farmer. Ben-Gurion later joined forces with those who organized a Zionist Labor movement that became a powerful political force in the emerging state.

On May 14, 1948, David Ben-Gurion raised a manuscript and read the following proclamation:

> In the land of Israel the Jewish people came into being. In this land was shaped their spiritual, religious, and national character. Here they created a culture of national and universal import and gave the world the eternal Book of Books.[1]

Ben-Gurion described the hope that Jews throughout the centuries had nurtured concerning their return to Palestine and establish a state of their own. "This was," he said, "the self-evident right of the Jewish people to be a nation, as all other nations, in their own sovereign state."

Then he concluded,

> With trust in the Almighty, we set our hand to this declaration at this session of the Provisional Council of State, in the city of Tel Aviv, on the fifth day of Iyar, 5708, the fourteenth day of May, 1948. Let us all stand to adopt the Scroll of the establishment of the Jewish State.[2]

Ben-Gurion penned his name, just as Americans had done on July 4, 1776. He invited his colleagues to come forward in alphabetical order and sign the scroll. Thus was the state of Israel declared by the Zionist leadership, but not as yet recognized by the world community. The proclamation nevertheless was carried by radio across the land and news spread to every continent. Jews from Tel Aviv to London and New York danced the hatikva and celebrated the occasion. In a month, U.S. president Harry S. Truman changed his position after intense lobbying from intimate Jewish friends. Eventually the United States and other major powers pressured smaller nations to follow suit at the United Nations.

Palestinian Arabs, still constituting the vast majority of the population in Palestine, (over 60 percent) sat stunned and felt betrayed by the world community. Many feared what might happen to them. They sensed the tragic history that began to unfold in events beyond their control. Most were unaware and were simply swept along by events. A tiny minority planned to take up arms in self-defense, hoping the world would not allow them to be destroyed.

On May 14, 1948, the very day the Zionist leaders proclaimed their new state to the world, another event transpired in rural Palestine without international attention. In the Palestinian township of Beisan, just a two hour drive north-east of Tel Aviv, the Zionist militia organization, the Haganah, (later to be named the Israeli Defense Forces) was completing its expulsion of Palestinian residents.

The Haganah had entered Beisan on May 12. Naim Ateek, presently the Anglican Canon of St. George's Cathedral in East Jerusalem, was a boy of seven when Beisan fell. He described this dreadful day to our tour group, a tragedy he summarizes in his book *Justice and Only Justice.* "We had no army to protect us. There was no battle, no resistance, no killing; we were simply taken over." [3]

On the morning of May 14, according to Ateek, the Haganah summoned all the male leaders to the center of the town and told them they had two hours to pack and vacate their homes. Naim remembers those frightful moments when, as children, they had to decide in a matter of minutes what to take on their journey. In the panic, his brother forgot his prized possession, the family radio, and ran back to the house to retrieve it. The father pleaded with the militia leaders, "I have nowhere to go with my large family. Let us stay in our home." [4] But the Israelis offered no exceptions to the orders.

The family packed their most important possessions, papers, and enough provisions for two days of travel. When they boarded the bus, the father could not account for the jewels and few valuables they kept hidden in the home. He asked the Haganah officer if he could go back, but the request was denied. He was able, however, to persuade the bus driver to pass by the house on the way out of Beisan and wait five minutes for him to retrieve the jewelry.

When the buses left Beisan, the residents were told that Christians were being shipped to Nazareth, and Muslims taken to the Jordan River and dropped off in the desert. Canon Ateek summarizes the experience, "Within a few hours, our family had become refugees, driven out of Beisan forever." [5]

The Ateek family, like the rest of Beisan, was not aware that their experience was being repeated throughout Palestine according to a strategy drawn up by the Zionist leaders. The plan, code-named Plan Dalet (after the fourth letter in the Hebrew alphabet), has now been made public through the opening of Israeli Defense Forces files of this historical period. The strategy behind the plan was to (1) to depopulate key Palestinian population centers so as to reduce the Arab citizenry of Israel; (2) clear other land for annexation into the new Jewish state; and (3) to open prime agricultural areas for Zionist control.

Between April 1948, and July 1949, the United Nations reported that 758,000 Palestinian civilians were forcibly expelled from their homes while Israel seized an additional 23 percent of the land designated by the United Nations for an eventual Arab state. The actual number of refugees is a highly debated issue and may be higher than the United Nations figures. Whether the total number of Palestinians who became refugees is 660,000, 770,000, or over 800,000, this catastrophe (*Al-Nakhbah* in Arabic) is remembered today as the greatest tragedy in the Palestinians' sad history. It marks the beginning of the Palestinian refugee crisis which still remains unresolved.

There is convincing evidence that many Zionist leaders began to consider the massive transfer of a significant percentage of the Palestinian population as early as the mid-1930s. David Ben-Gurion, often viewed in the West as a progressive Israeli, suggested this as early as 1937. In October 1937, Ben-Gurion wrote to his son Amos that if the Palestinians did not leave voluntarily, the Zionists would be compelled to use violence against them. "We must," argued Ben-Gurion, "expel the Arabs and take their places . . . and if we have the means to use force, not to dispossess the Arabs of the Negev and Transjordan, but to guarantee our own right to settle in those places, then we have to force them at our disposal." [6]

Ben-Gurion, like the other leaders, was careful to avoid public references to the Zionist strategy, knowing it would alienate British and U.S. supporters. For this reason he often stated in public that he opposed the concept of "transfer" (a euphemism for massive population expulsion), a public relations maneuver common among all politicians. When testifying before the British-sponsored Peele Commission in 1939, he expressed his outright abhorrence of the idea. [7]

Ben-Gurion's true position on the matter was fully demonstrated in July 1948, when he had an opportunity to decide whether or not to expel the vulnerable and unprotected Palestinian population in the townships of Lydda and Ramle. A young commander named Itzhak Rabin (destined to rise the highest leadership positions in Labor Party politics, becoming Prime Minister on two separate occasions), asked Ben-Gurion what they should do with the Palestinian population once he gained control of the villages. The steely eyed Ben-Gurion pointed toward the Jordan River and bluntly stated, "Drive them out!" [8] Today Israel's Ben Gurion International Airport is built on the ruins of Lydda!

Another incident occurred in the first week of December 1947, just four days after the November 29 United Nations partition to divide Palestine into Jewish and Arab states. Hostilities in the region were still relatively low. Ben-Gurion told a gathering of the progressive Mapai Party that the biggest problem facing the new Jewish state was the Palestinian population. The issue was not security related. Ben-Gurion's remarks reveal that the basic issue in the transfer campaign was simply to depopulate the land of its Palestinian inhabitants in order to prepare the area for future Jewish expansion in territory "free of Palestinians."

As Ben-Gurion warned, "There can be no stable and strong Jewish state so long as it has a Jewish majority of only 60 percent." [9] His answer was very simple: Expulsion! The phrase popularized in the 1990s to describe Serbian atrocities in Bosnia applies to Israel's Plan Dalet and other measures taken to "cleanse" the land.

The Plan Dalet cleansing effort left approximately a 40 percent minority of Palestinians in the new Jewish state. It was well known that their birth rate was considerably higher than the Jews if they were to remain then within ten years the Jews would become a minority in the Jewish state.

In recent years I have developed a close friendship with the Palestinian evangelical leader Rev. Audeh Rantisi, founder and director of the Evangelical Home for Boys in Ramallah. Audeh was born and raised in the Palestinian Christian township of Lydda, where his family traces their roots back to the fourth century C.E. On one of our many visits to the orphanage that Audeh and his wife, Pat, run in Ramallah, we sat and listened carefully to his story.

"I was eleven years old when the Israeli soldiers entered our town on July 5, 1948. We had been kept indoors for one whole week. We didn't know the reason at that time but afterward understood that the army generals who took over Lydda didn't know what to do with us. When they asked Ben-Gurion, he pointed with his finger: 'Out!'

"So it was on July 12 Israeli soldiers knocked at each door in the town and demanded that we should leave our homes open and go. We thought at the time they were going to search the homes and we could return later, because that is what happened in 1936 when the British ordered the people to leave their homes and go to a certain area for the day.

"This time it was an exodus without return. My parents, three brothers, and two sisters decided to go to St. Georges' Church in Lydda. At the turn of the road that led to the church, Israeli soldiers were posted. They forbade us to go to the church and demanded we follow the stream of people leaving town. We were not allowed to take the main road but led through a narrow opening that led to the mountains." [10]

Although Audeh had told his story several times, I could tell that there was still incredible pain and agony as he spoke.

"I walked hand in hand with my grandfather, who carried our only remaining food—a small tin of sugar and some milk for my aunt's two-year-old son, sick with typhoid. I remember many terrible sights. Mothers lying exhausted on the roadside with their children. I will never forget one mother who died from exhaustion. The daytime heat often was well over one hundred degrees. Her tiny baby was crying, trying to nurse at the dead mother's breast.

"Another incident occurred just outside Lydda when we were leaving. The Zionist soldiers ordered everyone to leave their money and valuables on a blanket and the soldiers would take it for their own. One young man and his wife of six months were close friends of our family. He refused to give up his little money and their wedding rings. A Zionist soldier pulled out his gun and simply shot our friend to death, right in front of us.

"There was no appeal. It was simple cruel murder. His young wife screamed and we all cried. I felt nauseated at once, my whole body numbed from the shock. This is how the journey began. By the third day of the march, many people were staggering and weary. I recall the wife of my father's cousin saying she was tired and could not go on. Suddenly she collapsed and died in front of us.

"We could not carry her so we took her body to a tree and left her there. She found peace and was spared the agony that we have continued to live as Palestinians." [11]

The Rantisi experience, like that of countless other Palestinians and the Jews before them, fulfilled the desperate words of the sage in Ecclesiastes: "And I thought the dead, who have already died, more fortunate than the living" (Eccles. 4:2).

After three days, Audeh Rantisi's family reached the outskirts of Ramallah, a Christian Palestinian city north of Jerusalem. His family, like the others, lived in a refugee camp on the outskirts of Ramallah. They were given only tents. Eventually the United Nations took responsibility for their survival. His father kept the key to the Lydda home around his neck for years, never letting go of the life that his family, like his Rantisi ancestors for 1,600 years, had known in Lydda.

Later, the Rantisis learned that Israel gave their home to two Jewish families but they, the original owners, were prevented from returning, or receiving compensation for their losses. Thus, reparations and the "right of return" have been granted to Jews but until now it has been denied to Palestinians.

Audeh Rantisi has tried to convert the pain of the 1948 period into a ministry of compassion and justice. He recently published his memoirs, *Blessed Are the Peacemakers,* where he writes,

> After more than four decades, I still bear the emotional scars of the Zionist invasion. Yet, as an adult, I see what I did not fully understand then: that the Jews are also human beings, themselves driven by fear, victims of history's worst outrages, rapidly, sometimes almost mindlessly searching for security. Lamentably, they have victimized my people. Four years after our flight from Lydda, I dedicated my life to the service of Jesus Christ. Like me and my fellow refugees, Jesus had lived in adverse circumstances, often with only a stone for a pillow. As with his fellow Jews 2000 years ago and the Palestinians today, an outside power controlled his homeland—my homeland. They tortured and killed him in Jerusalem, only ten miles from Ramallah, my new home. He was the victim of terrible inequities. Nevertheless, Jesus prayed on behalf of those who engineered his death, 'Father, forgive them. . . .' Can I do less? [12]

For decades, Israeli public relations experts have explained the Palestinian exodus in 1948 as a product of the appeals of Arab leaders who instructed the Palestinians to leave. In 1961, British journalist Erskine Childers investigated all radio broadcasts in the vicinity of Palestine, using the archives of the BBC. Childers learned there was not a single broadcast of this kind. In fact, the Arab leaders had told the people to remain in their homes.[13]

A new generation of Israeli historians has begun to examine the recently opened Israeli Defense Forces (IDF) archives of the 1948 period. They have concluded that the primary reason for the Palestinians' departure was sheer terrorism and a calculated strategy to depopulate the lands through force.

Since 1988, five Israeli historians have written studies of the 1948 events. Among them are former *Jerusalem Post* writers Tom Segev (*1948, The First Israelis*), and Benny Morris (*The Beginning of the Palestinian Refugee Problem*), plus Simha Flapan (*The Birth of Israel*). They have confirmed that, in most cases, the Palestinians fled neither of their own volition nor in response to appeals by Arab leaders but due to Zionist terrorist tactics.

Unfortunately, most of these authors are unwilling to recognize that Plan Dalet included the massacres that were eventually the most efficient instruments of the depopulation strategies. They claim that such massacres as Deir Yassin were exceptional cases and work of extremists. However, the noted British journalist David Hirst presents another perspective.

> Deir Yassin was an integral part of Plan Dalet, the master-plan for the seizure of most or all of Palestine. In the first phase of the military campaign that followed the partition "recommendation," the Zionists, their forces not yet fully mobilized, contented themselves with a holding operation in which they simultaneously "softened up" the Palestinians, engaged such fighting men as they did possess, and undermined, through terror, the morale of the civilian population. That was the essence of Plan Gimmel. Nothing was officially disclosed about Plan Dalet, Gimmel's successor, when it went into effect on 1 April, although Ben-Gurion was certainly alluding to it in an address six days later to the Zionist Executive: "Let us resolve not to be content with merely defensive tactics, but at the right moment to attack all along the line and not just within the confines of the Jewish State and the borders of Palestine, but to seek out and crush the enemy wherever he may be." [14]

Bertha Spafford Vester, a Christian missionary working in Jerusalem most of her life and very close to the Israeli government, was a witness to one of these tactics in 1948. She describes how, following the terrible Deir Yassin massacre, the Israeli jeeps and trucks drove through the small villages with microphones mounted on the trucks, intimidating Palestinian villagers to flee immediately or they would become the next Deir Yassin.

Deir Yassin was a small Palestinian village near Jerusalem that had signed a nonaggression pact with neighboring Jewish towns. It had no armed resistance. Menachem Begin's Stern Gang entered the village one night and massacred 254 men, women, and children. This fact was confirmed by Red Cross inspector Ryees.

In 1949, Spafford took a manuscript based on her memoirs to a New York publisher who happened to be Jewish. The publisher decided that he could not publish the memoirs unless she deleted the paragraphs that confirmed the above facts about Deir Yassin. She eventually relented and granted the wishes of the publisher. Her book *Our Jerusalem* is still distributed by the *Jerusalem Post* and is occasionally given to new subscribers. But Spafford also took the manuscript to a small company in Beirut, Lebanon, and published the entirety of her memoirs. Unfortunately, the later edition had a severely limited distribution.

The final figures of the Palestinian diaspora, counting those who fled between December 1, 1947, and the armistice in July 1949 will never be known. The United Nations has placed the number at approximately 758,000. Many Palestinian scholars have placed the actual number at 800,000. Israelis, such as historian S. Katz, suggest "no more than 440,000." [15] In addition, according to the Israeli League for Human and Civil Rights, over four hundred entire villages and towns were demolished. Some were turned into forests or parks, others hotels, still others into kibbutzim. The Palestinians diaspora created a nation that would need to struggle outside of its borders for dignity and self-determination.

From the earliest days of this crisis, the Christian churches of the Middle East and the West have wrestled with a legitimate response and eventual resolution of the Palestinian tragedy. Appeals went forth from the Anglican (and other) bishops of Jerusalem and the official Mediator of the United Nations, calling on the churches of the world to take a responsible position.

There have been two opinions that shaped the two different strategies on the matter. The first position taken by most Western churches, modeled by Elefan Rees, was that the Palestinians were refugees but had no political rights. Rees had been involved with the settling of East European Jews in Palestine for several years and was effective in delivering immediate tents, blankets, and food. This "Palestinians as refugees" approach dominated Protestant and Catholic thinking and that of the international community for decades.

Edwin Moll, who directed Lutheran World Federation activities in the Middle East for several years, urged Christians to go beyond relief efforts. In a speech presented at a conference on the Palestinian situation in Beirut, Lebanon, in September 1950, Moll said,

Three years—and there are those of us who have been here all of those years, of torturing refugee life with no prospect that the torture will come to an end. . . . It is my conviction that the Christian church has the means and the power to furnish the wherewithal so that we may demonstrate a big compassion. Could and should not Christian forces in the world exert their influence in the realm of justice? [16]

However, the World Council of Churches general secretary Dr. W. A. Visser't Hooft went further in his presentation. Visser't Hooft called for a "rediscovery of solidarity" "because it is precipitating the work of the Lord Himself." Citing Paul's 2 Corinthians letter, he read, "As a matter of equality your abundance at the present time should supply their want, so that their abundance may supply your want, so that there is equality." [17] Christians cannot be divided one from the other, for as one part of the body suffers, it all suffers.

Challenged by these presentations, the conference delegates issued a declaration, noting that they were "shocked by the plight of the refugees from Palestine" and felt responsibility "must be shared by many nations and political groups." The Palestinians were owed "a debt of restitution by their fellow men [sic], especially those who in any way shared responsibility for their present plight." The delegates concluded that there could be no permanent solution to the refugee crisis until there was a political settlement between Israel and the Arab states.

Today, going on fifty years after the Palestinian tragedy of 1948, the situation remains unresolved. Many of the original refugees have died and their grandchildren are growing up in refugee camps. Others have been displaced from country to country, three or even four times. Still the Palestinians have held together in articulating their case and finding various mechanisms to keep the search for justice alive in the international community.

What is the response of the Christian churches? It seems that there has been little progress in implementing the four options that presented themselves to Christians and the world in 1950: 1. Palestinians are refugees and in need of humanitarian relief efforts; 2. Palestinians deserve justice so we must improve their human rights under occupation; 3. Palestinian need to have a political solution if they are ever to have true freedom, justice, and peace, including the right of self-determination in their independent state; 4. Palestinians must be granted the "right of return," like the Jews of the world, and/or receive compensation for their land, losses, and psychological abuse.

Because Palestinians are one people facing these complex challenges, the Palestinian Christian community faces these same themes concerning their survival. Western Christians must now wrestle with the challenge to stand with Palestinians and Israelis to reverse these long-standing wrongs, to secure the future security of both peoples. A political resolution has an urgent moral responsibility attached as bloodshed continues to haunt both Palestinians and Israelis.

As for Christians, they must consider the realistic possibility that if Palestinian Christians have no state they will have no future, and the West will sit by and watch the Palestinian Christian presence die out during this present generation.

12

Stuck in Old Patterns: Will Peace Ever Come to the Holy Land?

. . . . Visiting the iniquity of the parents upon the children and the childrens' children, to the third and fourth generations.

(Exodus 34:7)

I sat on the south lawn of the White House at 11:00 a.m. on September 13, 1993, amazed that the event was unfolding on schedule. After more than seventy years of bloodshed, with more than fifty thwarted peace proposals since World War I, and periodic slaying of diplomats pursuing peaceful negotiations, there was still time for something to go wrong. Would there be a last-minute hitch in the plans that would postpone the signing ceremony? Would PLO Chairman Arafat be blocked from entering the White House? Or would there be an attempt by an Israeli or Palestinian extremist group to commit a terrorist action in the United States similar to the bombing of the World Trade Center in New York City?

Anything was possible in the countdown to Monday, September 13, 1993. But the reluctant handshake between Arafat and Rabin did take place, and the document was signed before one of the largest international television audiences in history.

The event and content of the peace agreement left me with mixed reactions. On the positive side, having invested nearly fifteen years working for peace and justice in the Middle East, I could not help but celebrate even a staged reconciliation between these two embittered enemies.

Rabin and Arafat were the symbolic expressions of two Semitic peoples whose collective suffering and intense insecurity had driven them into perpetual cycles of violence since World War I. Rabin's people had become the stronger party, thanks in large part to the military and economic support of Western nations. The Palestinians were the weaker party and the one with the most to lose. Would today's White House ceremony be another step in the "Balkanization" of the Palestine question or a true breakthrough for peace based on justice?

As I sat on the lawn, I thought back to a morning almost eleven years before to the day, when I entered the Palestinian refugee camps Sabra and Shatila (southern suburbs of Beirut, Lebanon) on September 20, 1982. A few hours earlier, Lebanese militias operating under Israeli military authority had massacred an estimated 2,500 unarmed Palestinian refugees. I entered the camps holding a handkerchief filled with cologne over my nose to keep me from choking on the stench of death that permeated the air. Red Cross emergency crews, fully equipped in gas masks, were still pulling mangled corpses from the rubble that had been their homes. I stood beside a mass grave with over 500 bodies beneath me, tears rolling from my eyes as the suffering and pain registered in my spirit.

The United States had promised Arafat and the PLO that their civilians, particularly those in the refugee camps, would be protected if the Palestinian army would withdraw from Lebanon, signaling an end to the bloody three-month war. No protection was provided, and Arafat paid a heavy political price for trusting the United States and Israel. Was he falling into a similar trap twelve years later? Some of his own people feared this was the case.

I thought back on my visits to Auschwitz, Dachau, and the Terezin Nazi concentration camps during the mid-1970s, when I led high school and college young people through Europe on two tour-study programs. We were so devastated by our experience at the camps that we wondered if Jews would ever overcome what had been done to them. Moreover, centuries of Western anti-Semitism provided the tragic historical context for this genocide, and Christians had much to confess in this regard. How could this pain ever be healed? Would the need for security and respect drive these two "cousins" apart forever and feed the daily hostilities that had dominated their lives for two generations?

Over fifty peace proposals connected to the Middle East have been submitted to various international agencies since World War I. Every proposal has failed to bring security and a just peace to the Israelis and Palestinians. The high degree of frustration and anger that evolved from each failed peace proposal usually resulted in significant bloodshed and at least seven wars in the region since 1948.

Seeing this endless cycle of violence, many people have taken the position that peace is beyond the reach of the Arabs and Israelis due to some character defect or a perpetual hatred between Jews and Arabs. Most doubt that they will ever be able to live in peace, so it is useless to try to help these eternal enemies.

There is a cynical joke about the Middle East that has been told in various forms for several years. It seems that a scorpion and a camel were swimming across the Jordan River one day up near the Sea of Galilee, where the headwaters are relatively wide. Suddenly a storm arose; the water became turbulent.

The scorpion called out to the camel, "Help me! I can't make it with the wind and the waves."

The camel shouted back, "No way, my friend. You will sting me and we both will die."

The scorpion called back, "Why would I do that? I need your help. Please let me climb on you."

The camel took pity and invited the scorpion to climb on board. Quickly they moved toward the Jordanian shore.

When they were within a few feet of the other side, the scorpion stung the camel, whose body began to weaken immediately from the poison.

"Why did you do that?" asked the camel. "Now I will drown and you will die with me."

The scorpion replied, "Welcome to the Middle East."

This negative humor is representative of many of our Western attitudes as we think about this region. So often I have heard, even from my own family, "Why do you waste your time on the Middle East? These people have been fighting since Cain and Abel and will never change. There is nothing that you can do about it with your limited influence."

I find this attitude reflected in the secular press and in much of the Christian literature available on the Middle East. In these arenas the Arabs are usually the "bad guys," and the authors assume that there is something inherently violent about Arab culture or Islam. The highly acclaimed volume *From Beirut to Jerusalem*, by *New York Times* Pulitzer Prize winner Thomas Friedman, is filled with this attitude, particularly in his overstated use of the concept "Hama Ethics."

My purpose in this chapter is to provide a historical context by which we might evaluate the present peace accords and raise the following questions: Have the Oslo Accords taken us back to the 1920s? Are we returning to an enforced peace or will the Declaration of Principles lead to justice and a lasting settlement for both sides? What is our task as Western Christians or people committed to justice and peace?

Phase One: 1915-1923

In *Culture and Imperialism*, Edward Said argues that during most of the nineteenth century, a Western colonial orientation dominated virtually every aspect of the West's relationships with Africa, South and Central America, and the Orient, including the Middle East. This influence can be analyzed today by looking closely at such fields as political alliances, economic interests, missionary activities, and literature.

Said examines nineteenth- and twentieth-century novels in the United States, England, and France. He begins by citing the astounding fact that by 1885, England and France controlled over half of the land and people on the planet.[1] The percentage grew as the years moved on and World War I arrived. The earthshaking events that evolved after the Great War left significant problem areas that the major powers failed to resolve. One region involved Serbian-Christian vs. Bosnian-Muslim hostilities in the former Yugoslavia, a delayed time bomb that exploded in the 1990s. Another conflict involved the Israelis and Palestinians, and can be traced to the same period.

One of the most objective accounts of this history is *The Chariot of Israel* by the British statesman Sir James Harold Wilson. Wilson was viewed as a significant "friend of Israel" during his term as prime minister of England and remained so until this book appeared. Now out of print and curiously unavailable, his record of the period from 1915 through 1948 is especially useful and is the source of much that follows. To a lesser extent, I will draw on the British historian David Fromkin's *A Peace to End All Peace: Creating the Modern Middle East 1914-1922.*[2]

Wilson is aware of the considerable influence of the revived evangelical Christian millenial theology on the British public and such influential statesmen as Lord Shaftesbury, Lord Balfour, and David Lloyd George. In chapter eight I developed the thesis that these early expressions of evangelical Christian Zionism helped to prepare British politicians and the British public to adopt modern Jewish Zionism as an answer to the Empire's colonial aspirations for the Holy Land and the Middle East. Beneath the colonialist attitudes and political motives of the Western powers was a strong religious conviction that God had originally given the land to the Jews, and restoring it to them would bring God's blessing on the British. Wilson's account underscores how domestic British political concerns converged with this evangelical Christian theological aberration. These trends also converged with the British Empire's colonial interests in its "jewel," India, and developing a shorter passage through the Middle East. The Zionist movement seemed to provide the political and religious answer that many high-ranking British officials were seeking in order to achieve their goals.

Less persuaded by religious arguments in deference to the imperial dreams of England was Winston Churchill. A major figure in Britain's campaign against the Ottoman Turks, Churchill was later stationed in Palestine during the early Mandate years. He was impressed by the Zionist movement and saw it as an important instrument for the Empire to fulfill its aspirations. In the mid-1920s, he received a scroll of the Torah and planted a tree at the future site of Hebrew University on Mt. Scopus (Jerusalem). He told a Jewish audience, "Personally, my heart is full of sympathy for Zionism. This sympathy has existed for a long time, since twelve years ago, when I was in contact with the Manchester Jews."[3]

His reference was to Chaim Weitzmann and his support staff, who maintained a close relationship with Lord Balfour and Prime Minister Lloyd-George. Although Churchill went on to state that the Jews must support "the moral and material benefit of all Palestinians," he believed that the political power and control of the land should be with the Zionist leadership. This is the crux of the issue in the Israeli-Palestinian conflict. Churchill, like his political colleagues in London, failed to see the consequences of these assumptions and their effect on the Palestinian majority.

Among the most problematic of the maneuvers undertaken by the British in relation to the Arabs was their promise of future independence for Arab territories, as stated in the McMahon correspondence of late 1915-1916 (see Appendix A). Sir Henry McMahon, British High Commissioner for Egypt, was the official designated by the Foreign Office to convey certain promises to the Arabs to enlist their support in the war against the Ottoman Turks. McMahon drafted a series of letters to the Sharif Hussein of Mecca, later king of the Hejaz and great-grandfather of the present King Hussein of Jordan. Hussein was the foremost leader of the Arab masses and became the central character in Lawrence of Arabia's effort to unify the Arabs in the war against the Turks.

The McMahon correspondence stated that the Arabs would receive independence once the Turks were defeated. One of McMahon's letters designated zones that would be excluded, such as Aden, western Syria (eventually Lebanon), and Kuwait. The remainder of the Middle East was to be granted independence in return for the Arabs joining the British war effort—or so the Arabs were led to believe.

But Hussein and the Arabs were unaware of the extensive relations and promises made to France, England's colonial competitor. On May 16, 1916, the British secretly signed the Sykes-Picot Treaty, which promised to divide the Middle East into two spheres of influence, or Mandates, that would be granted to the British and the French. The League of Nations granted to England the Mandate for Palestine, Iraq, and Transjordan. France received Syria and Lebanon.

Under the Mandate system, the colonial powers were obliged to nurture their subjects toward independence within a short period of time. This course was followed for all nations with the notable exception of Palestine. In Palestine, another strategy was the driving force in that future trouble spot. Behind the scenes was the close political and religious alliance between the British elite and the proponents of Zionism.

The secret Sykes-Picot Treaty was followed by the Balfour Declaration of November 2, 1917, whereby the British granted for the first time a questionable form of international legitimacy to the still small and somewhat obscure Zionist movement. Few Jews in Western Europe or the United States supported Zionism at that stage. By publicly declaring their intent to create "a homeland for the Jews," without providing for the political legitimacy of the Arab majority of Palestine's population, the British violated the principles of the League of Nations. They took one party's side in a dispute that would negate the aspirations of over 90 percent of the population.

To clarify the significance of the British decision, we note that when the Balfour Declaration was issued, approximately 600,000 of the residents of Palestine were Arabs (Christians and Muslim). They constituted 93 percent of the population. Arabs owned over 98 percent of the land.[4] The words of the Jewish author Arthur Koestler seem appropriate in summarizing the legacy of the Balfour Declaration: "In Palestine you have the case of one party giving another party's land to a third party."[5]

The Arabs were not informed of the secret agendas of the British, the French, or the Zionists until the Bolsheviks released the documents in December 1918. When Hussein learned of the British double cross, he protested to the Foreign Office, which sent a special envoy to repair the damage. In the encounter with Hussein, British commander D. C. Hogarth stated that the new British declaration on Palestine would not assist the Zionists if it was not "compatible with the existing population," nor would Britain even contemplate the establishment of a Jewish state in Palestine.[6]

Unfortunately for his Arab constituents, Hussein made the mistake of accepting the British promises at face value without insisting on written guarantees, timetables for the independence of the Arab regions, and means of maintaining accountability concerning the Zionist-British agenda. He clearly underestimated the influence of the Zionist leadership in England and the intimate relationship between British political elite and the Zionists. These tragic miscalculations would have dire consequences.

At the same time, Arab leaders in Syria were pursuing another strategy. They assembled in Damascus during July 1919 for the Syrian National Congress. After several delays, they announced on March 8, 1920, the establishment of an independent Syrian state that would include today's nations of Syria, Lebanon, Jordan, Israel, and Palestine. Faisal, son of Hussein, would be king of the proposed constitutional monarchy. The initiative demonstrated the national aspirations of the Arabs, including Palestinians, during these critical years.

But the British, French, and Zionists opposed the Arab proposal for a Greater Syria because it challenged the agendas that were quietly underway. On May 5, 1920, the Allied Powers met at San Remo to resolve the future status of the defeated Ottoman territories. The proposals that emerged from San Remo were similar to the Sykes-Picot Agreement. The vision of the Arabs for Palestine was not included at San Remo.

Meanwhile, the League of Nations understanding of the former Ottoman territories, as influenced by U.S. President Woodrow Wilson, were developed according to a series of principles designed to combat colonialism and move indigenous peoples toward self-determination. Wilson's Fourteen Points and the Covenant of the League of Nations formulated many of the first internationally accepted norms of human rights law, including the principle of self-determination.

According to the Covenant, various classifications of transitional government (called "Mandates") were prescribed for the former Ottoman territories. The more developed peoples, including the Palestinians, were designated as Mandate "A" and would be given a period of tutelage under Western powers before realizing full independence. The text of the League of Nations' Covenant states this principle of "provisional" independence.

> Certain communities formerly belonging to the Turkish Empire have reached a stage of development where their existence as independent nations can be provisionally recognized subject to the rendering of administrative advice and assistance by a Mandatory until such time as they are able to stand alone. The wishes of these communities must be a principle consideration in the selection of the Mandatory.[7]

Given the fact that most of the population of Palestine was Palestinian Arab, and that the League of Nations was publicly committed to facilitate self-determination for the indigenous peoples of these regions, one might conclude that the Palestinian Arab majority and a Jewish minority should receive one state in Palestine—not two states, and not an ethnic Jewish or Arab state.

However, when the Western powers met at San Remo for the conference that would shape the agenda for a post World War I settlement, they pushed the clock backward. They adopted the Sykes-Picot formula for Palestine rather than one consistent with the Covenant.

The Paris Peace Conference of 1922, which ratified the San Remo decisions, formally granted the Palestine Mandate to the British. At the insistence of Zionist leaders and their advocates among the British political elite, the Paris Peace Proposals included the very language of the Balfour Declaration in its final text. Paragraph III of the Preamble to the Mandate stated, "Whereas recognition has thereby (through the Balfour Declaration) been given to the historical connection of the Jewish people and to the grounds for reconstituting their national home in that country."[8] Zionist leader Weitzmann had lobbied for the phrase "recognizing the historic rights of the Jews to Palestine," but the British Foreign Secretary, Lord Curzon, dropped that language believing it to be both factually inaccurate and presumptuous on the part of the Zionists.

Nonetheless, the political damage had been done concerning the exclusion of Arab aspirations for Palestine and the virtual negation of Palestinian political legitimacy, self-determination, and future statehood. The Zionists had scored a major victory, and the Palestinian majority had lost by default their first and most important political battle. The die had been cast for inevitable bloodshed and favoritism toward one party at the expense of the other.

Moreover, when the British received the Mandate from the League of Nations, it was stipulated that the Jewish Agency would assist the British in developing Palestine. The World Zionist Organization had created the Agency and the Jewish National Fund in 1901 as mechanisms to purchase and hold land in Palestine for exclusively Jewish settlement. The recognition of these bodies by the British granted them *de facto* international legitimacy and authorized them to purchase and control land for exclusively Jewish colonization. These Zionist policies became the focal point of conflict from 1920s through the 1940s.

Unfortunately, the Mandate did not allow for a parallel Palestinian Agency to be created to assist the majority of the population, even though this extending of the right of self-determination was a central tenet of the League of Nations.

Today, over seventy years after the Paris Peace Accords were signed and implemented, the Palestinian Arabs have yet to see their promised self-determination and independent state. The Zionists' agenda, as defined by Theodor Herzl and Chaim Weitzmann, and implemented in part by the British, had no place for Palestinian self-determination, the development of the economy and resources of the Palestinian Arab sector, and certainly no room for a binational or independent Palestinian State. The British, for the most part, were willing to live with this arrangement because it fulfilled their colonial interests and satisfied those who had adopted the pseudo-Christian premillennialist arguments. Lord Balfour summarized his support for Zionism as clearly as one could articulate it.

> For in Palestine we do not propose even to go through the form of consulting the wishes of the present inhabitants of the country, though the American Commission has been going through the forms of asking what they are. The four great powers are committed to Zionism and Zionism, be it right or wrong, good or bad, is rooted in age-long traditions, in present needs, in future hopes, of far profounder import than the desire and prejudices of the 700,000 Arabs who now inhabit the land. In my opinion that is right.[9]

Why would this high British official support Zionism, "right or wrong"? Because Zionism fit the "age-long traditions and future hopes" of the British, both in political and religious terms. Again, the Christian Zionist orientation had met its match with British colonial interests to form a strong bond of political action.

Experts in international law, such as professors Thomas and Sally Mallison of the George Washington University Law School, have evaluated the documents of this period and concluded that the primary authority for interpreting the Class A mandate designation (as in the case of Palestine) rested with the League of Nations Covenant. The Covenant itself superseded the language of the preamble and thus the inclusion of the Balfour Declaration. The Mallisons state,

> The Mandate for Palestine was, under the primary authority of the League of Nations Covenant, the basic constitutional document for the interim government agreed to by the League of Nations. Its provisions, therefore, are of particular importance in implementing the juridical limitations imposed by the Balfour Declaration as an integral part of the Mandate.
> It is fundamental that no part of the Palestine mandate could be valid if it were in violation of any provisions of the League of Nations Covenant.
> The Covenant was the preeminent constitutional instrument of the organized world community of the time and the Palestine Mandate was authorized to it and subject to its limitations.[10]

This legal provision is underscored by the strict principles of the prime mover of the League of Nations, Woodrow Wilson, and by the historical evidence of the period. Wilson's chief adviser on foreign affairs, Colonel Edward Mandell House, was deeply troubled by the content and spirit of the Balfour Declaration when he received an advanced copy on May 18, 1917. On seeing the British and French strategy to divide the Middle East between them and ignore the desires of the indigenous peoples, House remarked, "It is all bad and I told Balfour so. They are making it (the Middle East) a breeding place for future war."[11]

Wilson, a highly principled academic and son of a Presbyterian clergyman, was committed to the human and national rights of indigenous peoples. The British, French, and Zionist agendas were contrary to his wishes, although he was not always aware that this was the case. If he lacked certain skills in the area of realpolitik, Wilson was consistent in his devotion to ethical principles. Thus, on February 11, 1918, he spoke to the U.S. Congress concerning the implication of his "Four Principles" upon which a peace settlement could be realized. Wilson's second and third principles were the following:

> 2. That peoples and provinces are not to be bartered about from sovereignty to sovereignty as if they were chattels or pawns in a game, even the great game, now for ever discredited, of the balance of power, but that
> 3. Every territorial settlement involved in this war must be made in the interest and for the benefit of the populations concerned, and not as a part of any mere adjustment or compromise of claims amongst rival states.
> In the President's mind and spirit, the rights and needs of the indigenous peoples was first and foremost in the order of priorities, or in his words: "Every territorial settlement . . . must be made in the interest and for the benefit of the populations concerned."[12]

On July 4, 1918, Wilson was even more clear in defining the ends for which the United States and others were fighting. These included:

> The settlement of every question, whether of territory or sovereignty, of economic arrangement, or of political relationship, upon the basis of the free acceptance of that settlement by the people immediately concerned, and not upon the basis of the material interest or advantage of any other nation or people which may desire a different settlement for the sake of its own exterior influence or mastery.[13]

Without question, President Wilson's principles set a high standard. But the reality of hard-nosed politics and greed by the major powers was to supersede the principles for decades.

Fearing British support for the Zionist agenda, the Palestinian leadership in Jerusalem expressed its desire to the King-Crane Commission that the Mandate for Palestine be granted to the United States. The San Remo decision of April 20, 1920, granted the Mandate to the British. In March 1921, the British ceded territory east of the Jordan River to the Emirate of Transjordan, whose leaders remained in a close semi-dependency upon the British.

Sensing problems in the Palestine case, Woodrow Wilson dispatched the King-Crane Commission to evaluate the issues of the region. After several months of painstaking interviews and meetings with Arabs and Jews alike, the Commission recorded that the overwhelming number of Palestinians wanted Palestine to remain under the sharif of Mecca and become an independent state. The territory of the state would include Syria, Lebanon, and Palestine. In addition, the King-Crane Commission warned against "the extreme Zionist program for Palestine of unlimited immigration of Jews, looking finally to making Palestine a Jewish state."[14]

Not only was the King-Crane Commission report ignored by the League of Nations and major powers, it was not released to the public until late 1922, nearly three years after their visit to the Middle East. It is, nonetheless, significant that this official U.S. presidential inquiry into the conflict, the first major U.S. governmental involvement in the Palestine-Zionist problem, formulated conclusions consistent with the Palestinian majority and the spirit of the League of Nations Covenant. That the recommendations were ignored by the British, the United States, and the international community was detrimental not only to the Palestinian majority, but also to the future of peace and justice in the region. These decisions foreshadowed the processes that dominate this even today.

Palestinians chose a policy of nonparticipation in the various British and Zionist strategies developed during the Mandate. As a result, they excluded themselves from influence in articulating their case to the British during the Mandate. This left a political vacuum that the Zionists were able to fill and control for decisive early years of the Mandate period.

Prior to this period there were no significant incidents of Palestinian

Arab-Jewish violence in the Holy Land. Problems had been growing in recent years due to Zionist colonization, but actual violence did not become a concern until the Zionist program was adopted by the British and actual implementation commenced in the 1920s. Palestinians increasingly sensed the danger of Zionist colonization and the degree of betrayal by the British. Isolated attacks were reported as early as 1921 in the Jaffa-Tel Aviv district. By 1929 there were full-scale massacres of Jews by Palestinians in Hebron. These assaults were more than symbolic reminders that the option of peaceful coexistence in the Holy Land was rapidly fading. The source of the problem and means of resolving it should have been evident to all who had more than a passing interest in these lands and peoples.

Phase Two: 1923-1949

A British census in 1922 revealed that there were 589,000 Muslims and 71,000 Christians in Palestine, with 83,000 Jews. The Jewish community had grown from approximately 7 percent of the population in 1918 to 14 percent in 1922. The Peel Commission, sent by the British Parliament in 1936, showed the Jewish increase had reached nearly 400,000, or about one third of the population. The settlement process had moved forward at a remarkably fast pace.

At the heart of this process was the new legitimacy that the Jewish National Fund had achieved under the British Mandate following the San Remo and Paris Peace Conference. The JNF rigorously adhered to two principles in its purchase and holding of land in Palestine. First, all land would be purchased but the title held by the JNF for exclusively Jewish use. Second, only Jews could live on these lands.

The Peel report illustrates the growth of Zionist settlement policy with the case of Petah Tikvah, the new Tel Aviv suburb, which had grown from 700 acres and a population of 125 in the 1890s to 5,000 acres and a population of 4,000 in 1925. Tel Aviv itself grew from 2,000 in 1914 to a city of 30,000 in 1936, which the Peel Commission described as "the only town in the world which is wholly Jewish."[15] The Jewish Agency maintained control over the lands under its authority so that the settlements were exclusively Jewish. The Histradut (the General Federation of Jewish Labor) provided jobs for Jews only.

Palestinian Arab anger over Zionist settlements and British complicity in the arrangement began to turn violent during the 1920s. Clashes developed at the Wailing Wall and Dome of the Rock (Haram al-Sharif) Plaza with disastrous consequences. The Peel Commission estimated that 133 Jews and 116 Arabs were killed during this period. Sir Walter Shaw of the British Colonial Office reported,

To the Arabs it must appear improbable that such competitors (Jews) will in years to come be content to share the country with them. These fears have been intensified by the more extreme statements of Zionist policy and the Arabs have come to see in the Jewish immigrant not only a menace to their livelihood but a possible overlord of the future.[16]

The report went on to document the understandable resentment Palestinians were expressing as their best agricultural land was sold to Zionist organizations and settled exclusively by Jews. It also noted that the Arab population was beginning to experience economic consequences from the Jewish settlements and support granted by the British Mandatory Government in Palestine. It warned that Jewish-Arab tensions would only increase if the ambitious policies of the Zionists were to continue. The massacre of more than forty Jewish settlers in the Hebron region in 1929 underscored the case.

In the 1930s and 1940s, the two communities pulled further and further apart. The Zionist agencies were by then drawing on significant international economic and military assistance while their agricultural and industrial sectors grew in remarkable ways. Jewish immigration increased. Due in part to Hitler's accession to power in Germany, between 1933 and 1938 over 217,000 Jews entered Palestine to strengthen the Zionist cause. By 1939 the Jewish population had risen to 429,605, or 28 percent of the total.[17] Palestinians saw that their land and hope for an independent state were slipping away, due in large part to the British-Zionist alliance.

In 1936 the Palestinians launched a series of boycotts, strikes, and demonstrations. Soon armed conflict with the British authorities followed, leading to an open revolt by Arabs throughout Palestine. The British crushed the rebellion in a decisive and brutal fashion, killing over fifteen thousand and imprisoning or killing most of their leadership.

The total defeat of the Palestinian community following the 1936 revolt had three major side effects. First, the Zionist militias received increased military training from the British during the revolt. Much of this was coordinated by a British evangelical Christian, Colonel Orde Wingate, who personally trained the young Moshe Dayan and a generation of Israeli military officials. Second, both the morale and leadership of the Palestinian community were destroyed, setting back their cause for approximately thirty years. Third, the bitterness between the Jews and Palestinians became so deep-seated that potential marriage seemed to be inconceivable.

Within this atmosphere, the Zionists turned to a maximalist program. No longer was a single democracy or binational state worthy of consideration by the Jews, a concept promoted by such luminaries as philosopher Martin Buber, Albert Einstein, and president of Hebrew University Judah Magnes. Hard-line Zionists such as David Ben-Gurion had won the day.

During this period the British sent a series of royal commissions to investigate the growing crisis in Palestine. Perhaps the most noteworthy was the Peel Commission of 1936, which Sir Harold Wilson calls the most important report on record of this era. The Peel Commission concluded that Palestine must be partitioned into an Arab and Jewish state, the first major international statement of this proposal. Both the Palestinians and the Zionists rejected the proposal. The Jews preferred one Jewish state in Palestine. The Palestinians favored one of two proposals—one parliamentary democracy in Palestine whereby Jews, Christians, and Muslims would be equal; or the Greater Syria program would be enacted as articulated above.

Harold Wilson adds that the British Colonial Office and those who implemented policies in Palestine under the Mandate were gravely insensitive to the needs of the Palestinian Arabs. Referring to the missed signals given by Palestinian leadership and the violent protests in Palestine, Wilson comments,

> What was emerging, and highlighted by the Arabs' resort to violence in 1929-30, was the fact that Whitehall and Parliament had for so long underrated the Arabs' deep hostility to Jewish immigration, and had in fact over many years too easily accepted the comfortable doctrine that anything that was good for the Jews would be good for the Arabs. As Peel was to report six years after this uprising, British inability to appreciate the reasons for Arab resentment of Jewish immigration and land purchase was based on the "old original assumption that the two races could and would learn to live together."[18]

We might add that this was not a simple case of two people learning to live together. In fact, they had been living in Palestine for generations prior to World War I. Rather, the problems commenced with the implementation of the Zionists' political strategy in relation to the land of Palestine, a strategy that was fully supported by the British Government. Prior to World War I, the conflicts were manageable but the shift in power and the introduction of the Zionist element changed the course of Palestine. Zionist policy toward the Palestine question solidified on their demand for a single Jewish state to be created in Palestine, a position that became the operational consensus among Zionists during the famous Biltmore Declaration in New York in 1943.

The Partition, Birth of Israel, and Catastrophe

The situation in Palestine deteriorated rapidly during the 1940s. The British found themselves waging a three-way war; while they fought against the Palestinians and their former clients, the Zionists, they were fighting for their national survival in World War II. By 1947, the British decided to depart from Palestine and hand the situation over to the United Nations, which in turn formed the United Nations Special Committee on Palestine (UNSCOP). The Partition proposal was adopted by the UN General Assembly in November 1947.

The Jews quickly accepted the Partition ruling. But the Palestinians rejected it for several reasons. First, the Palestinians had long suspected British duplicity in their dealing with the Arabs. Second, the Zionists still constituted only 30 percent of the population of Palestine. And despite all the maneuvers by the World Zionist Organization to seize the land, Palestinians still owned most of the land.

But this overwhelming superiority of the Palestinians in terms of land ownership and numerical superiority might have given them an illusion of dominance. Certainly the Palestinian leadership seems to have operated in a realm of prolonged political fantasy, apparently incapable of grasping the power that the Zionists had seized. Moreover, several Arab nations promised to liberate the Holy Land for the Palestinians, a promise that had more bravado than reality. Palestinians also rejected the Partition because they had long supported a single democratic state in Palestine, with equality for Jews, Muslims, and Christians.

In the period immediately following the 1949 armistice, Israel had increased its holdings from the proposed 55 percent to 78 percent of the land. In addition, between 725,000 and 775,000 refugees were expelled to the neighboring Arab countries while the Zionists assumed control of their land. The Zionists controlled over 77 percent of Palestine by 1949. The Palestinians were in total disarray; they had lost most of their land, lost control of their economy and destiny, and were without the political structures and benefactors necessary to realize their national aspirations. They were now a nation of refugees, living under Israeli (or Arab) military occupation.

The Denial of Palestinian Rights: 1967 to Present

The Palestinians had known severe occupations throughout their history, but now they faced four additional problems. First, they had lost their political rights in the decisions of the previous fifty years. Second, a significant percentage of the population had been forced from their land and were now destitute refugees. According to United Nations figures, approximately one quarter of a million Palestinians lost their homes, land, and livelihood in this period. Third, the Palestinians lost over half their land in the 1947 Partition decision, then an additional fourth in the Israeli military operations of 1948-1949. In 1967 they would lose the remainder of Palestine. Fourth, the new occupying army, Israel, had as part of its political agenda the negation of basic Palestinian rights and national aspirations. In their weakened and dispersed state, it was questionable if the Palestinians would survive as a people with national aspirations.

In the Galilee, Israel pursued a policy of containment and Judaization (settlement by Jews) of the land from 1950-1967. A new and more efficient form of this strategy was refined and applied to the West Bank, East Jerusalem, and Gaza Strip following the June 1967 War. In an effort to provide a historical-political shorthand of these years, I will summarize the policies in terms of *five strategies of negation*.

Negation of the Land

The most vital dimension of the Israeli-Palestinian conflict had always turned on the question, "Who controls the land?" Throughout history, most populations or nations that controlled the land survived. From its earliest formulations, the Zionist movement has consistently pursued the policy articulated at the first World Zionist Congress in 1897—creating a Jewish state recognized by law.

The early theme of Zionist father Theodor Herzl stated, "A land of no people for a people with no land." The assumption was that the land was (a) uninhabited, or (b) exclusively given to the Jews even if inhabited. The dogged pursuit of land has been consistently adhered to by Zionist leadership prior to the creation of Israel and has continued until today. Following the hostilities of 1948, the new state of Israel destroyed a minimum of 418 Palestinian villages and expelled the residents to adjacent villages or other Arab countries.[19]

A recent case illustrating the land issue involved a leading U.S. cleric and a major Zionist agency. In the spring of 1994, the Jewish National Fund approached Joseph Cardinal Bernardin, archbishop of the Roman Catholic Archdiocese of Chicago, with what appeared to be a distinguished honor. The Cardinal accepted. The offer was that Cardinal Bernardin be presented the Tree of Life Award by the JNF, followed by the establishment in Israel of the Cardinal Bernardin Forest.

I and another peace advocate in Chicago contacted the archdiocese to see if they were aware of the ethical implications of this decision and whether they had investigated the possible consequences for the Palestinian Christian community. After a series of conversations and exchanges of documents, it became clear to us that the issue was more complicated than the archdiocese was initially aware. We requested that Christian organizations in Palestine begin an investigation into the potential fallout on local Christians should the cardinal accept the award and forest in his name. We also asked the Galilee-based Arab Association for Human Rights to research the proposed site of the Cardinal Bernardin Forest.

My private conversations with the Chicago archdiocese quickly made clear that the Jewish National Fund had misrepresented itself, the nature of its land acquisition procedures, and the nature of the Bernardin Forest. The archdiocese was initially offered a forest site in the Jerusalem region, which it wisely declined, knowing that the status of Jerusalem land was still unresolved in international law. Further, if the archdiocese had accepted the construction of a forest in the greater Jerusalem region, it would probably have been built over the ruins of one of the 418 villages Israel destroyed after 1948. The local Christian community would have been deeply hurt and angered by a decision of Christian leaders in Chicago that was insensitive to their history and present condition. In addition, such a decision, when made public by Israel, would place local Christians in a compromising position before their Muslim and secular colleagues.

A few weeks before the award was to be granted to the cardinal, the JNF proposed another site for the Bernardin forest, in the Tiberias district of Galilee. At this point I contacted Catholic leaders in Galilee and the Nazareth based Arab Association for Human Rights and requested they conduct research on the proposed site, with particular concern about the acquisition of the land and whether it was on the site of a destroyed Palestinian village. As of this writing, it appears that the proposed site of the Joseph Cardinal Bernardin Forest is adjacent to or contiguous with the Arab village of Lubya and the Jewish settlement of Lavi. The land is in the possession of the Jewish National Fund and Lubya is one of the 418 destroyed villages.

Israel has repeatedly built a number of enterprising projects over the destroyed villages, a matter of severe Christian (Jewish and Muslim) ethical consequences. Not only are these villages covered by forests, shopping centers, parks, or Israeli settlements, but money is raised by the JNF to continue similar operations. Our appeals to the cardinal's office for a delay in accepting the award and forest were not heeded.

The director of the Association, Mansur Kardosh, sent me the following reply, which I forwarded to the Cardinal's office in Chicago one week prior to the award ceremony.[20]

The story of Lubya has its parallels in Father Chacour's village of Biram and Reverend Ateek's village of Beisan, (see chapters 10-11) also occupied and destroyed in similar Zionist campaigns.

The pattern of confiscation and control of the land has continued in Galilee and the West Bank, East Jerusalem, and the Gaza Strip until today. Since 1967, Israel has concentrated on the occupied territories to the extent that today over 60 percent of the land has been confiscated or declared state land, and its jurisdiction has been automatically transferred to either the government or other proper authority. This representative case demonstrates how central the issue of land has been for Palestinians (Christians and Muslims) and how Israel and the Zionist organizations have worked to deny Palestinian control over the land. Further, the case of Cardinal Bernardin reveals how Western Christian leaders have been used to advance Zionist strategies.

Peoplehood and International Legitimacy

As late as 1969, Israeli Prime Minister Golda Meir could state in public that "there are no Palestinians." Israel's aim has been to deny Palestinians their national identity and thus their legitimate claims as a people. One strategy was to state that Palestinians are not an identifiable people with a claim and should be absorbed into the Arab nations. Some officials, most recently General Ariel Sharon and other militant members of the Knesset, have recommended that Palestinians be expelled to Jordan to set up a state there.

However, Palestinians trace their roots in the land of Palestine to the early Semitic tribes of Canaan, including the Jebusites whose King Melchizadek welcomed the Patriarch Abraham and Sarah when they arrived in approximately 2000 B.C. The Palestinians have been an identifiable people with national aspirations since the turn of the last century. Despite their political and land losses to the Zionists and British, Palestinian claims to the land and their identity as a people remain a fact. The recent Oslo Agreements are a step toward supporting these claims, but doubts linger as to their capacity to deliver all that was promised on September 13, 1993.

Self-Determination

For a people and a nation to survive, they must be granted legitimacy by the international community. Otherwise, their claims to land, freedom, and self-determination will be lost in the corridors of diplomacy or on the battlefield, as in the case of the Kurds, Native Americans, and countless others. The League of Nations Covenant recognized this fact in the World War I era and proposed the concept of self-determination as a vital component for the prevention of future wars and the safeguarding of future states, indigenous peoples, and nations that would evolve from the former Ottoman Empire. One of those "nations in waiting" was the Palestinians.

However, we have also observed how the colonial politics of the British Foreign Office, British domestic politics, and the agenda of the Zionist movement combined to undermine the just claims of the Palestinian community. Their dream of an independent Palestinian state based on equality for Muslims, Jews, and Christians, with accompanying democratic procedures and institutions, was undermined over the successive two decades. When Israel was created and the resistance of the Arabs and victory of the Zionists was completed, the Palestinians had lost their state and over three-fourths of their land.

However, they did not lose their national right to self-determination, which includes a state of their own and the right to be represented in negotiations by their own leadership. These rights have been reiterated by the United Nations on an annual basis since 1948 and we explicitly understood in the terms of the Mandate Agreement. Since 1967, the positions of most nations in the world has moved toward a consensus that the Palestinians, like Israelis, must have an independent state of their own, based in law and international legitimacy. The formulas for this are found in United Nations resolutions 242, 338 (see Appendixes B and C), and 38-58 C. These outline an Israeli withdrawal from East Jerusalem, the West Bank, and the Gaza Strip; the commencement of an international conference under the United Nations Security Council's authority; and negotiations leading to a Palestinian state in these territories beside the state of Israel. Israel's rights and security would be guaranteed through law and subsequent treaties.

Time after time various nations and international forums have proposed alternative representatives for the Palestinians in negotiations determining their future. Noteworthy are the Camp David Accords with Egyptian President Anwar Sadat representing Palestinian concerns. More recently, the issue of political (a people with political rights) legitimacy for the Palestinians became an issue in the Madrid Peace Process, initiated by the Bush Administration following the Gulf War. At Israel's insistence, Palestinians affiliated with the PLO or Palestinians from Jerusalem could not participate in negotiations, thus raising the question of legitimacy. In these instances, Israel was able to decide who could or could not represent the Palestinians whereas Palestinians could not decide the matter for themselves.

Leadership

Throughout Palestinian history, the Zionist movement has denied legitimacy to Palestinian leadership and proposed alternatives to the Western decision makers. There are numerous cases of the Palestinian leaders being eliminated by Israeli assassins or through internal military or governmental procedures, such as expulsions, house arrest, or imprisonment. Consider the case of Dr. Hanna Nasser, president of the prestigious Birzeit University, was illegally expelled from the West Bank to Jordan in the middle of the night in 1975. Hanna Nasser happens to be a pacifist and devout Anglican Christian (Episcopalian) layman. His wife, Tanya, became a leader in the international YWCA movement and was lead soprano in their church choir. Their pastor and bishop in the new church home in Amman, their new place of exile, was expelled from Jerusalem by Israel in 1967. Bishop Elia Khouri went on to become, not only Anglican bishop of Jordan, but also a member of the PLO Executive Committee and a close adviser of Chairman Arafat. Well over 2000 Palestinian leaders have been expelled by Israel since 1967, a practice that violates all standards of international law, including the Fourth Geneva Conventions (1949) of which Israel and the United States are signatories.

The questions of leadership and legitimacy have surfaced repeatedly in various regional and international diplomatic procedures related to the Middle East. One case involved the Camp David Accords, where the Palestinians were excluded in matters pertaining to their situation and Egypt's Anwar Sadat represented them, at the insistence of Israel and the United States. More recently, the Madrid Peace Process, initiated by the Bush Administration in November 1991, allowed Israel to decide who would represent the Palestinians. Israel refused to allow any Palestinian officially related to the PLO and Palestinians from Jerusalem to participate in negotiations. These restrictions raised the question of legitimacy, which Israel was able to secure for themselves and deny to the Palestinians.

Such a strategy might be compared to a farmer in Pennsylvania whose land was illegally stolen by a more powerful, wealthy farmer in a neighboring township. When the courts met to decide the fate of the poor farmer, he was not allowed to speak for himself. Instead, the courts decided to bring in an "expert" from Washington, D.C. As it turned out, the expert knew nothing of local laws, history, and the importance of the land to the local farmer. In fact, the expert took financial payments from the wealthy farmer and ended up opposing the case of his client.

The wealthy farmer then received the land of the poor farmer and ordered him to be expelled from his property. He was forced at gunpoint to collect his belongings immediately, load his family in their car, and vacate the property.

The poor farmer still carries the deed to the land in his wallet and believes a grave injustice was committed. His appeals to the legal system have been rejected, and he lacks the means to pay legal expenses. Today he lives with his family in Iowa and must endure the pain of his loss and the injustice his family has suffered. He draws strength from his belief in a just and loving God who one day will reconcile all injustices.

Negation of the Palestinian Economy and Resources

Among underlying principles of the Zionist movement, its major institutions, and the state of Israel, has been maintaining the economic controls that sustain the Jewish state and keep the Palestinians in a subservient position.

The issue of water illustrates this point. In the Middle East, water is essential but scarce and thus a more precious commodity than oil. Throughout history, communities and nations in the Middle East have established themselves on the basis of available water. With the rapid growth of Middle Eastern populations in recent decades and the absence of enforceable conservation methods, water has become an ever shrinking resource.

In Israel and the occupied territories, the issue of water is reaching a crisis point. Israelis tend to have a relatively careless pattern of water use. Statistics demonstrate that Palestinians are far more conscious of protecting what is available. However, Israel maintains control over Palestinian land and is able to create laws or issue policies that restrict the Palestinian community, while giving generous water rights to Jews. Such is the case within Israel proper and in the occupied West Bank and Gaza Strip.

In the territories, the acceleration of exclusively Jewish settlements has brought the matter to a head. While military and settlement construction gives Israelis control of over 60 percent of the West Bank and 45 percent of the Gaza Strip, Israelis control over 80 percent of the water usage in each case. Water reserves in the West Bank are the highest in the region, making the West Bank capable of meeting the needs of its population if normal controls are enforced. However, with the virtually uncontrolled use of water by Israeli settlers in the occupied territories, reserves are dropping rapidly. In addition, Israel is now diverting West Bank water to Israel proper, where old habits are not changing.[21]

Some experts are predicting that if Israel does not alter its excessive consumption of water, it will demand new sources. The obvious sources are Lebanon, Jordan, and Syria. Lebanon and Syria represent two of the four countries in the entire Middle East with sufficient water reserves to meet their needs. This tension, some claim, will be the source of future wars in the Middle East, unless it is corrected by law and behavior modification.

The Next Phase: The Oslo Peace Accords and Beyond

When Yasir Arafat and Yitzhak Rabin shook hands and their respective foreign ministers initialed the Declaration of Principles (Oslo Peace Accords) in Washington, D.C., on September 13, 1993, most international observers believed that peace had finally come to the Israeli-Palestinian conflict. I took a position of "hopeful cynicism," hoping on the one hand that if specific steps were taken to rectify the injustices, peace might be possible over a five-year period. At the same time, I found the Declaration of Principles (DOP) severely lacking in a number of basic areas. It was clear that the DOP was a flawed agreement. If it was not upgraded soon to a treaty consistent with existing United Nations resolutions on the question of Palestine, the process would inevitably break down.

There are several positive aspects of the DOP. Israel's official recognition of the PLO as the sole representative of the Palestinian people, and official recognition of Israel by the PLO, was a major breakthrough made possible by the DOP. Throughout their history the Israelis and Palestinians had refused to accept the legitimacy of each other, often living in political illusion concerning the alleged "nonexistence of the other." This significant flaw has been corrected, at least for the present.

In addition, the DOP provided a specific formula for the Palestinians to receive a portion of their land back, albeit in a small district, allowing them to run municipal affairs, police their community, and hold local elections. Perhaps of equal importance was the opportunity given to Arafat and the PLO to gain access to urgently needed economic assistance through the World Bank, U.S. AID, and other institutions. Conditions in the Gaza Strip had grown so impoverished that the PLO was desperate to deliver relief or lose its base of political support.

Unfortunately, a series of delays between the PLO and Israel, beginning on December 13, 1993, stalled the economic relief, caused significant suffering in the occupied territories, and led to Arafat's loss of considerable support. Frustration grew in the West Bank and Gaza Strip to such an extent that support for the DOP dropped from a popularity of over 75 percent in September, 1993, to just under 40 percent by February 1994. The decline of support within the Palestinian community is likely to continue.

The massacre of Palestinian worshipers at the Ibrahmi Mosque in Hebron on February 25 turned more Palestinians against the DOPs. They recognized that the critical issue of protection for the Palestinian community was not covered by the DOP. Immediately, the Islamic movement Hamas retaliated with subsequent attacks inside Israel to drive home its opposition to the accords and to revenge the Hebron massacre.

The following concerns over the DOP represent some but not all of the criticisms that have arisen since September 13, 1993. First, the Palestinian leadership did not involve the community in the process leading up to the DOP. As a result, Palestinians who had long attempted to practice elementary forms of democracy, even under occupation, became immediately suspicious of the veil of secrecy in which the negotiations were conducted. When I visited the West Bank in November 1993, just over two months after the signing, I was shocked by the number of former Arafat supporters, including Christian clergy, who had turned against him. Many believed that, out of desperation to make a deal, Arafat had compromised essential principles with a much stronger partner and the Palestinians had lost any hope of an independent state.

Second, Israel did not accept the international consensus that had been adopted by every nation in the world by the mid-1980s. The basis of a settlement was United Nations Resolutions 242 and 338 (Appendixes B and C), and the applicability of the Fourth Geneva Conventions (1949) to protect the civilian population in the interim period.

Third, Israel held a structural political advantage in the negotiations due to the weakness of the PLO and the partiality of the United States to Israel. Israel functioned virtually as a "senior" partner with the Palestinians in a far inferior position. The United States, host of the final signing ceremony, was more than willing to support Israel and maintain this imbalance. Critics of the DOP could convincingly describe the accords as "an Israeli document."

Fourth, the DOP allowed Israel to maintain military and political control over the land, including those areas designated for autonomy in the Jericho district and Gaza Strip. This created a situation called "split sovereignty," which grants the Palestinians control over limited aspects of their affairs but Israel retains control over the land, security, and essential political authority over the territories. With this arrangement, Israel can always return to occupy the land if they deem the situation a threat to their security. A change in government from Labor to Likud could return the West Bank and Gaza Strip to Israeli military occupation.

Fifth, the problem of Jewish settlers living in the West Bank and Gaza Strip would continue to present a significant security problem for the Palestinians and an ongoing point of tension between the communities. In addition, Israel continued the construction of illegal settlements in the occupied territories, in defiance of international law. The presence of Israeli settlers and the ongoing settlement process will be major points of confrontation and violence in the future.

Sixth, inherent in the question of settlements and many of the above concerns is the question of authority and the rule of law in the new Palestinian autonomous regions, in the West Bank, in the Jewish settlements, and within Israel proper. The DOP is vague on most practical aspects of the rule of law. For example, if an Israeli settler massacres or assassinates Palestinians in the Gaza Strip and flees into Israel, who will have the legal authority to prosecute the case? What is the role of the Palestinian police or of the Israeli Defense Forces if the assassin is captured? Where will the trial be held? Would the assassin be extradited to the Palestinian authority and put on trial there? If a Palestinian assassin kills Jewish civilians in Israel, and flees to the Gaza Strip, who has the authority to extradite, imprison, and bring the person to trial?[22]

Finally, the question of the future status of Jerusalem has been delayed by the DOP, leaving Israel the time and opportunity to seize additional land and build settlements within the expanded boundaries of Jerusalem, creating a situation that Judaizes the Arab sectors of the city. With Israel in control of both East (Arab) and West Jerusalem, it has defied international law and blurred the distinction between the two cities while at the same time it has declared it to be "the eternal capital of Israel." Despite an August 1994, agreement granting Jordan authority over Islamic holy places in Jerusalem, the entire Islamic world will continue to resist Israel's approach and unless resolved, Jerusalem will become a major source of tension and terrorism.

Naseer Aruri, a widely respected Palestinian American academic and former member of the Amnesty International Board of Directors, has added to the growing voices of criticism of the DOP. Aruri and other critics doubt that the DOP can lead to a Palestinian state and is simply occupation under another disguise. Aruri summarizes his argument.

> The agreements, let us call them Cairo I, II, and III, have also demonstrated that the Gaza-Jericho First model is not likely to improve during the next phase. After all, there is no ambiguity about the fact that, during the interim period, the status of the Gaza Strip and the 'Jericho Area' will be identical to the West Bank. Article IV and Annex II of the DOP make this quite clear. Cynics have been saying, since September 13, 1993, that Gaza-Jericho First will also be the Last.[23]

Critics of the DOP and a growing list of prominent Palestinian intellectuals have gained popularity at all levels of society. They see the imbalance of power in the negotiations and urge the PLO to wait and try to secure more results in future diplomacy. These critics believe that Arafat and his diplomats have secured a poor agreement and could have done much better. Because the Palestinians are negotiating from such a weak position, they have been forced into a series of compromises that will only bring tragedy. While they see South Africans gaining their independence, many Palestinians see a retreat to establish a new apartheid regime in Israel. What they will receive in the end is comparable to the reservations given to Native Americans or the bantustans once offered to South African blacks.

I agree with many of the above criticisms of the DOP, but one fundamental question haunts me. What is the alternative for Palestinians? The options available to Palestinians at this moment are unjust and limited. However, the Palestinians must choose to participate and demand as much as they can negotiate concerning the international norms for peace (UN Resolutions 242, 338, and the enforcement of the Geneva Conventions). If the Palestinians are able to bring relief to some of the most severely oppressed segments of their community, namely Gaza, they may gain additional followers in the international business and political communities.

In addition, we never know when a massive, popular movement will erupt from the people themselves. A people like the Palestinians can never be repressed for so long a period and forget the freedom that others have today. They will seize a moment that the finest diplomats and scholars could not consummate. Like the Intifada, a popular uprising or another breakthrough could occur that will turn the tables on today's occupiers.

What is the responsibility of the church? The church must stand with the weak. The church must initially join those organizations and movements that would feed, clothe, and heal the most severely damaged sectors of the Palestinian population. Let Matthew 25 be their guide, for truly the Lord will be there as the "sick, maimed, imprisoned, and dying." And the church must stand with those Jews and Palestinians Arabs who will pursue peace in every activity.

Pope John Paul II summarizes our discussion.

Why is there so much violence around us? Have we perhaps preferred a peace "as the world gives"? A peace consisting of the silence of the oppressed, the powerlessness of the vanquished, the humiliation of those—individuals and peoples—who see their rights trampled upon? True peace, the peace which Jesus has left us, is based upon justice and flourishes in love and reconciliation.[24]

Conclusions

Are there parallels between the Declaration of Principles and what occurred among the British, Zionist movement, and Palestinian community during 1915-1923? The following parallels between the DOP and the

World War I period must be considered for there to be any semblance of justice and peace between Israel and the Palestinians.

First, from 1915 through 1923, colonial competition between the British and French led to the British adoption of the Zionist movement and many of its goals. The Palestinian majority was virtually excluded from the most important decisions concerning their future and particularly with regard to the land. A similar situation has emerged in the 1990s, as Israel with the support of its benefactor the United States has been able to forge a peace process that has avoided the United Nations resolutions and been more in compliance with the Labor Party platform of Israel.

This process has led to serious divisions in Israel and more so in the Palestinian community. Palestinians in particular view the DOP as imposed on them by the West to favor Israel and prevent an independent Palestinian state from becoming a reality. The Western nations also seem to operate by a double standard, whereby they favor the Israelis and grant them significant economic, military, and political support while they abandon the Palestinians and other Arabs. The selective use of the United Nations and United Nations resolutions is an example of the Arab's grievances. The United States rallied the world to attack Iraq and liberate Kuwait in 1991 but has not implemented United Nations Resolutions for the Palestinians that have been before the world since 1949. Lebanon is a similar case. The Oslo Accords and the attempt to sidestep the full "land for peace" proposal of UN resolutions 242 and 338 (see Appendixes B and C) are the latest repeat of the same phenomenon that we read above concerning the League of Nations and its Covenant from 1917 to 1922.

Second, the Oslo Accords have demonstrated some improvement in the question of legitimacy as it applies to the Palestinian leadership and their representative, the PLO. As a result of the DOP, the PLO is somewhat accepted by Israel and the United States as the sole representative of the Palestinian people. However, the recognition is often limited and will continually be demonstrated by the limited authority granted to the PLO by Israel. The refusal of the World Bank to release the desperately needed funding for the Palestinians in Jericho and the Gaza Strip is one illustration of the limitations, which held true as the first anniversary of the DOP approached. Israel, however, receives over $4.5 billion from the United States alone on an annual basis, with no conditions or requirements for accountability. There is improvement over the League of Nations and British dealings with Palestinian legitimacy. But there is significant room for growth.

Third, of great importance is the question of land. The problems for the Palestinians began with the Zionist movement successfully convincing the British to adopt their model during the World War I era, to the extent that the Balfour Declaration's language and principles were included in the Paris Treaty. The British then allowed the Jewish National Agency to receive official status and purchase and develop Palestinian land for exclusive Jewish settlement and housing.

This phenomenon has continued since the 1920s to the extent that it is a sophisticated and highly developed science by the state of Israel. Today Israel is developing East Jerusalem and the West Bank with exclusively Jewish settlements and other means of land confiscation. This major imbalance in relation to control over and use of the West Bank, East Jerusalem, and Gaza Strip will inevitably delay future negotiations and prevent a just and peaceful future for both Israelis and Palestinians. Continued settlement of these lands by Israel is a violation of existing international law (the Hague Conventions, Fourth Geneva Conventions 1949, etc.) and official United States policy.

Unfortunately, the United States is operating in a manner similar to England during its Mandate Period. The DOP delays discussion of the settlements and a final resolution of the land issue until 1998; that may be too late to prevent a bloody confrontation.

Fourth, a major flaw in the DOP which parallels the British Mandate period is that of security for Palestinians in relation to security for Jews. Due in part to the large population of Palestinians in relation to Jews in the 1920s and 1930s, the British give protection to the Jewish communities and began to train many of the Jewish militias. Jewish forces were trained and fought with the British against the Palestinians during the revolt of 1936-39.

The tragic massacre of Palestinians at prayer in Hebron on February 25, 1994, reminded the world that Palestinians are not secure. The failure to resolve the settlement question and its implication on Palestinian security is a major flaw in the DOP. Until this is resolved in an equitable and significant manner, such incidents as the Hebron massacre will lead to increased instability for Palestinians and Jews alike.

A final problem, perhaps the major question in both the DOP and the World War I negotiations and British Mandate era, is the imbalance of power in relation to the Zionist agenda and the Palestinian agenda, with an accompanying lack of accountability for both parties. Both British policy and the Paris Peace Treaty favored the Zionists and advocated their agenda. The Palestinian agenda was not represented, and they had no advocates, power base, or representation at Paris.

The DOP is a significant advance in this regard. However, the Oslo Accords are structured in a manner that favors the Israeli agenda. With the United States serving as the host and "guarantor" or the DOP, rather than an international body such as the United Nations Security Council, the power has shifted significantly in Israel's favor. Israel has been able to prevent the implementation of UN resolutions 242 and 338 (see Appendixes B and C), has maintained its settlement of Jerusalem and the West Bank while transforming the demography, and has been able to maintain control over the land, resources, and economy of the Palestinians through a variety of procedures implanted during its occupation.

Until the DOP and the negotiations shift to the United Nations or another international body, and until the basis of a negotiated settlement returns to the international consensus of United Nations resolutions pertaining to the Israeli-Palestinian conflict, there will not be an opportunity for a just and durable peace in the Holy Land. With the weaker Palestinian party having to make repeated concessions on major issues, it is not likely that full peace will be realized. More extreme leadership and movements will rise up in both societies to polarize the issues, and another war will be inevitable. Caught in the midst of these unresolved issues and crises is the ever-diminished Christian community and the churches of Palestine, who call out to us to help facilitate a future that is free and peaceful.

Nahum Goldmann, a great Jewish thinker of the past generation and a president of the World Zionist Organization, once said: "It seems to me that diplomacy in the Middle East is the art of delaying the inevitable as long as possible."[25] Such is the case with the Declaration of Principles as it relates to such pivotable issues as Jerusalem, the Jewish settlements, full Israeli withdrawal from the West Bank, and the establishment of a Palestinian state with full security guarantees for Israel. It is my conviction that a Palestinian state is the best security agreement for Jews in Israel for the long term. The delay of a state through diplomatic maneuvers by Israeli and U.S. politicians is seeding resentment and violence. It is at this level that the Christian churches can join hands with concerned Jews and Muslims around the world to reiterate "the things that make for peace." In the Israeli-Palestinian case, over ninety percent of the nations in the world and most mainline Protestant, Roman Catholic, and Orthodox Churches are united in their support of UN Resolutions 242, 338, and 38/58 C of the UN General Assembly. The latter forms the basis for all states in the Middle East, including Israel and a new Palestinian state, to recognize each others fundamental rights to security, self-determination, and independence. Partial solutions, such as the Declaration of Principles of September 1993, may be seen as significant steps along the path to peace but they are inadequate. For the sake of the future Middle East let the churches rekindle their spirits and act prophetically to keep the vision for justice alive for all of God's people in the Holy Land. There can be but one standard of justice, and diplomatic maneuvers and legal loopholes should not dilute that standard. Perhaps a remnant of concerned Christians, Jews, and Muslims will heed the call to peace based on justice in the Holy Land, and the words of the psalmist will ring again in our hearts.

"Let me hear what God the Lord will speak, for he will speak peace to his people, to his saints, to those who turn to him in their hearts. Surely his salvation is at hand for those who fear him, that glory may dwell in our land. Steadfast love and faithfulness will meet; righteousness and peace will kiss each other." (Ps. 85:8-10, RSV)

13

The Incredible Shrinking Church

A problem cannot be solved
on the same level in which it was created.
Albert Einstein

I regularly visit Riah Abu-al-Assal when I travel independently or with groups to Palestine. Archdeacon Riah was until January 1994, the pastor of Christ Evangelical Anglican (Episcopal) Church in Nazareth, an old, small church that is a striking contrast to the magnificent Church of the Annunciation, just one block away. Governments and congregations around the world poured millions of dollars into this beautiful edifice, making it a showcase for tourists. But the fundraisers did little for the dying Christian community and the needs of the poor in Nazareth.

On entering Christ Church you will see a simpler, older, and far less impressive sanctuary. Those able to look beyond surface appearances will discover a deeper message in the dusty old church, for on the altar cloth in large Arabic script is the passage that served as the text for Jesus' first sermon upon returning to his hometown.

The Spirit of the Lord is upon me,
because he has anointed me
to bring good news to the poor.

He has sent me to proclaim release to the captives
and recovery of sight to the blind,
to let the oppressed go free,
to proclaim the year of the Lord's favor. (Luke 4:18-19)

Jesus read these words from Isaiah 61 when he entered the synagogue in Nazareth and began his public ministry. There is no question that he deliberately selected this text to demonstrate the direction of his ministry, which would be one of bringing the gospel of salvation, freedom, and new life to those who were marginalized and outcast. The contrast between Jesus' message and that of the synagogue establishment provoked the latter's hostility to the extent that they threatened to throw Jesus off the large cliff at the edge of town. Somehow Jesus passed through their midst and continued on his journey.

I am reminded of the contrast that exists today between the local Palestinians, represented in the poorer churches and mosques, and the Jewish establishment in Israel. In many ways the two churches are a contemporary parable of the Palestinian Christian condition in the Galilee and the rest of Israel/Palestine. Considerable funds, regular visits from Christian tourists and favored status from the government of Israel have been granted to the Church of the Ascension and to various Christian Zionist organizations in Israel. If the Western churches sing the praises of Zionism, they will be viewed positively by the government. Such is the religious game played in Israel and occupied Palestine today.

Local Palestinian Christians, the living churches and communities, are usually ignored. They receive few if any tourists, no income from the visitors, and minimal support from Christians around the world. However, there are many poor but vibrant churches worshiping and ministering within a few feet of these pilgrims, who unknowingly miss profound opportunities for spiritual and personal enrichment. Instead of visiting the "living stones" (1 Peter 2:5), they tour the archaeological ruins and historical sites of by-gone eras.

In this chapter I will examine several of the challenges that face the Palestinian churches. Again, I am using the case of Palestinian Christians to demonstrate what is occurring throughout the Middle East, with the realization that each country has its own unique set of problems but trends found in Israel/Palestine can be found throughout the region.

The Shrinking Church in the Holy Land

"We are the 'living stones,' " proclaims Father Elias Chacour, quoting 1 Peter 2:5. "We are the Christians who never left Palestine since Pentecost. But it hurts us to see so many Western Christians visiting our land and only stopping at the ancient ruins. We, the body of Christ in the Holy Land, urgently need your fellowship, prayer, and support during these trying times in the Middle East."

Jean Zaru, an articulate Palestinian Christian from Ramallah (ten miles north of Jerusalem) and active in international church circles, spoke to one of our tour groups in October 1992. Zaru reflected on the mixed blessing that Eastern Christians experience in their relationships with Western Christians. She cited many of the positive contributions that Western Christian missionaries brought to the region but at the same time she raised serious questions.

For example, Mrs. Zaru told us that the influence of Western missionaries encouraged Palestinians (and other Arab Christians) to assume a Western identity in terms of culture, dress, food, music, and even worship. As some Eastern Christians have adopted Western ideas and cultural expressions, they have provided a basis for Arab Muslims to raise the accusation that Christianity is a Western religion and aligned with the same colonial powers that denigrated Palestinians.

Jean Zaru went on to identify four major tasks that Palestinian Christians must face immediately if they are to be faithful to their calling in their own land.

> 1. To witness in the midst of our Muslim neighbors, concerning the love of Jesus Christ for the world, despite the fact that both Muslims and Christians still hold the Crusades fresh in our memories. 2. to witness to this same love among Jews, who assume that most Christians are anti-Semitic; therefore, we must demonstrate that we are sincerely committed to the well-being and security of our Jewish neighbors. 3. We must express our faith in a way that will respond to the challenges of Israel's occupation and oppose those Western Christian theologies and policies of governments that claim God gave to Israel all the promises of the land, ethnic superiority, and power. These Christian groups, such as the International Christian Embassy, love Israel more than they love the church of Christ, and they hate Palestinians; this is contrary to the gospel as I read it. 4. We must care for our own spiritual renewal as individual Christians and as churches who are primarily Arab, Eastern, and have significant resources and traditions that date back to Jesus and the disciples at the day of Pentecost. We have many untapped resources and gifts to offer Christians everywhere, if they would only stand with us now in this hour of trial and share the journey. I know that God will bless us all as we learn to travel together.[1]

But will the Christians in the West and around the world become awakened to Jean Zaru's challenge and opportunity? Perhaps of immediate concern is this basic question: will there be enough Palestinian Christians left in the land in twenty years to even address her agenda for the churches? There are many leaders, including Israeli Jews and Muslims in the Arab world, who fear that the rate of attrition is so high that the living church will become extinct by the year 2025. Several analysts are stating that if the present trends continue in the "holy" land (and elsewhere), Christianity will be no more than a museum piece, a relic of the past, as is the case in Turkey and North Africa today.

Christians have been leaving the Middle East in large numbers for several years. Hundreds of thousands left Lebanon during its fifteen years of civil war (1975-1990) and the majority may never return. Others have fled Egypt, Syria, Iraq, and Jordan due to economic problems and political instability. The Sudan, although in Africa, should be of serious concern due to the tension between political Islamic terrorist groups, the government, and Christians in Southern Sudan. The Sudan has lost much of its Christian community due to starvation, civil war, various terrorist militias, and its extremist Islamic Government. The Gulf War, while popular in some Western evangelical circles, brought new catastrophes to Arab populations in Palestine, Jordan, Iraq. The increased economic blight throughout the Middle East served to accelerate a new wave of Christian emigration from the region.

Gabriel Habib, General Secretary of the Middle East Council of Churches, summarized the trends when he stated, "Fear, human suffering, and hopelessness" have caused so many Christians to emigrate that there is profound concern about the very "continuity of Christian presence and witness in this region." [2]

One of the most disturbing examples of this phenomenon is occurring in Jerusalem and the Israeli-occupied West Bank. In 1922, Jerusalem had 28,607 residents, of which 14,699 (51 percent) were Christians, according to British government statistics. In 1978, the Israeli Bureau of Statistics counted only 10,191 Christians in East Jerusalem, which is less than 10 percent of the Palestinian population. Christian researcher Bernard Sabella, of Bethlehem University, claims that the number has dropped to approximately 5000 today or approximately 4 percent. [3]

In 1948 the Palestinian cities of Bethlehem and Ramallah were overwhelmingly Christian. Today, due to political and economic pressure, over half of the Christian residents have left for Europe, North or South America, or Australia. More Palestinian Christians from Ramallah now live in Detroit, Michigan, and Jacksonville, Florida, than in their hometown. Local pastors note that Christians have had greater economic means and an orientation toward the West that helped to facilitate their emigration and eventual assimilation into Western societies.

The Anglican bishop of Jordan, Elia Khoury, expelled by Israel on dubious charges in 1967, sadly told me, "I give Christianity ten to fifteen years, no more, in Amman [Jordan] and the West Bank if these trends continue." [4] The prominent Israeli writer Amos Elon recently told *Time Magazine* that Jerusalem may soon become a mere "museum" for tourists, bereft of Christianity as a living religion.[5] The Church of the Annunciation (Nazareth), the Church of the Holy Sepulchre (Jerusalem), and the Church of the Nativity (Bethlehem) will continue to thrive as a result of foreign tourists, but in a few years there will be no living church unless present trends are reversed.

During the late 1980s and 1990s, Palestinian Christian leaders have sensed increased hostility toward their institutions and ministries from Israeli military authorities and extremist settlers. Easter 1993 brought events that reached a serious stage during severe military restrictions in movement from one city to the other. On Orthodox (Eastern) Easter, Christians living outside the boundaries of Jerusalem were forbidden to attend services at the Church of the Holy Sepulchre. Then as Christians gathered in Ramallah, Bethlehem, and Beit Jalla, to receive the "holy" light from the Holy Sepulchre church, many were attacked by the military during peaceful and even prayerful gatherings. In Ramallah, the Israeli military stamped out the holy light when it arrived by taxi for the priests and faithful who had gathered. In Bethlehem, police beat and abused a gathering who awaited the light on Easter morning.

A World Vision observer in Beit Jalla reported,

> Over 4000 people gathered outside the churches in Beit Jalla awaiting the light. From the early morning, soldiers parked a jeep in front of the entrance to the Santa Maria church, harassing the Christians waiting there. . . . The bells of the church began ringing as the procession with the light appeared. Soldiers shot live ammunition at the bells, the clock, and the cross of the church, and shot tear gas at the crowd.[6]

The son of a World Vision project partner who was arrested while carrying a candle described his feelings this way.

> The cross on the church represents me in this country. If something happens to this cross, I feel like my whole basis is shaken. Some people thought this spoiled Easter. But I think it gave pleasure to many of us since at that day we felt our identity as Palestinian Christians. This brought us back to the reality that all these fantasies like nice clothes, good food and what they represent were not as our own because they could be taken away from us at any moment.[7]

When we received word about these troubling anti-Christian actions, we asked several Christian friends across the United State to register their concern with the government of Israel. Many wrote, among them Norval Hadley, director of Evangelical Friends Mission. He received an indignant reply from the Israeli Embassy's counselor for church affairs, Avi Granot, who emphatically questioned whether the events even took place.[8] Having reviewed the case with eyewitnesses to the sad events of Easter 1993, we can safely conclude that thousands of Christians and Muslims witnessed these events. In addition, the Ramallah incident was videotaped.

The case of Easter 1993 underscores the pressure building for Palestinians in general and for the shrinking Palestinian Christian community in particular. Until there is a just and durable political solution, the Palestinian church will suffer, and its attrition rate will be higher than that of Muslims. Father Riah Abu al-Assal of Nazareth confirmed this when he told our group in 1991, "The only way to bring long-term security to Palestinians and Jews alike is to give the Palestinians their freedom and end the occupation. What we Christians over here need is for you in the United States to go back and tell your elected officials in Washington, D.C., that they must now implement the UN Resolutions on Palestine, just as they did with UN Resolutions on Kuwait. Then we will believe that Americans are truly seeking freedom and justice for all, regardless of whether they are Palestinian Arabs or Jews from Israel."

The Identity Crisis Facing Christians in the Holy Land

Palestinian Christians face several internal and external conflicts, all of which contribute to their eventual emigration from their homeland. A Palestinian professor from Jerusalem, Dr. Munir Fasheh, has reflected on the internal pressure that Palestinian Christians experience as a result of their loss of land and Israel's occupation. Fasheh says that

> as an Arab, as a Palestinian, and as a Christian, [I have been] trapped since I was born. Either I speak the language of the West, embody its ideology (including its Christianity), and am deformed—but then many would hear me—or I speak in my own voice, about my own experiences, including my indigenous Christian tradition that lived through the ages and was embodied by people like my parents—and risk the possibility many will not be able to hear or understand me.[9]

Munir explains how this trap leaves Christians feeling confused, lacking power, and burdened by a lack of self-worth. He then recalls the time he visited the Jerusalem home from which his family was expelled in 1948. His first opportunity to return to the home occurred in 1968 when he crossed the line to visit the house now occupied by a Jewish family. With a significant sense of embarrassment, he approached the front steps, knocked on the door, and asked if he could enter the home.

The startled woman asked who he was. "I am Munir Fasheh, and I was born here in 1941," Munir replied.

The woman answered, "Oh, but I was told that a Christian family lived in this house."

Munir said, "Yes, I am a Palestinian Christian."

"But you cannot be a Christian and a Palestinian. Palestinians are all Muslims," she said.

Somewhat startled, Munir responded, "Go and check with the neighbors, and see if the name is correct."

The woman locked the door and went out to ask the neighbors who confirmed that indeed the Fasheh family, Palestinian Christians, had owned the home. The woman returned but refused to allow Munir to enter. Then suddenly she volunteered, "Look, we did not push you out of the house. The government of Israel gave this house to me." [10]

Thus Palestinian Christians have the problem of constantly explaining who they are, often having to define their identity in contrast to Muslims or Jews. Even after significant effort, the Christian identity is denied, ignored, and often denigrated, largely out of ignorance. The consistent message to the Palestinian Christian is "You don't belong here."

One of the most outspoken leaders of the movement continues to be Canon Riah Abu al-Assal of Nazareth, who has decided to relinquish other political and ecclesiastical responsibilities to advocate this "Macedonian call." He told one of our tour groups, "We do not need your missionaries coming here. We need your help to declare the desperate need for a Christian 'Aliya'—an ingathering and return of Christians to Palestine. Given the present statistics, only such a movement and God's intervention will save Christianity from extinction in the 'holy' land." [11]

The Task of the Palestinian Church

In this final section of the chapter, we return to the haunting challenges of Jean Zaru stated at the outset. Reader are reminded that the Palestinian Christians are serving in this chapter as representatives of Christians throughout the Middle East. The overwhelming challenges this tiny community is facing today concern us all.

Christian Witness in the Islamic Context

In the "holy" land, where coexistence has been peaceful, Christianity has lived creatively with Islam since its inception in the seventh century. The story is told that when the great Saladin liberated Jerusalem from the Crusaders, he would not enter the Church of the Holy Sepulchre, choosing instead to pray outside its doors as a sign of the respect and dignity that Islam shows the Christian community.

Bishop Kenneth Cragg presents the challenge of "A Future with Islam?" as brilliantly as anyone has described it in his volume, *The Arab Christian*.

> The question mark can be removed, for there is no future for Arab Christianity except with Islam. Yet the interrogative remains. It is the quality of that future that is in perpetual question. The fifteenth Islamic century is only one decade on, while the twenty-first Christian century is only one decade away. What may the common century hold? . . . How will the task of survival decide the quality of what survives? [12]

Cragg begins his final chapter by stating that the revival of political Islam and its present tendencies raise serious concerns for Christians throughout the Middle East. We will not belabor the fears and concerns raised by the Muslim extremist movements in the Sudan and Iran (represented most crassly by Sheik Omar Abdel-Rahman's followers and the January 1993, bombing of the World Trade Center in New York City). But just as Christians would not wish to have the world judge Christianity by the terrorist and vulgar actions of David Koresh and the Branch Davidian sect, we in the West must not judge Islam by the actions of an extreme sect of Islam.

The future of the church in Palestine may not be the secular democracy that Palestinian Christians and Muslims have struggled to establish through the Palestine Liberation Organization and even before the PLO was born in 1965. The future Palestinian government, and even the limited Palestinian Self-Governing Authority now being discussed in international negotiations, may have a significant Islamic orientation.

Yet this does not mean that the Palestinian church will face imminent persecution and discrimination from Islam. On the contrary, if Christians are at the center of negotiations and pay the price of being involved in the planning process, the future state will provide for the protection and general well-being of Christians. The same scenario may hold for Lebanon, Jordan, Syria, Yemen, and possibly Egypt. Unfortunately, the same hope cannot be given for Saudi Arabia, North Africa, Iraq, and most of the Gulf.

As Jean Zaru warned, Arab Christians must demonstrate now that they are committed to the future of their people, especially the poor. They must witness through acts of love, service, and the struggle for justice and human rights. At the same time, they must keep their spiritual center in Jesus Christ and provide for the spiritual, pastoral, and economic needs of their own community. They must find a way to curb massive Christian emigration and ensure that their brightest leaders take positions of political and institutional leadership.

Palestinian Christians have had a significant influence within the PLO and in articulating the Palestinian cause to the West. In addition to church leaders such as Bishop Kafity, Father Chacour, Canon Naim Ateek, Riah Abu-al-Assal, Jean Zaru, and countless others, Palestinian Christians have been leaders in the fields of literature, politics, and human rights. Palestinian scholar Edward Said of Columbia University comes from a Jerusalem Christian family, as did the great Palestinian spokesmen of the 1970s, Kamal Nassar and Fayez Sayegh. Dr. Hanna Nasser, President of Birzeit University, has served as Treasurer of the Palestine National Council and oversees the development of his university. Perhaps the greatest living Palestinian artist is Kamal Boulatta, a devout Christian.

Dr. Hanan Ashrawi, a Christian from Ramallah, has been one of the most able Palestinian spokespersons to the West since 1990. And several PLO offices worldwide are staffed by Christians, such as the head of the London office, Afif Safieh. In human rights, the previously mentioned Jonathan Kuttab and his colleague Raja Shehadeh were the founders of Al-Haq (Law in the Service of Man), the award-winning West Bank affiliate of the International Commission of Jurists. The list goes on and on, to the point where Palestinians themselves feel it is irrelevant and counterproductive to emphasize the involvement of Christians.

Nevertheless, I believe that the times have changed and we must affirm the central role of Christians, both for the sake of the Arab Muslim masses and even more for the West. Everyone must know that Palestinian Christians are committed to a pluralistic solution based on full equality for all, and that their Christian faith is at the heart of their motivation.

It will only be by our actions and the fruit of our labors that the Muslim community (and the world) will know who we are and why we are involved.

A basic biblical text that reminds us of this task of credible witness and presence in Arab societies is Luke 7:18-23. There the disciples of John the Baptist challenged the ministry of Jesus. Jesus responded, "Go and tell John what you have seen and heard: the blind receive their sight, the lame walk, the lepers are cleansed, and the deaf hear, the dead are raised up, the poor have good news brought to them" (v. 22).

If the Palestinian churches do more than their part in ministering to the needs of the entire society in the land, Muslims and Jews included, the people of the region will respect them. As in Jesus' example above, the emphasis must be on the needs of the poor and the disenfranchised, the lepers and blind of our time. Political prisoners and victims of shootings and beatings in Israeli military attacks must be at the forefront today.

What a powerful witness to the gospel of Jesus Christ it would be if the churches of the world aligned themselves with the justice issues of the Palestinians, who have been the political lepers of our time. What a testimony to Muslims and Jews in the "holy" land it would be if Western Christians redoubled their sharing of economic and skilled professional resources to meet the needs of the poor in this society, Muslims and Jews included. Tangible actions will give rise to the verbal interpretation of the gospel, but today the emphasis must be on the witness through ministries of action.

Christian Witness and Presence in Israel and Palestine
In most Western evangelical circles, Christian witness in the Middle East connotes the ministry of the Messianic Jewish community in Israel or strategies to convert Muslims. Unfortunately this book does not have the space to give adequate treatment to Christian witness to the Jews. Instead, I will confine myself to address several of the more general concerns of the Arab Palestinian churches in Israel and the West Bank and the implications of their dilemma for Western Christians.

Briefly put, I will argue that the Western Christians must support and empower the Christians in Israel and occupied Palestine simply to survive—to survive with dignity, to extend their hands to affirm Jews who live with both real and exaggerated fears, and to avoid compromising their Christian faith and Palestinian identity despite pressure from the government of Israel and Zionist organizations.

First, the previous statistics and grim saga of recent Palestinian Christian history demonstrate convincingly that there will be little other than a skeletal Palestinian church within twenty-five years. If present trends continue, by the year 2010 less than one percent of the Palestinian population in the West Bank, East Jerusalem, and the Gaza Strip will be Christian. This tragic reality must be compared with the statistics of 1947, which reflect a Christian population in Jerusalem and Palestine in the neighborhood of 18 to 20 percent. Although the Christians in the Galilee may still number 10 percent of the Palestinian population, similar trends away from Palestinian Christianity are now evident in Israel itself.

Thus the first prerequisite of the church in Palestine and Israel is survival—a spiritual, demographic, economic, political, and practical mandate. Until now few Western Christian churches and organizations have given this urgent challenge the priority it merits. Those Catholic, Orthodox, mainline Protestant, and a mere handful of evangelical relief and development organizations that have begun to respond have done so rather late and with limited resources. I state this concern, not to invoke guilt and defensiveness, but as a challenge for everyone to pray, analyze, and mobilize the best of our resources to save Arab Christianity in the "holy" land.

Second, Palestinian Christians may have more freedom and options to build serious and lasting bridges to Israeli Jews, both as significant symbols of cooperation and as signs of the reconciliation between the two "cousins" that will inevitable occur someday. The gospel of Jesus Christ and a central theme of the New Testament is the breaking down of all barriers between Gentiles and Jews. Paul's development of the concept of reconciliation in 2 Corinthians 5 assumes that Christians have no option but to advocate a costly, sometimes painful, and creative ministry of reconciliation.

> So if anyone is in Christ, there is a new creation; everything old has passed away; see, everything has become new! All this is from God, who reconciled us to himself through Christ, and has given us the ministry of reconciliation; that is, in Christ God was reconciling the world to himself, not counting their trespasses against them, and entrusting the message of reconciliation to us. So we are ambassadors for Christ, since God is making his appeal through us; we entreat you on behalf of Christ, be reconciled to God. (2 Cor. 5: 17-20)

Christians have no option but to embrace and be embraced by the spiritual, practical, and the political implications of this challenge. It is a difficult word to Palestinian Christians who have lost their land and homes, and seen both their own futures and those of their mothers and fathers for three generations sacrificed at the altar of Zionism. We in the West cannot presume to ask Palestinians to reconcile with Zionist Jews. Nevertheless, Palestinian Christians must and are struggling to respond to the all encompassing challenge of reconciliation with Jews.

To cite but one of many examples, I remember my friends in the Palestinian Christian city of Beit Sahour (Shepherds Field). Early in the Intifada, Beit Sahour began to resist paying taxes to Israel, recalling the well-known theme of the American Revolution, "No taxation without representation." Deciding to make an international example out of the Beit Sahour tax revolt, the Israeli Defense Forces attempted to crush it brutally. The key leaders were carted off to prison on a variety of fabricated charges, businesses and homes were raided, machinery and bank accounts were confiscated, and many of the families were brought to economic ruin.

Our tour groups visit the friends in Beit Sahour every year and have heard their stories of imprisonment, suffering, and pain since 1988. Academics such as Professors Jad Isaak and Ghassan Andoni, or a businessman like pharmacist Elias Rishmawi, embrace for me the principle of New Testament reconciliation. They stand firm in their identity as Christians who demand respect and justice for their families. They make no concessions or apologies for the fact that their rights, their families, and their futures are violated by the state of Israel.

At the same time, these Christian friends have organized the Rapproachment Centre and various mechanisms to reconcile with those Jews willing to begin the painful journey. Since 1989 weekly meetings have been taking place in Beit Sahour between the leaders of the Centre and leaders of the Jewish peace movement, as well as some religious and political leaders. The meetings are simple, sometimes difficult in their bluntness, and often practical. At times they have received limited legal and financial support from their Israeli friends.

The Beit Sahour community still suffers and fears for its survival, but they have begun to live reconciliation as a central act of their community. The possible hatred of Jews in general has been reduced, and the Beit Sahourans have discovered channels of hope and support, limited though they may be. As one of them noted in our last meeting, "We can choose to hate or to live hopefully. We must light one small candle rather than curse the darkness that will surely lead to our destruction. We are not naive enough to believe this Centre and these activities will answer all of our problems, but we must work at this strategy with all our energy and trust that God will honor our efforts."

The witness of reconciliation to the Jewish community in Israel is a simultaneous statement that "we are here and must be respected as God's children," of equal value with anyone else. At the same time, the Christian community approaches the Jews with open hands of hospitality and openness to dialogue: "Come, let us sit and break bread together, and work creatively to find a way out of our conflicts and build a future together."

Perhaps the theme of reconciliation (with dignity and justice) is more pronounced in Christianity than in Judaism and Islam, although the historical record of the church for nearly two thousand years gives little testimony to this fact. Perhaps in the "holy" land, this tiny and embattled

Christian minority will create several models and develop the possibilities of true spiritual, political, economic, and interfaith reconciliation. If the Palestinian Christian community can begin to develop models for reconciliation, and if the Western churches will lend practical support, including significant economic resources, the gospel of reconciliation will indeed bring healing and advance the cause of peace in this strife-torn place.

Third, the Palestinian Christian community in Israel, Jerusalem, and the West Bank often appears to be hopelessly divided. Many Catholics do not cooperate with Orthodox, the Protestants are not accepted as a true church by many Orthodox and Catholic leaders, and all the indigenous Palestinian Arab Christians are alienated from the Western Christian fundamentalist Zionists (Bridges for Peace, International Christian Embassy-Jerusalem, etc., and many Messianic Jewish Christians). The internal conflicts among Christians are at least as serious as the external threats that Israel imposes on the local churches. Jesus warned, "A house divided against itself cannot stand."

Western evangelical author and activist Ronald J. Sider received a taste of this division when he visited the Church of the Holy Sepulchre on Western Easter Sunday 1993. He saw an Orthodox priest (Greek) take a candle from a Protestant and state that the candle was not an authentic representation of Christ's light because the only true expression was that of the Orthodox Church, which celebrated Easter Sunday the following week. Sider was rightly shocked and troubled by this tragic statement and action.

I share his concern but am not surprised. The Palestinian church is still weak and divided in many quarters, and the case cited above must be analyzed from the standpoint of an Orthodox Church dominated by foreign bishops, clergy, and a mentality of a bygone generation. There is a welcomed revolt in the Orthodox Church that is like a breath of fresh air from the Holy Spirit. Sider could have stood with Fr. George Makhlouf, the Orthodox priest from Ramallah, who on "western" Easter stood outside the Israeli military headquarters in a prayer vigil demanding the right of all the churches to travel to Jerusalem to celebrate Easter on both Sundays. Makhlouf was also with Rantisi and all the clergy and Christian leaders on Western Easter when the Easter light was received from Jerusalem and trampled underfoot by the Israeli army.

There is a new generation of clergy and laity in Palestine who respect each other's holy dates and find dramatic ways to cooperate under occupation. These same leaders put aside minor differences in theology to be faithful to God in their ministry to all the people of Palestine; and to live the gospel of reconciliation, forgiveness, and justice in Jesus Christ.

I believe the struggle of these Palestinian Christian leaders to assume leadership over their churches; to address the political, social, and economic crisis of their people; and to minister to the spiritual needs of the community will in the end be triumphant. The Anglican community, Lutherans, and Roman Catholics have made significant strides in the previous decade to indigenize the gospel and to empower an authentically Arab Palestinian Church. Two theological movements, one centered at St. Georges Anglican Cathedral under the leadership of Bishop Samir Kafity and Canon Naim Ateek, the other in Bethlehem under the leadership of Giryis Khoury of Bethlehem University, are providing the intellectual vision for the movement. Even these two movements are alienated from each other as of this writing. However, most believe that this separation will be short-lived and will in time be yet another sign of the healing and empowerment of Christians in Palestine.

Fourth, for the Palestinian Christian community to survive with dignity and make a contribution to their future society, they must "be wise as serpents" concerning the issue of power. We would be naive and irresponsible as servants of Jesus Christ if we did not note that the destruction of Palestine and the Palestinians is an issue of political power and control of the land. If there is not a political change in Palestine concerning Israel's usurpation of the land and the desperate need for Israel to negotiate some form of political power sharing in occupied Palestine, there will be no Palestinian Christian community.

The living church, both numerically and as a network of spiritual and institutional presence and witness in the "holy" land, will disappear so gradually that few will notice. Call it the "Lebanization" or "Armenianization" of Palestine, the future will be grim if characterized by a totally disempowered body of largely poverty-stricken Palestinian Arabs. These Arabs without country or political identity could end up living on Israeli-dominated reservations or Bantustans in what is now called the West Bank and Gaza Strip. In such a scenario, most Palestinian Christians will have fled to the West, to Australia or South America. Western churches and evangelical agencies will send missionaries and limited funds to minister to the "poor natives."

Such a tragic spectacle is not an exaggeration. The precedents exist on every continent, beginning with the Native Americans. While there is still an opportunity to raise our voices and work for a just solution, Western Christians must listen to the cries from the Palestinian Christians concerning the agendas needed today to ensure their survival tomorrow.

A young Lutheran pastor in Bethlehem, Mitri Rahab, stated it well in a 1991 lecture in East Jerusalem.

> The three monotheistic religions have to work for a political solution. Every political solution needs an analysis of the prevailing situation. The analysis of the Israeli-Palestinian conflict is not a matter of religious hate, but it is a problem of power imbalance. . . . The only just order in this case lies in the redistribution of power, and in the placement of law in its proper place and perspective, so that law and power will become the true instruments of justice. To work in this direction is actually a religious act by itself, because God is a

God of justice . . . God became [hu]man, so that [hu]mans will be like God, wrote the famous theologian Athanasius. This means that religion cannot be used in any way against human beings . . . If anyone harms a human being, he or she is harming God and everybody who serves [the needs of] human beings serves God through them. God and men and women are not divided any more.[13]

There is a great company of western evangelicals who took the gospel into the corridors of political decision making or led their churches in the struggle to end slavery or child labor abuses. They range from Lord Shaftesbury and William Wilberforce in Victorian England, to contemporary examples like former President Jimmy Carter and Mark Hatfield, senator from Oregon. Such great leadership will be replicated in Palestinian society. Those Christians called to address the power equations and injustices of their time are the modern Jeremiahs, Amoses, and Micahs whose prophetic voices challenge those controlling power (including all too often the church hierarchy).

Rev. Rahab ended his important address by reminding the audience that one of the primary areas of ministry for the church is with the poor. He cited Jesus' own recitation of Isaiah 61 concerning his ministry "to bring good news to the oppressed, to bind up the brokenhearted, and to proclaim liberty to the captives," as the biblical mandate.

Rahab recalled that the churches of the Middle East have been in the forefront of establishing hospitals, schools, orphanages, rehabilitation centers, and homes for the elderly. Then after 1967, the church in Palestine began to identify itself with the politically oppressed, the victims of torture and imprisonment. During the Palestinian Intifada, the church leadership took a principled stand on a political solution to their problem.

But Rahab rightly warns that the Christian's ultimate loyalty is not to Palestinian nationalism or a political system, but to God and God alone. "Every exercise of religious power and authority has to be accountable to God and at the same time accountable and answerable to the people on whose behalf they are exercised." [14] These guidelines are necessary in the charged emotional and political crisis that is the Israeli-Palestinian conflict, where the temptation to demonize the "other" is always nearby. However, these guidelines of simultaneous accountability to God and to those whom one is serving seem to be applicable both to the Palestinians themselves and to the Western Christians encouraged to walk this journey with them.

Justice is central to the church's life. Evangelicals need only turn to the Lausanne Covenant, adopted in 1974. The covenant is the largest creed under which any ecumenical body of Christians find common ground; it should be updated and studied. Point 13 of the covenant states,

It is the God-appointed duty of every government to secure conditions for peace, justice, and liberty in which the church may obey God, serve the Lord Jesus Christ, and preach the gospel without interference. We therefore pray for the leaders of the nations and call upon them to guarantee freedom of thought and conscience, and freedom to practice and propagate religion in accordance with the will of God and as set forth in the Universal Declaration of Human Rights. We also express our deep concern for all who have been unjustly imprisoned, and especially for our brethren who are suffering for their testimony of the Lord Jesus. We promise to pray and work for their freedom. At the same time, we refuse to be intimidated by their fate. God helping us, we too will seek to stand against injustice and to remain faithful to the gospel, whatever the cost. We do not forget the warnings of Jesus that persecution is inevitable.[15]

This powerful statement will have increasing relevance for evangelicals and the church at large in its relationship to Christians in the Middle East during the years immediately ahead. We have noted the suffering of the churches under Israeli occupation and must add that, since the Gulf War, the situation is extremely tense in every predominantly Muslim country. Egypt, where 8 to 9 million Coptic Christians live, has witnessed the burning of churches and violent attacks on Christians by Islamic extremists. The attacks increased from 1992 to 1993 but had been preceded by over a decade of sporadic attacks. Those Islamic groups that advocate a violent overthrow of the present Egyptian government and the institution of Islamic law (the *Shari'a*) have steadily gained power due to the extreme poverty, population explosion, and insensitivity of Europe and the United States to human rights issues in the Middle East.

In the 1990s, Western Christians will be called on to stand with those Christians under attack in the Middle East. There are many human rights cases, that are extremely sensitive, particularly those involving proselytizing Muslims and Jews (which is illegal in all Islamic states and in Israel). In most of these cases the local churches must be empowered to develop quiet and careful strategies.

However, when the local churches call for Western support and/or the involvement of respected human rights organizations such as Amnesty International, the churches in the West must be prepared to act. This will involve grassroots organizing for letter writing to the governments in question. This must be underscored by educational forums and fervent prayer campaigns across the nation. Periodic campaigns for Muslims and Jews who fall victim to human rights violations must also be adopted to demonstrate that the churches have one yardstick for justice.

A case in point occurred when Israel expelled 415 Palestinians from the Gaza Strip in December 1992. It quickly became clear that this deplorable action violated all standards of international law and would endanger the fragile peace process. Several evangelical leaders, including Leonard Rodgers of Venture Middle East and Brother Andrew of Open Doors, visited the Muslim leaders stranded in south Lebanon. The Presbyterian Church (U.S.A.) issued a strong declaration opposing the order and called for U.S. action to encourage Israel to return the men safely to their homes.

Christians, Muslims, and Jews will occasionally find common ground in advocacy issues. In the Babylonian Talmud, Rabbi Joshua ben Levi is reported to have said, "Great is peace, for peace is to the world as leaven is to dough." In the same source, Rabbi Simeon ben Gamaliel said, "By three things does the world endure: justice, truth, and peace." Rabbi Muna said, "The three are one, because if justice is done, truth has been effected and peace brought about." [16]

Leonard Rodgers, director of the Cyprus-based evangelical mission organization Venture Middle East, came under attack, January 1993, from the International Christian Embassy and others for visiting the 415 Palestinians expelled from Israel. He responded in a thoughtful and caring manner. After citing the illegality of Israel's action and how the men were not given a fair trial prior to their expulsion, he added,

> What we did say is that God loves the world, including people with political views you or I don't agree with. We did say that these men and their families are the objects of God's love and are not an exception. We did say it is appropriate for us to show them Christian concern and the same concern to anyone denied basic human rights. . . . I call upon you to find it in your heart to pray for your enemies; for these men and their families. Don't be so concerned to win an argument as to be an instrument of reconciliation. Be open to the prompting of the Spirit in allowing your heart to be touched for these men and their families as people for whom Christ died. At the same time, remember all those who suffer for their Christian faith in these lands of the Bible. [17]

During periods of darkness and persecution God has always done great things in the Middle East—and everywhere. We do not know what difficulties Christians will face in coming years in these ancient lands. We do know that renewal is taking place now in many churches throughout the Middle East. The powers of the cross and resurrection, which transcend all secular powers and political strife, remain alive and well.

Middle Eastern Christians have to teach a great deal in the West. Our secular culture is seductively challenging our very roots as spiritual people and in terms of our Christian identity. Arab Christians coming from life-threatening societies who cope with significant poverty and violence are traveling a different spiritual road. We have much to learn from them, and they need our support. Could it be that God is calling us together to heal each other, and in this way strengthen the unity of the one body of Jesus Christ?

I am reminded of the wisdom of the book of Hebrews, written during the intense persecution of Christians in the first century.

> But recall those earlier days when, after you had been enlightened, you endured a hard struggle with sufferings, sometimes being publicly exposed to abuse and persecution, and sometimes being partners with those so treated.

For you had compassion for those who were in prison, and you cheerfully accepted the plundering of your possessions, knowing that you yourselves possessed something better and more lasting. Do not therefore, abandon that confidence of yours; it brings a great reward. For you need endurance, so that when you have done the will of God, you will receive what was promised. (Heb. 10:32-36)

14

Signs of Hope

A harvest of justice is sown in peace for those who make peace.
James 3:18

*W*hy is there so much violence around us? Have we perhaps preferred a
peace 'as the world gives'? A peace consisting of the silence of the oppressed, the powerlessness of the vanquished, the humiliation of
those—individuals and peoples—who see their rights trampled
upon? True peace, the peace which Jesus has left us, is based
upon justice and flourishes in love and reconciliation.
Pope John Paul II, Ecumenical Vigil for Peace; Assisi, Italy, 1993

*W*hy is there so much violence in our world today? Cities in the United States seem gripped by an epidemic of gang-related violence, rape,
and senseless murders. Worldwide, there are now over forty wars or major conflicts that threaten to bring death and suffering to millions of people. Bosnia, Afghanistan, Sudan, and Somalia are at war. Ethnic wars rage
throughout the former Soviet Union, a threat that will hang over most of
Asia and Europe in the next generation. In Africa, the 1994 genocidal horror committed in Rwanda saw the execution of hundreds of thousands of
civilians. Shortly after he left Rwanda in 1994, Bob Seiple, president of
World Vision, wrote,

> I have seen many disasters, but the enormity of this one is staggering. Bloat-
> ed bodies, both whole and in pieces, drift by in a parade of tragedy. Too nu-

merous to count, they are silent testimonies to a world yielding to sin, a world increasingly incapable of dealing with humanity's deepest differences. No one can provide a rationale for what is happening. To date, no one can stop the slaughter.[1]

Perhaps it is simply the human psyche's defense mechanism when overloaded by a steady diet of death and despair, but there seems to be a growing loss of sensitivity in Western societies to such suffering.

In the Israeli-Palestinian conflict, we watched with hope and amazement as on September 13, 1993, Yasir Arafat and Yitzhak Rabin shook hands and the historic Declaration of Principles document was signed on the White House lawn. But the ray of hope so evident in September faded quickly and turned ugly on February 25, 1994, when thirty Muslim worshipers were massacred while praying at the Ibrahimi Mosque in Hebron. The cycle of violence returned as Palestinian militants then bombed two Israeli buses, leaving six dead.

When Palestinian police assumed control over Jericho and most of the Gaza Strip in May, few were in the mood to celebrate the occasion. Worse, Palestinians had lost trust in their leadership after witnessing repeated delays in the Israeli withdrawal and the deterioration of their daily lives. The majority of the West Bank lacked protection from the heavily armed Jewish settlers, unemployment was reaching 75 percent, and people were tired and depressed from nearly thirty years of a brutal military occupation.

The growing Western insensitivity to suffering has influenced Western perceptions of the Palestinians and Israelis. A friend at church told me, "This conflict will never be resolved because Jews and Arabs will always hate each other." Another friend added, "It has been like this since Adam and Eve and will continue long after both of us are dead and buried." A family member keeps telling me, "You should give up on these people. This conflict won't be settled until Jesus returns."

As our thoughts turn in this closing chapter toward the challenges we must address in the Middle East, the words of Pope Paul II provide a proper focus. "Have we perhaps preferred a peace 'as the world gives'? A peace consisting of the silence of the oppressed, the powerlessness of the vanquished, the humiliation of those—individuals and peoples—who see their rights trampled upon?"

What is the role of Western Christians in this situation? Why should we even be concerned? What can we learn from our sisters and brothers in the Middle East about relating to Islam, Judaism, and being faithful witnesses to Jesus Christ in situations of war and conflict? Do the Middle Eastern Christians have anything to share with us in the West, given our sophisticated technology and advanced culture?

Let us explore several general guidelines and directions as we begin to address these questions. First, we will reflect on why we should consider investing time, prayer, energy, and gifts in the chaotic Middle East. Second, we will examine several options facing Christians in the Holy Land during this increasingly urgent period. Finally, we will discuss in a preliminary manner responses we in the West might consider in relation to the churches in the Middle East. Again, we will concentrate on the Palestinian Christian community as representative of Christians throughout the Middle East.

We Have Enough Problems at Home

From time to time someone asks me, "Why are you as a U.S. Christian so involved in the Middle East? Why aren't you spending your energies and ministry on local issues, such as the problems in our cities? This emphasis on a region halfway around the world makes no sense to me."

These questions often haunt me. I regularly reflect on whether I am investing my time and energy faithfully. Having served an inner city church, I am sensitive to the needs in our cities today. However, for the present, I see several reasons why the Middle East deserves our attention.

First, the cry of the Christians in the Middle East, as we have experienced in the previous chapters through Palestinian Christians, is a challenge on both the personal and corporate levels. Paul's meditation on the church in 1 Corinthians 12 reminds us that "where one part of the body suffers, we all suffer." In the Holy Land, where Jesus walked and the church began in Jerusalem on the day of Pentecost, the indigenous Palestinian Christian population is shrinking at an alarming rate. Christians throughout the Middle East have called out to us for prayer, fellowship, and economic support, but until now there has been a limited response. We must not abandon them.

Second, those of us in the United States live in the sole remaining superpower and must urge wise use and caution as to the U.S. ability to shape world events. The United States was founded on such Christian principles as freedom, equality, and the dignity of the human being before our Creator. These values are being challenged and trivialized by a variety of secular pressures, as Stephen L. Carter argues so well in his volume *The Culture of Disbelief* (New York: Doubleday and Co., 1994). The image of America abroad is that of a violent, hedonistic, wealthy, and secular culture. Our religious institutions must rise to meet this challenge.

This leads to a third aspect of the issue, our significant political responsibility as Western Christians. Consider, for a moment how the people of the Middle East, a highly politicized population, view the United States. They see a government and a significant number of its citizens who have, for over fifty years, been major supporters of the Zionist movement and the government of Israel. They are well aware of the extraordinary military and economic assistance given to Israel by U.S. taxpayers and the political immunity provided by the U.S. Congress and the U.S. Ambassador to the United Nations when Israel violates international laws. The United States has taken sides in the Arab-Israeli conflict, and this has not been forgotten by the Arabs. But with this favoritism comes responsibility. Do we believe in freedom, justice, and human rights for all people or only the "special friends"?

Fourth, the Middle East has significant economic and strategic value to the United States, primarily due to being the source of relatively inexpensive and high quality oil reserves. The strategic and economic importance of the Middle East still makes it the first or second most vital region for the maintenance of current Western lifestyles. At the same time, the Middle East is the most volatile region on the map, the site of the only region since Vietnam in which the United States has engaged in major warfare. Those concerned about Israel and the future stability of the Middle East need to begin looking at alternatives to war and militarization of these societies.

Fifth, both Islam and Judaism present important challenges to Christians in the West and will continue to do so. The relationship with Jews is strong and relatively positive now, but there is always the threat of anti-Semitism (the anti-Jewish form as Palestinians are also Semites) that today raises its ugly head throughout Europe and the United States. Christians must fight anti-Jewish anti-Semitism and ensure that these crimes are not to be tolerated.

At the same time, a growing hatred of Arabs and fear of Islam is on the rise. One sees this in the anti-Arab movements among the right wing in France and Germany. We also hear it in testimony by U.S. senators and other elected officials, particularly after a Muslim extremist has been involved in a crime. Our churches, schools, government, civil rights, and the philanthropic community need to make significant investments in education and awareness to these other children of Abraham.

Finally, several biblical challenges such as Christian Zionism (see ch. 8-9), relate to this conflict, and popular misinterpretations of such biblical issues as land, people, covenant, and prophecy. Much of our theology must be corrected to avoid continuation of the agony.

The hour is late and time seems not on the side of the Palestinians. However, as the historical record makes clear, surprising developments can emerge in times of significant darkness. As people of faith, we believe that God is at work in quiet ways to prepare for a new era. Whether one looks at Abraham's journey to the Holy Land after the deterioration of humanity in the Tower of Babel, the return of the Jews to their homes after the Babylonian captivity, or the birth of Jesus Christ in the backwater town of Bethlehem, God has the last word. But the question before Israel and the Palestinians is this: Will there be another major war? Or will there be a new era of peaceful coexistence? The answers to these questions will shape the quality of life for everyone in the Middle East.

The task of the church is to be faithful in these times of darkness and to listen for the word of the Lord. The author of Hebrews, writing to the faithful in a decade of Roman persecution, wrote to the church, "Consider him who endured such hostility against himself from sinners, so that you may not grow weary or lose heart" (Heb. 12:4). The shrinking and beleaguered church in the Holy Land must endure hostility and not grow weary—but it has called Christians in the West to stand with it. How will we respond?

The Church Has a Stake in Peace with Justice

The fall of apartheid in South Africa was a massive undertaking, won by the blood and steadfastness of South African blacks and their supporters around the world. Many political, governmental, and religious movements are now highlighting the important role they played, and undoubtedly many of these reports are correct. The change to black majority rule in South Africa took three centuries, and the last two decades were particularly violent, as the vestiges of the apartheid system resisted change.

Among groups that played a major role were the churches in South Africa and others around the globe. Churches of every denomination and persuasion, with a few notable exceptions, reached the conclusion that apartheid was evil, contrary to the teachings of the Bible, and in violation of the dignity of the human being created in God's image.

One church group that took this position against racism in the 1960s, when it was still somewhat unpopular, was the World Council of Churches Program to Combat Racism. The Program and its leadership came under severe criticism, financial pressure, and smear campaigns from conservative Christians, journalists, and the government of South Africa. Among the critics were several U.S. Jewish Zionist leaders, who feared the same theological and political conclusions would be applied to Israel and Zionism.

On the twenty-fifth anniversary of the Program to Combat Racism, the Nobel Peace Prize recipient and Anglican archbishop of South Africa, Desmond Tutu, told the World Council of Churches Central Committee, "If we notch up a victory against apartheid, it is your victory." This illustration of Christian solidarity and affirmation is a note of inspiration to us all as we face overwhelming suffering, ethnic cleansing, racial hatred, and new wars based on ethnic and religious lines.

The church universal played a significant role in the struggle against apartheid, using such strategies as theological dialogue, economic boycotts, efforts to initiate education and reconciliation with the advocates of apartheid, providing economic support for the poor, and letting the black churches of South Africa know they were not alone. Sister church relationships, prayer support, mission exchanges, and providing a platform for Western Christians to hear the true situation in South Africa were among numerous spiritual and practical acts of Christian solidarity over many decades.[2]

A largely untold story is the vital role some evangelical Christian churches in South Africa played in the rapid changes South Africa experienced in the 1990s. Many of these churches had earlier provided the religious justification for apartheid. One leader of the South African government was former Prime Minister F. W. de Klerk. In addition to the political and economic pressures isolating South Africa from the community of nations, de Klerk was influenced by a growing conviction that on biblical grounds apartheid was evil. As prime minister, de Klerk became a prime mover for change within his party and among his peers in government. With Nelson Mandela, de Klerk became both a symbolic and real political force for change toward a more just social order.

The struggle for a just peace in the Middle East will be more difficult, possibly more bloody, and undoubtedly slower. However, the church and Christian organizations worldwide can learn from the South African experience. The Palestinian church may not be numerically strong, as in South Africa, but it has gained significant credibility among Palestinian Muslims and within the PLO. The Palestinian churches will continue to be a major factor but now need the Western churches to join them in significant ways.

Signs of Hope

Time and space do not permit an exhaustive catalog of responsibilities and directions for the church in the coming years. However, here are five general thrusts that may lead to mutual cooperation between Western and Middle East churches in the coming years.

Mission and Evangelism

Let us begin with a controversial issue—the challenge to proclaim the gospel to the world according to the great commission, "Go therefore and make disciples of all nations" (Matt. 28:19). As Christians we cannot ignore the fact that our Lord has called us to take the gospel to the ends of the earth. But what does this mean? Jesus' own life and ministry are sufficient testimony to the variety of methods. Consider the last judgment and its emphasis on feeding the hungry, liberating the prisoners, and clothing the naked (Matt. 25:31-46). The teachings of Jesus make it clear that we need to be faithful to the great commission by working toward economic development for the poor as well as the spiritual conversion of individuals.

When we consider the Middle East and our call to Christian mission and witness, the most important starting point is the local church (the *ekklesia*). Christians must respect the church created by the Holy Spirit to witness to the presence of God's realm. However, many Western mission agencies forget to include Middle Eastern churches or completely ignore them when planning for mission.

Two of the many problems that emerge in a discussion of the complex issue of Christian missions and evangelism in the Middle East are the following. First, there are unresolved historical matters. Middle Easterners live their history and have great pride in their historical, spiritual, and cultural roots. History is a living reality in this region where one walks each day in the steps of Jesus Christ, sees the Tombs of the Patriarchs, and observes the Dome of the Rock, where the Prophet Muhammad visited on his "night journey."

Some evangelical Christians utilize the language and strategy of the Crusades, which they see as a model of evangelization. But the Crusades are a negative symbol of Western colonialism; a reservoir of anger over the Crusades lingers among local Christians, Muslims, and Jews. We noted elsewhere that the European Crusaders entered the Holy Land killing Christians and Jews as well as their Muslim targets. The fact that the Crusades were represented as a form of Christian "mission" places an added burden on Middle Eastern Christians.

It is not by accident or merely for propaganda purposes that Saddam Hussein interpreted the Gulf War, as another Western Crusade against the Arabs. During the Gulf War, it was essential for Middle Eastern Christians to double their efforts in terms of solidarity and identification with all Arabs and oppose the Gulf War in the clearest terms, so the Muslim masses would not turn against the Christian community. The fact that the United States was orchestrating the war and President Bush invoked "Christian" language from time to time made the task of the Arab churches more difficult. Those Western Christian leaders who publicly opposed the Gulf War helped to save the Arab Christians and redeem the Christian witness in many countries across the Middle East.

A second problem concerns the missionary methodology of many Western Christian churches and mission organizations in the Middle East. In a region already hypersensitive to Christian missions, most missionary activity today is viewed with disdain by Muslims and Jews and by their governments.

In Israel, proselytism of Jews is punishable by up to five years in prison and a significant fine. In most Arab countries, where Islamic law governs the land, evangelizing Muslims is a serious crime. In Saudi Arabia, the death penalty can be applied for proselytizing Muslims. In Iran and Egypt, there have been recent arrests, imprisonment, and retaliation against local Christians.

Most churches in the Middle East fall under state law or an unwritten agreement not to proselytize. The recent growth and power of the political Islamic movements have put the churches on notice that proselytism will not be tolerated. The churches are monitored carefully by governments and the new Islamic movements.

Most Western missionaries, when arrested for the crime of proselytizing, will face arrest, possible fine and short-term imprisonment, and in certain cases expulsion. But the Muslim national who converts to Christianity will face significant punishment as a heretic, extensive prison sentences, family ostracization (which cuts off a person's identity in the community), and occasionally execution. In addition, a climate of restriction is often imposed on the local churches, limiting their hard-fought religious freedom and adding undue stress to an already difficult situation.

The problem of mission and evangelization is becoming increasingly serious as a new wave of mission organizations targets the Middle East as a primary mission field. Sadly, they forget that there has been a church there for nearly 2000 years; they operate as if it does not exist.

A new stategy among many of these evangelical agencies is the "Ten-Forty Window" (10 degrees north of the equator to 40 degrees north) which includes North Africa, the Middle East, India, China, and Southeast Asia. Islam is the primary religion of this region, with Buddhism and Hinduism close behind. Groups such as Mission Frontiers, the Cooperative Strategy Group (a coalition of 150 Western evangelical agencies operating in the Middle East), and many others are using this analysis and approach. Occasionally they meet under an umbrella called "The AD 2000 Movement" to plan major fundraising efforts, satellite television broadcasts, church planting, and various covert mission operations.

Such strategies are provoking a defensive reactions from Islamic nations and Muslim fundamentalist movements, several of whom benefit from oil-rich countries such as Saudi Arabia and Iran. If history tells us anything about Christian-Muslim relations, the new evangelical strategies are likely to be costly and ineffective. They will also cause the deterioration of the ancient Christian churches in the region.[3]

I believe that The AD 2000 and Beyond Movement has potential to awaken the West to missions, but I am concerned about their theology, Western orientation, and cultural insensitivity. A significant dialogue must begin, perhaps in the West, and then engage the Arab churches of the Middle East.

One forum for this dialogue has been the recent consultations called by Evangelical for Middle East Understanding (EMEU, which has worked in partnership with the Middle East Council of Churches and several evangelical agencies operating in the Middle East. Western evangelicals have found Middle Eastern church leaders to be deeply spiritual, Bible centered, Christocentric, rooted in prayer and Eastern spirituality.

Middle Easterners have often been surprised by the openness of the Western evangelicals, the authenticity of their spirituality, and their Bible-centered orientation; through prayer and fellowship many important relationships have begun through the conferences dialogue and programs of EMEU and MECC. The journey ahead is long and perhaps difficult, but significant common ground has been established between the ancient churches of the Middle East and the Western evangelicals through the EMEU movement.

EMEU has called on Western evangelicals and others to consider that mission programs or strategic theologizing must be conducted in full dialogue with the Middle Eastern churches. No matter how well the strategies are conceived or intended, they can not be developed in offices or churches in the United States, Canada, or Europe. They must be the product of considerable prayer, discernment, and debate in partnership with the Middle Eastern Christians. Bishop Aram Kishishian, a theologian of the Armenian Orthodox Church and a president of the World Council of Churches, told our 1991 EMEU-MECC consultation,

> If you hear people call the Middle East a mission field, remind them that it is the birth place of our faith. Our foreign mission agencies have failed here because they emphasize proselytism rather than building up the body of Christ and seeking justice for all. A mission agency that sets up structures that are parallel to local churches rather than in partnership is not authentic.[4]

It is a new day for mission and becoming the church of Jesus Christ in the Middle East. We must strive to become authentic partners with the churches of the Middle East. We will discover that God is already at work in Jerusalem, the West Bank, Beirut, Damascus, Cairo, Baghdad, and throughout this region. We will not only learn from our sisters and brothers in the faith in these lands, but we will find the true meaning of being the church in new ways that will honor our Lord and the gospel he gave to us.

Theological Concerns: Ecclesiology and Mission

The above problems in missiology, whether related to the Western evangelical orientation or mainline Roman Catholic and Protestant churches, are rooted in theological issues. On the Western evangelical side, mission has been interpreted primarily in terms of individual conversion and has often been limited to the preached word, radio or television evangelism, and Bible teaching and distribution. Some have embarked on church planting and relief for the poor. The goal has been to convert the unbeliever to the Christian faith.

Most Western evangelicals are weak in ecclesiology and total reliance on the Holy Spirit. Our Western secular culture breeds pragmatism, materialism, and a rugged individualism that often undermines Christian values. We also overlook both the historic spirituality of the Middle Eastern Christians and the necessity to work within the body of Christ. We fail to respect local Christian churches, local culture, political realities, and the overarching role that the dominant religions (Islam or Judaism) may play in relation to these churches.

On the other hand, most mainline denominational efforts have rightly emphasized such mission initiatives as social justice, human rights, relief for the poor, development of societies, and considerable support for the particular denominations' mission churches. However, many mainline or liberal churches have often been limited by their Western culture and approach to mission than they may think and have lost the spiritual dimension in their programs. Again, the theological assumptions are critical.

A recent incident will serve to illustrate the theological problems within Western mission approaches. In April 1994, the World Council of Churches convened a think-tank session near Chicago on the state of Christian missions and invited a broad spectrum of theologians and church executives. There was a healthy mixture of women and men, races, and representatives from every continent.

A Middle Eastern theologian reported to me that while the sessions were of high quality, the theologians asked to lead the sessions all reflected a Western orientation that Eastern Christians consistently encounter in the West. Roman Catholic and Protestant scholars rendered brilliant analyses of the political and sociological dimensions of missiology, and proceeded immediately to propose various strategies. The Middle Eastern theologian felt that these more liberal theologians were falling into another Western trap. They failed to bring the theocentric and Christocentric dimensions into their otherwise brilliant political and sociological analyses. They failed to address the primary dimension of Middle Eastern reality—its significant theocentric culture, language, and values.

The liberal ecumenists were approaching mission and the task of the church through such secular disciplines as anthropology, political science, or sociology. As a result, the liberal theological scholars fell into the same trap as the Western evangelicals. They jumped from their analyses to methodology without integrating Christian theology.

This Western theological tendency to approach issues from the perspective of either individualistic pietism or secular analysis fails to integrate the Holy Spirit into the process. It is the classic split of the spirit from the body. As a result, the liberal or ecumenical churches are lacking the transcendent dimensions of the gospel, whereas the evangelicals are either ill-informed or individualistic in methodology. Both approaches fail to present the gospel in its wholeness, with a commitment to empower the local church and to pursue both the humanitarian and the spiritual renewal of the community and the individual. We in the secular West must be careful to integrate the incarnation, the union of the human and divine, into our lives and ministries. This is a potential point of shared dialogue, mission strategy, and witness for all the churches in the future.

A Call for Dialogue and Missiological Reflection on the Middle East

Given the new wave of evangelical missions moving toward the Middle East, the unhealed wounds of Arab Christian churches in relation to the West, and the rising force of a more political and extremist Islam, Western Christian churches and mission agencies need to enter a period of careful theological reflection and prayer concerning their approach to the Middle East.

I urge mission leaders from all traditions to engage in substantive dialogue and prayer with Middle Eastern Christian leaders, particularly those from the historic Orthodox and Catholic Churches. They are the largest majority of the indigenous Christian communities. Whatever is done in their regions should at least involve dialogue with the leaders of these churches.

In the period leading up to the year 2000, Christians worldwide should evaluate their previous relationships and consider future plans that involve direct contact with the Middle Eastern churches. Those involved with strategy, funding, prioritizing, and theologizing mission should begin to make the changes necessary to make this dialogue and prayer take place, lest we fail again in our mission in the Middle East.

At the same time there will be a need for all churches, both in the Middle East and the West, to take a serious look at the question of religious freedom in relation to Islam and Judaism. These are complicated and significant issues involving cultural, theological, and political differences in interpretation and implementation. Christians have been reduced to insignificant minorities in Israel and most of the Arab world, and their programs and even worship are increasingly restricted. While Islam encourages its believers to be evangelistic as do some branches of Judaism, Christians will not have this privilege. They will need to address other ways of being faithful to the great commission. One important way is simply to survive and find unity with other Christians who remain in these lands. Their rights to worship and service must be protected. The West has an obligation to stand with them.

The United Nations Human Rights Commission has considerable interest in these issues and may be a neutral arena in which to negotiate the principles of religions freedom and deal with individual cases. The International Covenant on Civil and Political Rights emphasizes "the right to replace one's current religion" and states "the freedom to adopt a religion [is] protected unconditionally, even in time of emergency."

The practical implications of these principles will need to be tested, verified, and implemented as they are challenged by Arab (and other) regimes as well as by various Muslim and Zionist organizations. Not only Christian missionaries, but also relief and development and church agencies, will come under severe pressure in the coming years. All churches must stand by these principles of religious freedom and defend those undergoing persecution.

Christian Presence in the Middle East: The Witness of the Remnant

The Christian community in the Middle East is a tiny minority in comparison to their Muslim cousins, who will have approximately 250 million adherents in this region by the year 2000. There are only 14-16 million Christians and 3.8 million Jews in the Middle East. The Christian population is roughly half of one percent of the total population, and the numbers are falling due to emigration patterns. The Jews have their own nation in Israel, but Christians feel increasingly insecure in Israel and predominantly Muslim countries.

While some Christians are responding with understandable fear, others point out that this is not a new situation for Middle East Christians. It has been their fate to be a minority population, not only since the advent of Islam, but from the birth of Christianity. The church faced overwhelming odds during its first three hundred years under the Roman Empire. Despite considerable suffering, the early Christian community found amazing spiritual strength through its life of prayer, fellowship, worship, and serving the needy with acts of love.

During this initial phase of Christianity, the primary theological and spiritual focus was on the cross of Christ, the death and resurrection of our Lord, which gave definition to the everyday reality of the believer. Martyrdom became a path for many of the great Christian leaders and for the average believer. The saints and martyrs for the faith were looked up to as the most faithful of the faithful in the church.

These same themes are now being reexamined by Middle Eastern Christians in light of their increased suffering and shrinking status. This return to the cross is neither a depressing nor a passive experience, but one faced with renewed energy and strength. Choosing the cross is to testify that Christians do not have the options of military power, economic prosperity, and political solutions for the Middle East. In fact, these solutions have failed all the peoples of the Middle East.

Nobel Prize-winning Egyptian novelist Naguib Mahfuz often has his characters articulate the poverty and anger of the Arab masses. Their condition of powerlessness and anger at their inept institutions and leaders is reflected throughout the Middle East. Mahfuz captures the primal cry of the masses with a few words in his novel *Miramir* (New York: Quality Paperback Book Club, 1989) in which one character calls out, "Let the heavens fall . . . let all powers fall with them."

Bishop Kenneth Cragg, the great Anglican Islamicist and scholar with decades of experience in the Middle East, reminds us that alienation is the climate in which the gospel thrives. In his brilliant volume *The Arab Christian*, Cragg writes,

> [Alienation] is the context in which the gospel of love that cares and suffers and retrieves and does so as the truth of the divine name will most surely find itself. . . . the central conviction of Christian faith and Eucharist concerning the God who reigns in the meaning of the wounds of Jesus is where the divine unity and human situation come together.[5]

Bishop Cragg and Middle Eastern Christian leaders tell us that this coming together of the human and divine is the cross and resurrection. This is what Christianity has to offer the Middle East. It is what Middle

Eastern Christians know and love, for it has been at the core of their theology and experience since the Resurrection of Jesus Christ in Jerusalem. Affirmed is the power of love over death, and hope over despair.

Gabriel Habib of the Middle East Council of Churches expressed this reality as a Middle Eastern Christian when he addressed the Evangelicals for Middle East Understanding Conference in Washington, D.C., in February 1994.

> There is a feeling among Christians in the Middle East, maybe because they are in the minority, that they have lost power. Some would say it is a pity that we lost it. Others would say, Thank God we lost it, because power is, after all, not the power of Caesar but the power of the Holy Spirit, which is the power of the politically powerless. So the Holy Spirit is the power of the powerless.[6]

Habib then turned to the need to witness to the reality of Jesus Christ in places of conflict and suffering.

> You don't speak about it much, but it is in the collective historical memory of the Middle East that Jesus Christ was born in Bethlehem not far from most of us and not by accident. He came, he entered our history because that region was characterized by conflicts, war, divisions, hatred, and destruction. He came in order to give us, through the reconciling process of the incarnation, the seed for transforming hatred into love, division into reconciliation, and war into peace. So in their collective memory, Christians think and feel that they are peacemakers, agents of peace. We would like to demonstrate that Jesus Christ is the meeting place of God and the human being, partly because of the dichotomy between God and the human being that exists these days in Islam and Judaism.
>
> At times they consider that the human being became so powerful as to kill God, and therefore power and God have to be recentered so that God may kill the human being in his name; a kind of theocracy. This is why we (Christians) emphasize the fact that for us, Jesus Christ, the one born in Bethlehem, is the reconciliation between God and the human being; so there is no room for the one asserting himself at the expense of the other.[7]

The failure of Marxism and Pan-Arab nationalism to address the needs of the Arab masses, and the imposition of Western secular models of technology and state power reflected in the Gulf War and the U. S. support of Israel, have caused many Muslim leaders to react with force. The vision of many Muslim leaders, which is gaining influence among the masses, is of a return to Islam to restore Arab dignity. The more extreme political models of Islam, developed in Iran, southern Lebanon, and Sudan, have given inspiration to the older Islamic brotherhood movements in Egypt, Palestine, and Jordan.

Today Islam is filling the political and spiritual vacuum left by the failed ideologies and secular West. The temptation of many Arabs, including the church, will be to grasp for immediate results in their impoverished situation, and to ignore the more reconciling, long-term, democratizing path. The Christian church has this latter path to follow, filled as it is with suffering and weakness.

The challenges for Middle Eastern Christians will be manifold. First, they must encourage their people to stay, as they are emigrating in record numbers. Second, the churches and their leaders must provide the spiritual tools, theological rationale, and in some cases the economic incentives that will encourage Christians to remain or return in their homeland. Third, the people and leadership must be prepared to suffer with dignity and find within their spiritual heritage and fellowship in the church the means to go on.

For Middle East Christians, the coming decade will be a time of testing and opportunity. The growing minority status, the rise of militant Islamic movements, and the success of the Zionists in Palestine auger poorly for the future of Christianity. But while many Christians will leave the region, those who remain will be committed to their faith and dependence on the Holy Spirit. Power and strength derived from economic, political, military, or hedonistic success will be increasingly unattractive and will make room for the power of love through Jesus Christ.

To remain faithful, the Arab Christian community will need to overcome its temptation to emphasize the negative aspects of its divided history and cultural differences. Arab Christians will need to seek unity within the love of Jesus Christ. Until now, the tragic ecclesiastical and political divisions of the Middle East have prevented the church from realizing its potential in the society. Protestants mistrust the Orthodox, the Orthodox do not trust the Catholics, all mistrust the Protestants, and national churches such as the Syrians or Copts in Egypt are either isolated from others or dislike them due to regional differences.

However, the Middle East Council of Churches, a fragile but effective ecumenical body ministering to the region's Christians, has been working to overcome these divisions for twenty years. Born in Lebanon in the midst of the Civil War, the MECC has been forced to deal with adversity and political and theological strife from its inception. Somehow it has weathered the storms and has learned that its power comes from its capacity to unite the diverse traditions and peoples in the one body of Christ. MECC must stay on course and pursue its vision to unite the church of the Middle East, trusting that the region that gave Christians the church and the divisions of Christianity might now model healing.

Ironically, today the MECC is perhaps the only church council in the world to which the Orthodox (Oriental and Greek), Catholics (Melkite, Chaldean, Maronite, Coptic, and Roman/Latin) and Protestants (primarily Presbyterian, Lutheran, Anglican, and Reformed) all belong as full partners. The Roman Catholic community was the most recent to join. The next major challenge is that of the Western evangelical churches and movements, a matter being addressed already through Evangelicals for Middle East Understanding (see chapter 5).

The Growing Economic Crisis and Christian Response

As Westerners, our general impression of the Middle East is one of wealthy sheiks and oil-rich business executives with money to throw away on gambling, expensive cars, and jewelry. But this impression has little to do with the day-to-day reality of the Arab masses.

The Gulf War seemed to accelerate the deterioration of the economic situation in the Middle East. One of the most severe shortfalls befell the Palestinians. When Kuwait and Saudi Arabia terminated their considerable payments to the PLO, the effects in the West Bank and Gaza Strip were devastating. The extensive welfare payments, support for prisoners' families, teachers salaries, and university salaries were virtually stopped.

Up to 300,000 new Palestinian refugees fled Kuwait, many from lucrative businesses, all of which were lost on a matter of days. The Israelis used the Gulf War period to impose a shoot-on-sight curfew in the occupied territories, closing the doors on not only the economy but also on the well-being of over two million people.

The trend toward economic decline was severe throughout the Arab world during the 1980s. The Unified Arab Economic Report, a joint effort by the Arab League and Arab Monetary Fund (an affiliate of the World Bank), documented the alarming developments in a 1991 report. They noted that the gross national product (GNP) of all Arab countries had dropped from $440 billion in 1980 to $410 billion in 1990. The per capita GNP dropped by 43 percent during this period, from $3,283 to a staggering $1,879. The total Arab debt jumped from $90 to $220 during the same period. The disparity should be seen in contrast to the high population growth, which ranges from 2.7 to 3.0 percent in the Middle East.[8] In Egypt, a million persons are added to its runaway population every seven months, most born into impoverished conditions.

Why, one may ask, would a region with the largest oil reserves on the planet experience such a massive increase in foreign debt? The answer is simple: preparation for war and fear of future civil conflicts in most Middle Eastern societies. The Middle East spends a higher percentage of its GNP on the military than any region in the world, with about a fourth expended on militarization. The average number of soldiers in the region is fifteen per thousand of the population. The next highest levels are found in Latin America, with a level of four per thousand, and Africa, with three per thousand.[9] It is likely that Middle East military expenditures have increased since the Gulf War. Naturally those Western nations which are the major military industrial suppliers have been more than pleased to deliver more weapons.

These statistics only begin to reflect the depressing reality that the average Arab family experiences in a variety of ways. Most homes throughout the Middle East, from the slums of Egypt to the small towns of Syria and Iraq, are gaining access to television. An unpublished report by the Cooperative Strategy Group, an inter-mission effort involving over seventy mission organizations and ninety Arab church leaders, has demonstrated how new satellite television stations bring the latest news into Arab homes, including the most impoverished areas. In addition, Western films and sitcoms project Western values and materialism into the Arab living room.[10] The despair only grows as a result.

With frustration growing and the failure of recent political agendas to change their basic condition, the Arab masses are eager for a change. With the Western models giving power but no answers, the masses are turning to a political expression of Islam.

If the frustrations are expressed along the ever-widening lines of tribal, ethnic, or religion in the Middle East, as is the case in Africa and the former Soviet Union, the world is in for a major explosion. Because the Middle East receives more weapons than any other region, the next war will likely be regional and could be nuclear. If this proves to be the case, it will have serious implications for both the economies and the peoples of the world.

Western church agencies can help avert such disaster by addressing the economic challenges of the poor Arab masses. The church in the Middle East must be encouraged and given increased economic and practical resources with which to serve the poor, whether Christian, Muslim, or Jewish. The coming decade will require a conscious political and pragmatic choice to turn fighter jets into housing, missiles into food, and tanks into bread. The church can model through its mission programs the types of development options that are possible.

Signs of Hope Through Affirmation

Recent trends in business management and organizational theory emphasize the positive strengths of corporations. The tendency in the West has been to analyze problems in organizations and their personnel, with the assumption that problem solving will fix what is not working. Some management theorists now argue that this approach often limits new growth, imagination, and future development.

One new trend in management thinking is "appreciative inquiry," which is promoted by David Cooperrider and Suresh Srivastva. In their seminal volume, *Appreciative Management and Leadership: The Power of Positive Thought and Action in Organizations*, they say that

> the thesis explored in this paper is that the artful creation of positive imagery on a collective basis may well be the most prolific activity that individuals and organizations can engage in if their aim is to help bring to fruition a positively and humanly significant future.[11]

They show how organizations have failed to grasp the essential truth that, to find fulfillment and meaning, humans need affirmation and encouragement to envision a hopeful future. Cooperrider shows how Winston Churchill's leadership in World War II exemplified, in a dark time, the ability to see " 'what is' rather than 'what is not'."[12]

Is this not the role of the church? Is this not reminiscent of the faith of a nomad from the city of Ur in Iraq, then of the Chaldees, who first settled in the Holy Land some 4000 years ago? The author of Hebrews described his faith as "the assurance of things hoped for, the conviction of things not seen" (Heb. 11:1). Could it be that the appreciative inquiry methodology is a gift from God, using the language and management theory to turn people toward hope, mystery, and love?

Perhaps the Christians of the Middle East, who live in the lands that Abraham and Sarah walked, have retained many of these central ingredients of biblical faith. Many of these Christians have retained some freedom from the Western cultural pressures of efficiency, problem-centered analysis, and materialistic values. Most Middle Eastern Christians are more readily grasped by the spiritual dimension of everyday reality and find God everywhere. Could these small and weakened "remnants" have a message of several models, both contemporary and ancient, for us to study and apply to our situation?

But this is not the full story. As Cooperrider goes on to say, if we can recover the sense of mystery and hope, our futures will be opened to new possibilities, to hope, and to imagination:

> Appreciation not only draws our eye toward life, but stirs our feelings, excites our curiosity, and provides inspiration to the envisioned mind. In this sense, the ultimate generative power for the construction of new values and images is the apprehension of that which has value. . . . the appreciative eye actually seeks uncertainty as it is thrown into the elusive and emergent nature of organizational life itself. Appreciation is creative rather than conservative precisely because it allows itself to be energized and inspired by the voice of mystery.[13]

We in the West have lost our capacity for understanding the central role of mystery and the power of transcendence in our secular culture. The loss of mystery often takes with it the centrality of affirming love. Instead, we have relationships, values, and organizations that demand productivity and push us into various forms of denial or hedonism. Everything that could be of value—be it time, love, sex, people, or food—are reduced to what will bring instant gratification and can be purchased.

Middle Eastern societies have not yet fallen to our level of degradation, although some are turning in our direction. Most of the Middle East remains essentially simple, highly theocentric, and (with the exception of the oil-producing states) relatively poor. They can still see God at the center of everyday life. Middle Eastern Christians living in these societies may be able to share with us models of spirituality and of Jesus Christ amidst chaos and destruction.

As we in the West consider missions, peacemaking, and work for economic justice, there needs to be an additional word of concern, and here I speak autobiographically. Many of us expend our best time and energy on our jobs or a demanding travel schedule. We run to "faithfully serve the Lord" but at the expense of our inner spirituality, prayer life, relationships with children and spouses. Not only do we fail to be present to ourselves and to our families but to Jesus Christ.

There is an intimate connection between what we accomplish in our outward journeys of justice and peace and what we do in our personal lives. If we are to truly be peacemakers, we must have integrity in our homes and be about peace in our communities. It is always easier to be a prophet abroad than to work for peace at home. Most important, we must work at both public and private peace and justice. The remarkable openness to mystery and spirituality that dominates the Middle East will enhance reconciliation and peace wherever they emerge.

The Gospel and the Middle East Signs of Hope:

The potential for a reciprocal movement of the Holy Spirit, which gives gifts to the worldwide body of Christ, may be the unexplored territory God is calling us to share as we move toward the year 2000 and beyond. Rather than concentrating on winning every soul for Christ with high-technology methods, perhaps the focus should be on the church and how we can be the body of Christ in this broken region.

At the heart of being Christ's body in the Middle East is the power which lies at the heart of the gospel—reconciling love, which is what the region so desperately needs and lacks. Jonathan Kuttab, a Palestinian lawyer and Christian from Jerusalem, has been working for two decades as a human rights advocate. One of our delegations to the Middle East met with him in 1991 during the Gulf War. Iraqi scud missiles were still falling on Tel Aviv and the West Bank; the Israelis had imposed a brutal shoot-on-sight curfew on the Palestinians. Jonathan's appeal surprised many who expected to hear another angry speech about Israeli practices of torture and collective punishment.

> Before any solution is found for the question of Palestine, before all the political maneuvers and the shuttle diplomacies and negotiating with various leaders and the International Conference, there is one prerequisite: a healing of souls and a mending of broken bones. Such healing is only possible if Christians can look deep into their hearts and discover that at the heart of their faith is a cross and resurrection, giving them a capacity to bring hope and healing out of darkness and death. We must break down the dividing walls of hostility but we cannot do so unless we find justice for both parties, not a justice at the expense of the other, but through forgiveness to break the cycles of violence and find true freedom and community.[14]

If the small and weakened Christian community in Palestine and Israel can open themselves to this dimension of their faith and faithfully witness to God's reconciling love, God will honor them. They will also bring a much-needed dimension of life to a region that desperately needs the love and grace of Jesus Christ.

During the Crusades, Saint Francis came to the Holy Land to bring this love to the land of our Lord. His spirit was deeply troubled by what he saw —Western Christians killing Muslims and Jews in the name of Jesus. One day Saint Francis crossed the battle lines and asked to be taken to the tent of the great Muslim leader, Saladin. He came without weapons or pretense, and walked alone at great risk. The great Muslim leader responded, "What others have failed to gain by conquest, you have achieved by love." This is our mandate as would-be instruments of Christ's peace in the Middle East.

Progress will be discouraging, painfully slow. We may be tempted to give up when our efforts are not recognized and no fruit is in sight. The Trappist monk Thomas Merton wrote this to his friend Jim Forrest, then of the Fellowship of Reconciliation:

> Do not depend on the hope of results. When you are doing the sort of work you have taken on, you may have to face the fact that your work will be apparently worthless and even achieve no result at all, if not perhaps results opposite to what you expect. As you get used to this idea, you start more and more to concentrate not on the results but on the value, the rightness, the truth of the work itself. And there, too, a great deal has to be done though, as gradually you struggle less and less for an idea and more and more for specific people. The range tends to narrow down, but it gets much more real.
>
> In the end, it is the reality of personal relationships that saves everything. The great thing, after all, is to live—not to pour out your life in the service of a myth. If you can get free from the domination of causes and just serve Christ's truth, you will be less crushed by the inevitable disappointments. Because I see nothing whatever in sight but much disappointment, frustration, and confusion. . . . The real hope, then, is not in something we think we can do, but in God who is making something good out of it in some way we cannot see. If we can do God's will, we will be helping in this process.[15]

From my experience, our Arab Christian friends are more able to reach this state of leaving success and personal achievement behind and seeking the kingdom first. Middle Eastern culture places a high priority on hospitality and relationships. We will benefit by partnerships with them and at times we will remind them to remain focused on God's will, rather than "our cause" or our disappointment. Our responsibility is to discover, through prayer, partnerships, increased knowledge and sensitivity, and the surrender of our time and gifts to God, what it means to be lovers of God and all of God's children.

Gabriel Habib, of the Middle East Council of Churches, wrote a remarkable "open letter" to approximately 200 North American evangelical leaders in July 1987 (see Appendix G). He shared his personal faith and present concerns as an Arab Christian who feels both neglected and unequal in the eyes of Western Christians. He called for Middle Eastern and Western Christians to begin a journey of dialogue, prayer, mutual understanding, and possible partnerships as we seek to be faithful to Jesus Christ. The letter became a primary point of discussion and challenge to those who have participated in the Evangelicals for Middle East Understanding and Middle East Council of Churches programs.

Habib proclaimed,

> Let us seek means of proclaiming the truth of our Lord in the search for peace and justice in the region . . . . In solidarity, I am appealing for us first and foremost to be a bond of love which should destroy all racial, cultural, or confessional barriers between us, thus transforming mistrust or indifference into a common commitment in the search for our unity in witness to truth, love, and hope in the resurrected Lord, Jesus Christ.[16]

This paragraph perhaps summarizes our calling toward the love of Christ and the task to overcome the immense cultural, political, historical, and theological differences.

My wife and I have enjoyed attending performances by the Chicago Symphony Orchestra for more than twelve years. We have experienced the joy of listening to one of the great orchestras in the world as they perform beautiful music with sensitivity and incredible precision. I have little knowledge of classical music but have grown to love it. I sit back and relax after a long day and find myself uplifted by the interplay of violins, cellos, horns, and percussion.

We recently attended a performance of Beethoven's Third Symphony, directed by Daniel Barenbaum. I was sitting beside our close friends Lorrayne and Gary Brugh, both quite knowledgeable about classical music. Lorrayne is an accomplished church organist, professor of music, and has published several works of her own.

I asked her several basic questions, and she began to describe the background of the symphony, noting how the music was written for the opera *Fidelio.* "The 'Lenore' symphony is the most dramatic music that Beethoven wrote," she added, "beginning with the darkness of the prison cell where Floristan had been unjustly sent."

I thought of Arab Christians who have suffered through the ages for their faith. The music started and touched me deeply, even to the point of tears. My thoughts drifted to the Palestinians now imprisoned without just cause by Israel, and then to the Jews who suffered in concentration camps and were victims of Hitler's genocide.

A distant trumpet called out, announcing Floristan's reprieve. The flutes and violins lifted my feelings as I sensed the yearning for justice and freedom. Then I was reminded that if Lorrayne had not given me the brief background, I would have missed the point of the music. Certainly it would have been a relaxing and enjoyable evening on one level, but I would have missed the depth of Beethoven's message and its application to my ministry today. Without the lens of analysis and historical context, I would not have benefited so completely from the experience.

Perhaps this simple experience is applicable to how many of us in the West understand the Middle East and the possibilities to become involved in God's call for freedom, faithfulness, and peace. This complicated region is distorted by our media and the vast body of mythology that has been created by all sides of the conflict. Our analysis is usually superficial or we simply do not understand the complexities of the story, and choose to tune it out. Many of us have grown immune to the scores of wars and violence that dominate our news broadcasts.

However, a few insights into the history, our Scriptures, and relationships with the people of a particular region can make a significant difference. If we can begin to open our hearts and minds through prayer, the Bible, and our experiences, we will discover the richness of the people and of the region itself. We will be taken beyond the war and the violence to a powerful story that is unfolding today. For Christians, the key to these insights and experiences are the churches of the Middle East. They are our interpreters and our partners in understanding the symphony now being played in the Middle East.

Epilogue
A Call to All Churches Concerning Middle Eastern Christians

Recall the days gone by when you endured a great contest of suffering after you had been enlightened. At times you were publicly exposed to insult and trial; at other times you associated yourselves with those who were being so dealt with. You even joined in the sufferings of those who were in prison and joyfully assented to the confiscation of your goods, knowing that you had better and more permanent possessions. Do not, then, surrender your confidence; it will have a great reward. You need patience to do God's will and receive what he has promised.
(Hebrews 10:32-37; Jerusalem Bible)

"In the fullness of time," God chose the Middle East to enter history in the form of Jesus Christ (Gal. 4:4). Unfortunately, this region is not known so much today for its historic churches or Christian witness as for its oil reserves, wars, religious strife, and terrorism. Middle Eastern Christianity has for too long been viewed as a relic of the past, despite the fact that there are 14-15 million Christians in the Middle East seeking to live faithfully and creatively. We therefore ask Christians throughout the world to recognize the urgent call from Middle Eastern Christians to recognize their historic presence in this region and contemporary situation. The call to awareness is also a call for dialogue, solidarity, and sharing mutual gifts in mission and ministry.

From Pentecost to the Year 2000: A Rich Spiritual Heritage

Middle Eastern Christianity is usually evaluated according to Western Christian standards, which are flawed by political bias, Greek or Latin theological thought forms and assumptions, and a Western colonialist orientation. Although they are losing members due to various external and internal pressures, Middle Eastern Christians have a rich spiritual heritage that is not only alive but has gifts to offer the West.

Beginning with the day of Pentecost, when the people of God gathered in Jerusalem from Africa, Egypt, Libya, Lebanon, Syria, the Arabian Peninsula, Mesopotamia (Iraq), Persia (Iran), and beyond (Acts 2:8-11), the church of Jesus Christ had an Eastern orientation. Shaped by Jesus and Oriental spirituality, the church spread rapidly from Jerusalem to the ends of the Roman Empire (Acts 1:8).

Despite the severity of the Roman persecution, heresy, and division within the young churches, Christianity became a strong and durable living faith. However, as Christianity moved West, it lost much of its original cultural and wholistic spirituality identity as well as rich traditions that date back to the Pentecost era.

Still, there are up to 15 million Christians in the Middle East who have maintained the faith and are the present embodiment of this spiritual heritage. They are the descendants of the first Christians and proudly carry the responsibility to bear witness to the gospel in these ancient lands.

However, in recent years the accelerated emigration of Middle Eastern Christians from their homelands has weakened the Christian presence and witness in these lands. Christianity remains approximately half of Lebanon's population but is less than 10 percent and shrinking in Syria, Iraq, Iran, Jordan, Israel, and Palestine, and throughout the Gulf. Across North Africa and in the Arabian Peninsula, Christians account for less than one percent of the population. However, in Egypt the Coptic Churches have the highest number of Christians, approximately 8 million, and are experiencing significant renewal amidst renewed tension with Islamic extremist movements.

Today's Challenge to the Churches of the Middle East

Why are Christians leaving? They leave primarily due to economic and political strife and a persistent climate of war. In the Holy Land, the number of Christians among Palestinians in Jerusalem has dropped from 51 percent in 1922 to about 4 percent today. Middle Eastern church leaders are warning that in a generation there will be no living church in the Holy Land, only empty churches (museums) and archaeological sites for tourists to visit. The "living stones," the living church (1 Peter 2:4) will have emigrated to Europe, North America, South America, or Australia.

Those Christians who remain are increasingly a "remnant" (Isa. 10:20-22; Amos 5:4-9) but at the same time they may be a potential source of renewal and building blocks for the Holy Spirit to use in faithful service in the future. What pressures will this remnant face in the coming years? Since the Gulf War and the collapse of the Soviet Union, the Middle East has witnessed several religious and political developments that will shape the future. How are these changes affecting the churches of the Middle East?

First, the political ideologies that shaped the past several decades in the Middle East have fallen into disarray. Pan-Arab nationalism, Marxism, and humanism did not deliver on their promises to the people.

Second, the gap between the very poor and the rich is growing rapidly, as is the population. Most Arab countries, such as Egypt, have exploding populations with a median age of fourteen to fifteen years. If their cries for justice and equal rights are not heeded, bloodshed and civil strife will characterize the future. Third, the Middle East is the most heavily armed region in the world. Its ratio of fifteen soldiers per thousand population is the highest in the world, as is its military spending (26 percent of GNP). The introduction of nuclear weapons into the Middle East by Israel and possibly other countries raises the threat of nuclear war.

Fourth, in this political and spiritual vacuum the masses are turning to religious fundamentalism for answers. In Israel it is a religious Zionism that elevates Israel above all other nations as the chosen people of God. In the remainder of the Middle East, political Islam is shaping these societies as they call for a return to Islamic governments; the institution of the *Shar'ia* (Islamic law); and fierce opposition to Western secular, political, media, religious, and economic influences. Unfortunately, Christianity is often portrayed by the media (especially the present venue of Western evangelical Christian programming), as a legacy of Western intervention since before the Crusades, to reflect Western colonial and secular influence.

Middle Eastern Christians and Islam

Historically, the Middle Eastern churches predate Islam and are indigenous to the Arab world and its culture. As indigenous Arab Christians, they share a common monotheistic faith through Abraham and Ishmael; have common spiritual, ethical, and cultural values; and share a common language. These Middle Eastern Christians are the primary source of reconciliation and understanding between Christianity and Islam today. As Islam grows into a major religious and political force worldwide, those unfamiliar with Islam will benefit from the Middle Eastern Christians' 1300 years of experience.

Options Facing Middle Eastern Christians Today

Middle Eastern Christians face four options amidst the above challenges to their future presence and witness to the gospel. First, many are choosing to emigrate, a phenomenon accelerating throughout the region. Christians are leaving due to the economic blight and political instability that shapes much of the Middle East.

Second, Christians can choose to retreat into isolation as the civil strife increases. This defense mechanism was successful in previous periods of persecution but it is doubtful that in today's world of advanced military technology that isolation will prove effective.

Third, Christians can choose the military option, as some Maronite Christians did in Lebanon during the 1970s and 1980s. Thus far this choice has been disastrous, and the Maronites have lost significant ground.

Fourth, Christians can decide to stay and remain a creative witness to the gospel of Jesus Christ, to be true peacemakers and forces for equality in their societies. The Middle Eastern churches are the natural bridges between the Jewish and Islamic faiths and between Israel and the Arab nations. This latter challenge offers many opportunities for the Western churches to learn from these Middle Eastern Christians and indeed support their continuing presence and witness to the faith.

An Agenda for an Authentic Middle Eastern Christian Presence and Witness in the Middle East Today

Middle Eastern Christians are raising serious questions concerning the quality and future of their presence in the Middle East. The Middle East Council of Churches, the ecumenical umbrella under which the majority of the Christians of the region are seeking the unity and witness for the gospel, has become the forum for these concerns since its inception in 1974. The following issues are now being debated, experienced, and prayerfully studied for a faithful response.

1. How do Middle Eastern Christians maintain their identity amidst the immense pressures and turmoil now present in their societies? Do Christians have an authentic role to play? Or will they be marginalized as "bit players" with no influence on the powers?

2. How can Middle Eastern Christians be faithful to the gospel when they live as restricted minorities in increasingly hostile situations? Will the Christian future be one of suffering for the gospel, even facing martyrdom, in their search to be faithful? How can they creatively draw on their rich history of suffering and faithfulness in ways that will provide inspiration and creative witness?

3. How can the unity of the churches be strengthened in this region known for a history of theological and ecclesiastical division? Pope Shenouda of the Coptic Orthodox Church (Egypt) is fond of saying, "From the Middle East, Christianity emerged and became divided, so from here

we must now exemplify the greatest unity."

Although the Middle East Council of Churches (MECC) is a relatively new movement and somewhat fragile, it has already brought the majority of the churches into a structural, theological, and practical expression of their unity in Christ. The MECC is one of the most inclusive ecumenical bodies in the world and includes these churches as full members: Eastern or Greek Orthodox, Oriental Orthodox; Catholic (Latin, Maronite, Melkite, Armenian, and Coptic), and Protestant or National Evangelical (Presbyterian or National Evangelical, Lutheran, and Anglican). For the Middle Eastern churches to be a credible witness at this time of significant emigration and the weakening of the churches, the unity of these churches will be important.

4. How will Middle Eastern Christians conduct their mission and evangelism during this period of increased religious and political tension? The ancient churches are challenged by two opposing forces. On the one hand, the Jewish and Islamic governments are hostile toward proselytism of their communities by Christians. They often punish local Christians for incidents conducted by Western evangelical agencies. On the other hand, a new wave of Western evangelical and fundamentalist missionaries are now underway in the Middle East. What is the role of Middle Eastern churches caught between these opposing forces?

5. As many Middle Eastern societies return to forms of governance based on more conservative religious ideologies (religio-political Zionism in Israel and Islamic political fundamentalism in much of the Arab world), it will be necessary for Middle Eastern churches to form alliances that will facilitate pluralism, equal rights, and democracy throughout the region. In these situations, Middle Eastern Christians will increasingly be called on to develop skills in such fields as human rights, participatory democracy, and institutionalizing the basis for equality of all citizens in these nations.

6. How will Middle Eastern Christians maintain their historical continuity in ways that are both inspirational and renewing for the faithful—rather than romantic or nostalgic retreats into the past? Can the rich history of Middle Eastern Christianity be a source of constant renewal, even during times of persecution and war? Or will the temptation to become nostalgic leave the church impotent and marginal?

7. What forms of partnership in mission, relief and development, biblical study, and other dimensions of Christian life are possible today between Western churches and the Middle Eastern churches? After three waves of missionary activity that eventually weakened the local Middle Eastern churches, the local Christians are sensitive about Western forms of missionary activity, evangelization, and media strategies that do not consider their presence or existence.

Will the Middle Eastern churches continue on the road that leads them to recover their identity, power, and spiritual vitality in the lordship of Jesus? Will they recognize that their power is in the Holy Spirit and the power of Jesus coming alive in their communities? Can they withstand the temptation to be seduced by military, material, or secular forms of power? In this time, when there is both a spiritual and political vacuum in the Middle East, Christians can effectively bear witness to the gospel by drawing closer to Jesus and his church. This steadfast love of God in Jesus, love committed to serve the poor and the outcast while it turns suffering into redemption, can draw previous enemies to reconciliation in the God of love. If the Middle Eastern Christians remain focused on this road toward unity, renewal, faithfulness amidst suffering, loving service, and spiritual vitality, they have a key role in building a new Middle East and significant gifts to share with the West.

The Call to Western Christians

Christians in the Middle East must not be abandoned as they strive to be faithful during these demanding years. Their task is both overwhelming and urgent as their options rapidly close. At the same time, Christians in Western societies, who have known significant freedom and economic prosperity, are now called prayerfully to discern how they might share the burden of Christian witness and service with Middle East churches.

In the spirit of mutual responsibility in the one body of Christ, we urge Western Christians to enter a time of dialogue and spiritual discernment with Middle Eastern Christians concerning the future of the church in the Middle East. The following issues merit serious consideration in the years immediately ahead.

1. A Call for Mutual Prayer and Discernment in the Body of Christ:

The search for renewal and faithfulness should begin with prayer in both the Middle Eastern and Western churches. Prayerful submission to Jesus Christ, seeking fervently to hear the will of God in the present situation, should be the starting point in this common search for future service and mission. The following suggestions for mutual prayer support might be considered.

a. As Middle Eastern Christians clarify their priorities for mission and witness, or when there are periods of significant suffering that demand mutual support, the churches of the Middle East will need the prayers and support of the churches throughout the world. Now is the time to establish global prayer networks and relationships, making prayer a top priority for the churches and individual Christians in the Middle East and worldwide.

b. During times of crisis or as individual cases arise, Western churches can be alert to prayer requests from the Middle East to demonstrate spiritual solidarity and build the bond of support. Both existing prayer networks and new movements for intentional prayer for the Middle East can be used. The murder of three Iranian Christian leaders in early 1994, possibly by government authorities, combined with repeated attacks on Coptic Christians in Egypt, are examples of the urgent need for prayer and response networks on every continent.

c. Middle Eastern Christian leaders may be itinerated across the Western countries to raise awareness and call for prayer for specific issues. These Christians can share their own prayer traditions while they interpret specific concerns.

2. A Call to Middle East Christian Education at All Age Levels:

a. Western Christians are encouraged to heighten awareness of their members concerning the historical life and witness of Middle Eastern Christians. Through vehicles as Sunday school curricula, videos, film, books, travel, short-term mission experiences, and meeting Middle Eastern Christians on the personal level, awareness and fellowship will grow.

b. Of immediate importance is the future role of television and particularly satellite communications in the Middle East. Television is accessible to approximately 90 percent of the population in most countries. The introduction of Western satellite television broadcasts creates both an opportunity and a significant challenge for the church. If new forms of Western evangelistic strategies are undertaken in ways insensitive to other religions or the future security of local churches, the new technology could bring disaster to indigenous Christians. In addition, the new technologies are costly and should be carefully evaluated before commitment of diminishing resources to media.

c. Western Christians have a specific responsibility to educate contemporary Christians on the historical roots, teachings, and false promises of what is called "Christian Zionism" (see chapters 8-9). It is essential that Western Christians bear the major responsibility for this basically Western phenomenon. Christian Zionism should be considered a Western heresy detrimental to peace and understanding in the Middle East; contrary to the biblical witness of Jesus Christ to the Gentiles and the New Testament call that the church be one in Christ; and hostile toward the Arab Christian churches in the Holy Land.

3. A Call to Form Partnerships in Mission Between Middle Eastern and Western Churches:

a. Recognizing a history of insensitivity and the need to heal old wounds that date back to the Crusades, we call for a two-to-three-year period of exhaustive theological dialogue, prayer, and mutual planning concerning the future of Christian mission in the Middle East. The finest Middle Eastern and Western missiologists should be commissioned to prepare a comprehensive study that will consider the future of mission in the Middle East.

b. Western churches are reminded that the unity and integrity of the Middle Eastern churches is a sacred trust that must be respected and preserved. The future of Christianity in this region depends upon it. We affirm that in the end, all Christian mission is in some way linked to the local *ekklesia*. This factor must shape all mission strategies and practices in the years ahead.

c. Many Western Christians interpret mission in individualistic terms of proclamation and conversion, matters that are highly controversial and illegal in Israel and many Muslim countries. Western mission agencies must consider the ramifications of their policies on local Christians and find means of dialogue and cooperation in mission.

4. A Call to Affirm Middle Eastern Spirituality:

a. One of the great gifts that the Christians of the Middle East have to share with the West is approximately 2000 years of a Christian Eastern spirituality, including traditions of prayer, Middle Eastern Christian meditation, and a spiritual identity different from our Western experience. Most of these practices were developed in the first 300 years of the church, particularly during the Roman persecution. This Eastern Christian spirituality may be a healthy corrective to the predominantly secular Western values and lifestyles that have become dominated by materialism, technology, hedonism, and militarism.

b. With the dominance of secularism as an alternative form of belief in the West, Christian values and spirituality are being challenged in significant ways. North American and many of the European societies have been dominated by secularism for the previous 350 years, thereby shaping the basic identity and theology of both individual believers and religious institutions. Because the Middle Eastern churches have always lived in theocentric cultures, they have been able to maintain the spiritual practices and centeredness lacking in the West. Middle Eastern Christians may have important analysis, experiences, and spiritual gifts to share with the Western churches.

c. Western secular culture is generally death-denying and unable to cope with pain and suffering. Middle Eastern Christians have an entire history of dealing with suffering, persecution, and death. Today the Christians of this region are facing similar situations of persecution and even martyrdom. Again the Middle Eastern experience will have vital gifts to share with the Western Christians.

5. A Call to Advocacy:

a. It will be necessary for Western Christians to join Middle East Christians in their quest to build new societies that are democratic, pluralistic, and affirmative of equal rights for every citizen. The new forms of democracy and civil liberties will be somewhat different from those in the Western democracies. And the Middle Eastern churches may play an important role in mediating and promoting these values which are consistent with the gospel. At the same time, many Middle Eastern countries are moving toward ethnic or religious societies with particular communities receiving favored status over others. Christians must work with Muslims and Jews as well as secular agencies committed to democratic societies based on equal rights for all citizens.

b. The struggle for human rights will be an important arena where Western Christians can join the Middle Eastern Christians in the next decade. In the delicate matter of religious rights and freedom in the Middle East, it will be essential for Western Christians to maintain a degree of tolerance for standards different from their own while maintaining vigilance and advocacy when asked by their Middle Eastern colleagues.

c. The Middle East has known five major wars in less than fifty years; the region remains in a constant state of turmoil. With many nations becoming capable of nuclear warfare and with fewer enforceable means of accountability, the Middle East should be declared a "nuclear free zone" immediately, with no exceptions given to any nation. With the likelihood of another major war in this region at any time, Christians in the Middle East and the West should be in the vanguard to prevent nuclear war.

d. With the martyrdom of Christians in the Middle East becoming an increasing phenomenon—as events during the 1990s in Egypt, the Sudan, and Iran indicate—there will be an urgent need for Christians around the world to pray, network, and act in their defense. It will be necessary to contact government officials in countries responsible for the churches' security, as well as mobilize significant Western Christian leaders, government officials, and leaders of other faiths (particularly Muslims and Jews) to join us in demanding security for the churches in the Middle East.

6.   A Call to Partnerships in Relief and Development:

a. As new societies emerge or rebuild from their ruins, and as other nations emerge from devastating poverty, the churches of the Middle East must be involved with the poor. Matthew 25:31-40 says Christians will be judged according to their acts of love and compassion toward the poor, the imprisoned, the hungry; and according to their capacity to see Christ in the faces of their neighbors."

b. The Christians of the Middle East may be called to stand in the middle of armed conflict through service to the poor and "expendable" members of society. During times of war, the church must serve those who are victimized by various forms of political, economic, and military oppression, whatever their religious faith.

c. In addition to the compassionate response necessary during emergency situations, the churches East and West must think strategically about long-term development programs that will enhance the quality of life and encourage democratic societies to emerge. In a time of diminishing resources for mission and development programs, the churches in the Middle East and West will need to be more precise in establishing their priorities and sharing the shrinking sources of economic support. Extreme caution may need to be exercised with regard to receiving funds from institutions or governments that may have ulterior political motives and could eventually discredit or undermine worthwhile programs.

d. Through interfaith dialogue, peacemaking with Muslim and Jewish institutions and leaderships, the Christians in the Middle East can bear witness to Jesus' call to be peacemakers and to build new societies of justice.

7. Dialogue with the Middle East Council of Churches, Mainline Protestant and Catholic Churches, and Evangelicals:

a. For many decades the mainline Protestant and Orthodox churches have developed significant ecumenical partnerships and a variety of structures for doing so. These partnerships must be strengthened, expanded, respected, and studied by others. At the same time, new forms of ecumenical cooperation may now be available as old barriers fall and new forms emerge. The next families of churches likely to become involved in ecumenical partnerships are the Roman Catholics and Western evangelicals.

b. The MECC and a network of Western evangelical agencies called Evangelicals for Middle East Understanding (EMEU) have been involved in dialogue since 1987, as well as theological discussions, and some forms of partnership. The annual MECC-EMEU conferences may be useful models for other churches and agencies to follow or adapt. These events should be continued and made available to other churches, mission and Western evangelical organizations, and the broader church.

c. Middle Eastern Christians will have as their mandate the need to become a force of love and reconciliation during the next decade of inevitable alienation, bloodshed, and war. As they stand on the front lines of conflict, war, and service to the poor, they will need considerable spiritual and economic support in this vital witness to the gospel of love. Western churches and other Christians must become involved in significant ways to strengthen this mission.

*   *   *

Gabriel Habib of the MECC wrote to Western evangelicals in 1987. He gave the following appeal at the close of his letter.

> The historical moment is crucial, not only for the volatile politics of our troubled region, but for the future of Christian witness here. May the Holy Spirit help us discern the signs of the times, understand our call, and define our common responsibility in response to the gospel of Jesus Christ in the Middle East today. In solidarity I am appealing for us first and foremost to be a bond of love which should destroy all racial, cultural, or confessional barriers between us, thus transforming mistrust or indifference into a common com-

mitment in the search for our unity in witness to truth, love, and hope in the resurrected Lord, Jesus Christ.

Perhaps Christians in the West will be judged, according to Matthew 25, on the basis of their response to their sisters and brothers in the Middle East who need their support today to remain in these lands with justice, peace, and dignity. How will we respond? Let us ponder the wisdom of the proverb, "Rescue those being led away to death; hold back those staggering toward slaughter. If you say, 'But we knew nothing about this,' does not he who weighs the heart perceive it? Does not he who guards your life know it? Will he not repay each person according to what he has done?" (Prov. 24:11-12).

May God grant us wisdom as we consider the case of the Palestinians and all the Christians of the Middle East. May our Lord grant us his compassion and model as we respond to those in his own land. And may the power of the Holy Spirit infuse us with truth and strength in our journey of faithfulness. AMEN.

Appendix A

Second Note from Sir Henry McMahon to Sharif Hussein of the Hejaz, 24 October 1915 (Cmd. 5957, 1939)

It is with great pleasure that I communicate to you on . . . behalf [of the goverment of Great Britain] the following statement, which I am confident you will receive with satisfaction—

The two districts of Mersina and Alexandretta and portions of Syria lying to the west of the districts of Damascus, Homs, Hama and Aleppo cannot be said to be purely Arab, and should be excluded from the limits demanded.

With the above modification, and without prejudice of our existing treaties with Arab chiefs, we accept those limits.

As for those regions lying within those frontiers wherein Great Britain is free to act without detriment to the interests of her ally France, I am empowered in the name of the Government of Great Britain to give the following assurances and make the following reply to your letter—

1. Subject to the above modifications, Great Britain is prepared to recognize and support the independence of the Arabs in all the regions within the limits demanded by the Sharif of Mecca.

2. Great Britain will guarantee the Holy Places against all external aggression and will recognize their inviolability.

3. When the situation admits, Great Britain will give to the Arabs her advice and will assist them to establish what may appear to be the most suitable forms of government in those various territories.

4. On the other hand, it is understood that the Arabs have decided to seek the advice and guidance of Great Britain only, and that such Europe-

an advisers and officials as may be required for the formation of a sound form of administration will be British.

I am convinced that this declaration will assure you beyond all possible doubt of the sympathy of Great Britain towards the aspirations of her friends the Arabs and will result in a firm and lasting alliance, the immediate results of which will be the expulsion of the Turks from the Arab countries and the freeing of the Arab peoples from the Turkish yoke, which for so many years has pressed heavily upon them. . . .

Appendix B

United Nations Security Council Resolution 242 22 November 1967

*T*he Security Council,

Expressing its continuing concern with the grave situation in the Middle East,

Emphasizing the inadmissibility of the acquisition of territory by war and the need to work for a just and lasting peace in which every State in the area can live in security,

Emphasizing further that all Member States in their acceptance of the Charter of the United Nations have undertaken a commitment to act in accordance with Article 2 of the Charter,

1. *Affirms* that the fulfilment of Charter principles requires the establishment of a just and lasting peace in the Middle East which should include the application of both the following principles:

(i) Withdrawal of Israel armed forces from territories occupied in the recent conflict;

(ii) Termination of all claims or states of belligerency and respect for and acknowledgment of the sovereignty, territorial integrity, and political independence of every State in the area and their right to live in peace within secure and recognized boundaries free from threats or acts of force;

2. *Affirms further* the necessity

(a) For guaranteeing freedom of navigation through international waterways in the area;

(b) For achieving a just settlement of the refugee problem;

(c) For guaranteeing the territorial inviolability and political independence of every State in the area, through measures including the establishment of demilitarized zones;

3. *Requests* the Secretary-General to designate a Special Representative to proceed to the Middle East to establish and maintain contacts with the States concerned in order to promote agreement and assist efforts to achieve a peaceful and accepted settlement in accordance with the provisions and principles in this resolution;

4. *Requests* the Secretary-General to report to the Security Council on the progress of the efforts of the Special Representative as soon as possible.

Appendix C
United Nations Security Council Resolution 338
15 October 1973

*T*he Security Council

1. *Calls upon* all parties to the present fighting to cease all firing and terminate all military activity immediately, no later than 12 hours after the moment of the adoption of this decision, in the positions they now occupy;

2. *Calls upon* the parties concerned to start immediately after the cease-fire the implementation of Security Council resolution 242 (1967) in all of its parts;

3. *Decides* that, immediately and concurrently with the cease-fire, negotiations shall start between the parties concerned under appropriate auspices aimed at establishing a just and durable peace in the Middle East.

Appendix D
Message of the Vth General Assembly of the Middle East Council of Churches

By the grace and mercy of Christ, the Vth General Assembly of the Middle East Council of Churches gathered in Nicosia, Cyprus, January 22-28, 1990. Two hundred people participated—delegates, guests, observers, and staff. The majority of the delegations were led by the heads of churches, this being an expression of the importance of this historic meeting, the first of its kind for centuries.

The General Assembly was inspired through its prayers, reflections, and discussions by the apostle Paul's directive: *"Keep the unity of the Spirit in the bond of peace"* (Ephesians 4:3). It renewed its commitments to continue the march towards unity in the one Spirit and one mind.

The proceedings of the General Assembly were accompanied by representatives of different churches and ecumenical organizations, who offered words of greeting, love, and solidarity. Particularly important were those coming from the General Secretary of the WCC, and a delegation representing the Pontifical Council for the Promotion of Christian Unity, who brought a letter from H. H. Pope John Paul II.

The Fifth General Assembly of the MECC was characterized by the Catholic Churches joining as a "fourth family" of churches.

It is our duty, at the end as well as the beginning, to thank God for His

Grace and express the great joy, not only in our hearts, but in the hearts of all the faithful in our region and throughout the world.

This church gathering is an affirmation of Christian presence in the region and is a sign of our authenticity, which is the authenticity of Christianity itself, in this part of the world, where Christ was born, where he died and resurrected, and from which Christianity spread throughout the world. We shall not abandon this region nor long for a substitute irrespective of historical changes and turmoil. We shall stay in these lands according to the will of God—this is where we belong and where we are rooted.

As we gather ecumenically in this Council, we do not question the distinct identity of churches nor depreciate their uniqueness. Unity is enriched by the particular identities as well as enriching them. Unity brings our specificities together. However, our distinctive character should not be a cause of division. We have to consider that our renewed authenticity invites us to bear hope in the midst of the suffering of our people, and to be instruments in the service of our people. Our meeting together is not directed against any community in this region enjoying a similar authenticity, and aspiring, with us and like us, to live in concord and friendship. Our renewed dynamism is an additional motivation for our solidarity with our people, and an invitation to enhance our efforts in their service.

People in our region face, in many instances, different forms of political humiliation, social divisions, economic needs, religious ignorance, and moral decadence. Our ecumenical march will not fulfil its spiritual aim unless it participates, sincerely, in liberating our people from poverty, ignorance, racial discrimination, and religious fanaticism. The implementation of human rights is a commitment to which we are called by our Christian faithfulness. Human beings are created in the image of God, and in His likeness. The church of Christ cannot achieve its goal outside the dignity of those who were made brothers and sisters in the incarnation of God. He also chose among them the poor and the oppressed.

The General Assembly reviewed the various situations where our people suffer, and where peace and justice in the region is threatened, and adopted the following five resolutions:

Resolution on Palestine

The Vth General Assembly turns its thoughts and prayers toward the Palestinian people expressing its solidarity with the people in the midst of their suffering and their Intifada for freedom, justice, and dignity.

It affirms that the Christian calling to unity can not be dissociated from the Christian responsibility in making peace based on justice and leading to reconciliation.

It renews its support of the right of the Palestinian people to self-determination and the establishment of an independent state in its homeland, in the framework of a comprehensive settlement that guarantees peace and security for all states, nations, and peoples in the region. The Assembly urges governments and peoples in the region and throughout the world to contribute effectively toward the implementation of those rights. It looks to Jerusalem, as the focus of our common spiritual pilgrimage and as a symbol of encounter and harmony between all religions. It also emphasizes that the destiny of Jerusalem lies at the heart of the message and witness of the Christians of the Holy Land.

As it hopes that justice and peace prevail in the land which was sanctified by the life and ministry of Jesus Christ, the Assembly calls for the promotion of dialogue between the people of the three great monotheistic faiths. It salutes all Jews who work for peace and support the human and national rights of the Palestinians.

The Assembly calls upon churches in the world to join efforts in working toward a durable and firm solution of the conflict and refers more particularly to the recent initiative supported by the MECC calling for Christian solidarity in prayer and action for peace in the Holy Land.

Resolution on Lebanon

The Vth General Assembly reaffirms its solidarity with the people of Lebanon, who have been suffering now for fifteen years as a result of the violence imposed upon them. The Assembly supports the following demands of the Lebanese people:

1. The rejection of violence as a means to solve the Lebanese problems, and the promotion of dialogue between all Lebanese, leading to a comprehensive national reconciliation.

2. The affirmation of Lebanon's unity within internationally recognized borders, and the rejection of partition, or of the annexation of any part of Lebanese territory.

3. The recovery of total national sovereignty, through the exercise of Lebanese state authority on all Lebanese territory.

4. The return of all displaced persons to their homes, and the restoration of historical bonds between different Lebanese communities.

5. The preservation of the mode of Christian-Muslim coexistence, which has made Lebanon's uniqueness and determined its role in the Arab world, as well as its cultural contribution and significance for the world.

In order to fulfil these aims the General Assembly calls on all member churches to organize a week of prayer for Lebanon, expressing solidarity with its churches, and calls upon the Presidents of Arab states and members of the international community to spare no effort to help Lebanon recover its peace and vitality.

Appendix E
La Grange Declaration I

In May 1979, a significant conference on the Middle East was held in La Grange, Illinois; "Human Rights and the Palestine-Israeli Conflict: Responsibilities for the Christian Church." Among other actions, this conference prepared a statement, now called the La Grange Declaration, which is printed below. The initial signers, including conference participants and others who have since added their names, represent an ecumenical group of Christians—evangelical, mainline Protestant, Catholic, and Orthodox.

As believers committed to Christ and his kingdom, we challenge the popular assumptions about biblical interpretation and the presuppositions of political loyalty held so widely by fellow Christians in their attitudes toward the conflict in the Middle East.

We address this urgent call to the church of Jesus Christ to hear and heed those voices crying out as bruised reeds for justice in the land where our Lord walked, taught, was crucified, and rose from the dead. We have closed our hearts to those voices and isolated ourselves even from the pleading of fellow Christians who continue to live in that land.

We are anguished by the fact that countless Christians believe that the Bible gives to the modern state of Israel a divine right to the lands inhabited by Palestinian people and divine sanction to the state of Israel's policy of territorial acquisition. We believe such an understanding must be judged in light of the whole of biblical revelation affirming that in the revelation of Jesus Christ God's covenants find their completion. Therefore, we plead for all Christians to construct a vision of peace in the holy land which rests on the biblical injunctions to correct oppression and seek justice for all peoples.

Forthrightly, we declare our conviction that in the process of establishing the state of Israel, a deep injustice was done to the Palestinian people, confiscating their land and driving many into exile and even death. We are further grieved by the ongoing deprivation of basic civil rights to those Arabs who live today in the state of Israel.

Moreover, for 13 years large portions of the holy land and its people, including the West Bank of the Jordan River, Gaza, and East Jerusalem, have suffered under foreign military occupation, even as in our Lord's time. Land is seized from its inhabitants. Water for farming is rationed and restricted. Schools and universities are closed by the Israeli military authorities. And 100,000 people have been arrested, in large part for speaking their convictions. Of these, some have been subjected to brutal torture, described by the U.S. Consulate in Jerusalem as "systematic" and documented beyond any question.

We confess our silence, our indifference, our hardheartedness, and our cowardice, all too often, in the face of these dehumanizing realities.

Earnestly, we pray for a new anointing of the Spirit in our hearts, creating us into a more faithful people used to break every yoke of oppression and let the broken victims go free.

We extend our hearts to our Jewish brothers and sisters, common sons and daughters of Abraham. Like us in the United States, their corporate national spirit is being corroded by the weight of their government's reliance on rampant militaristic policies and actions. We would pray for them, and with them, for a vision of security rooted in expanding channels of trust rather than escalating arsenals of armed might.

Historically and today, the state of Israel's territorial ambitions have been justified as security needs. Through the decades, this has instigated a cycle of violence and counterviolence that still continues, engulfing all sides, and leaving none unblemished from the spilling of innocent blood. We pray with the Psalmist for every bow to be broken and every spear to be snapped.

Too many of us have been lulled into the shallow hope that peace can be built in the Middle East through the U.S. supply of more weapons, with the continued military occupation of the West Bank, Gaza, and East Jerusalem, and while basic human and political rights of the Palestinian people are denied. We call on Christ's followers to repent from their complicity—through either their indifference or their uncritical embrace of U.S. policies—in the continuing cycle of Middle Eastern violence, accelerated by our tax dollars and our government's political decisions.

The Arab people and their land have been plundered for centuries by Western Christendom. We acknowledge and confess a continuing legacy of prejudice evidenced today toward Arab people, both Christian and Moslem.

We repudiate with equal and uncompromising fervor the enduring prejudice toward the Jewish people still present this day in our society and in our churches (those churches include, ironically, many of those churches with staunchly pro-Israeli biases, drawn from their versions of biblical interpretation).

Overcoming these divisions and hatreds, we affirm, as God's revelation declares, our common humanity with all.

We believe that any biblical hope for peace and security for all peoples in the Middle East must encompass some form of restitution for past wrongs. Life, peoplehood, and land are all God's gifts. These gifts enjoyed by the Jewish people of Israel have been denied to the Palestinian people. Therefore, we yearn and we call for the building of a peace that includes the clear expression of political self-determination and justice for the Palestinian people. This includes leadership of their own choosing and a sovereign state. Our firm conviction is that through asserting these rights the way can be opened for Israeli people and Palestinian people to find peace and true security in that land.

We pledge ourselves, and we invite others, to an urgent devotion to see God's purpose of peace, justice, and reconciliation realized in this land. In that spirit, we call upon all Christians to join with us in reexamining assumptions regarding biblical revelation and views of the conflict in the Middle East; we commit ourselves and our resources to active and ongoing dialogue with other Christians on these questions; and, we pray that the body of Christ will extend its life as a humble, sacrificial, and unswerving servant of peace/salaam/shalom in the land where God sent his son to live among us.

LaGrange, Illinois; May 1979

Appendix F

Open Letter to Middle East Council of Churches General Secretariat, Limassol, Cyprus

July 3, 1987

Greetings in the name of our risen Lord, Jesus Christ.

It has long been my desire to write you this letter to initiate an exchange about Christian presence and witness in the Middle East. Today, the urgency of our current situation and the imperative requirements of Christian witness have compelled me to do so. After all, we have much in common through our faith in Jesus Christ. Christ is the center of our lives, and irrespective of our different theological perceptions, we are called, through the Scriptures which we all follow, to be members of his Body, the Church. The commonality of our faith is, therefore, a bond which should transcend any geographical, cultural, or historical differences. My fervent prayer is that the Holy Spirit will inspire your steps in response to my appeal.

Allow me first to share something of my own Christian journey. I was born and baptized in the Orthodox Church of Antioch, the church where Christians were first called Christians (Acts 11), the church in which I continue to be an active member. Since my youth, I have been a member, and then a leader, of a renewal movement in my church aimed at deepening the spiritual quality of the Christian community in view of a more authentic witness to Jesus Christ in our society. It is through this experience that I discovered to what extent the historic divisions among Christians have been detrimental to our witness in the religiously pluralistic society of the Middle East.

The dilemma that many of have faced has been how we could claim to bring the message of love and peace to people of other beliefs while we believers in Jesus Christ, who is the incarnation of God's love and peace to all creation, continue to accuse each other of betrayal of the biblical faith or of cultural or political bias. I cannot but be reminded of Jesus' words in John 13:35: "By this will all men know that you are my disciples, that you have love one for another."

It is important to recall in this respect that in Christian history the intervention of human political power and philosophy in the life of the church has led Christians in the East and in the West into the temptation of adopting the logic of worldly power and reason instead of love and sacrifice. This has caused many Christians to hate and make war even against each other instead of living God's love and peace between themselves, and among all peoples and nations. The Crusaders, for example, who supposedly came to save the Holy Sepulchre from the Muslim conquerors massacred some Eastern Christians whom they considered heretics, and therefore non-persons. It is significant that some Christians were saved from the Crusaders by Muslims; also, Muslim conquerors were received by Christian communities in the coastal Mediterranean area as liberators from the Byzantine Empire.

My personal experience and this history [just mentioned] have convinced me that the unity of believers in Jesus Christ celebrated in the Holy Communion and expressed through love and sharing is absolutely fundamental to our mission. Jesus clearly stated: "A new commandment I give to you, that you love one another, even as I have loved you, that you also love one another." (John 13:34)

This conviction has been strengthened through my experience with the Middle East Council of Churches (MECC). The Council is the place where the majority of the churches of the region meet to rediscover each other through prayer, spiritual sharing and common witness. In obedience to the Gospel's message, and in all humility, we try to discern ways of cooperation in mission and service (diakonia). Approximately 12 million Christians from the Oriental Orthodox, Eastern Orthodox, and Episcopal and National Evangelical churches are represented in the MECC. A deepening relationship and growing cooperation with the Catholic churches promises an even greater expression of the unity needed for Christian witness in the Middle East today.

Today, due to the ongoing politico-religious developments in the region, we are facing critical challenges to the present basis of our society and to our national identity. Resurgent fundamentalist movements are rejecting the secular, legal, and social developments of the last few decades. This rejection is founded on the conviction that these developments are based on criteria borrowed from European nationalism and Western Christian cultural experience. Such trends are exacerbated by regional wars as well as by the conflicting interests and strategies of the international powers. These challenges and confrontations are causing violence, economic hardship, the displacement of people and the relocation of some in inhuman refugee camps, political and religious factionalism, and fanaticism.

All this affects the people of the region without distinction as to race or religion, causing suffering, fear, and despair. Christians are sharing these tribulations, and as a religious minority, are becoming increasingly vulnerable and are exposed to marginalization and emigration. These critical challenges to the continued Christian presence in the region where God was revealed and [the] Scriptures were born must elicit from us a common concern about the future of Christian ministry here. The churches of the Middle East are called, through these trials, to witness to Christ, the giver of hope and peace to all peoples and nations. They are looking for ways to participate with other communities and groups in establishing a society that respects religion and religious differences and guarantees human rights, justice and peace. Our aspiration is that, through a living faith, we can transform the power of hatred and destruction in our region into the potential for love and creativity and thus become living signs of hope in Christ's love and peace to all the people of the region.

Toward this end, the churches of the Middle East are seeking the understanding and cooperation of Christians all over the world. Unfortunately, some evangelical Christians hinder rather than help this process. The result is to make the local church's presence and witness even more difficult. We realize that certain Western evangelical Christians remain unaware of the local church and its witness in the region. However, at times we are convinced that others deliberately ignore the fact that Christianity began in the Middle East and formed the local church, which continues to exist here. As a result, the particular ministry and vocation of the churches here are often overlooked when Western evangelical Christians plan their involvement in the region. Moreover, some Western evangelical Christians come here and attempt to carry out forms of witness and evangelism considered inappropriate by local or national churches. All this tends to create further division among Christians and also provokes strong reactions from other [non-Christian] religious communities.

What is disturbing is the realization that such behavior towards Middle Eastern churches and people is doing a disservice to Christ and Christian ministry. This presents a face of disunity and confusion that distorts the very meaning of Christ's message of love, compassion, understanding, and unity. This diminishes rather than glorifies Christ's name.

I therefore appeal to you to make evangelical Christians in your country aware of the necessity of reviewing some of their basic assumptions and attitudes with regard to the people and the churches of the

Middle East. Many Christians here are perplexed by the influx of Western evangelical mission groups operating in the region. Most of them, if they do not ignore our very existence, tend to consider us "not Christian enough" or "insufficiently biblical" or not "Christ-centered" and therefore unable to evangelize. In reality, since Pentecost, and despite suffering and martyrdom resulting from both outside challenges and internal divisions, Middle Eastern churches survive. Our faith in the resurrection remains alive and active through the power of the Holy Spirit. Moreover, we hope that under your guidance, evangelicals in your country will be able not only to overcome their ignorance of the Middle Eastern Christian reality but transcend prejudices and stereotypes with regard to Middle Eastern people in general [which were] created by particular historic circumstances or modern sensationalist media. For us, this is an essential Christian requirement when dealing with people of other cultures, religions, or even churches, as all are members of God's creation.

It is hoped that through these efforts your people will discover that we indeed share with you a strong Christ-centered belief and a deep faith in the Lordship of Jesus Christ who is the Alpha and the Omega of our life and witness. The importance we sometimes give to tradition, which we understand as the accumulated spiritual heritage of the church and community, does not make us sacralize cultural or ethnic identity at the expense of our identity in Jesus Christ. For us, the Bible is not only the Word of God in a printed book, but the way in which this is lived through the people of God. These are two aspects of a single reality that must always be held in tension in order not to deny the ongoing work of the Holy Spirit.

I hope that we can begin new relations and a search for joint ministries based on a greater understanding of the life and vocation of local churches in the religiously pluralistic society of the Middle East.

The first requirement in this respect is to *realize the spiritual renewal* that is developing within our churches and is being enhanced by the MECC. This renewal is aimed at deepening the spiritual life of the individual and the community in order to respond to the present challenges using the mind and spirit of Jesus Christ rather than any religious or political ideologies or the power of the sword. This renewal is also aimed at enabling Christians here to continue to be a faithful witnessing community within their own society. I pray you will agree that the priority is to nurture those seeds of renewal and creativity in our churches.

The second requirement is to *appreciate the search for unity* undertaken by the majority of the churches in the region. The movement of Christian unity in the Middle East must be understood as the way of proclaiming the Gospel message of love and unity in a polarized and divided region. It is a fellowship of love in search of full communion in Jesus Christ through prayers, repentance, and common witness. This unity should not be confused with ideas of institutional uniformity or uniformity of theological expression. Nor is it a political coalition or a front against any person, group, or community. I hope that you can pray for these efforts and help evangelical missionaries coming to the Middle East contribute to these endeavors and not to discredit them.

The third requirement is to *understand and respect the witness of the local churches.* For us, this involves communicating the Gospel of Jesus Christ through our life and through ways appropriate to the churches here. These churches are sharing the same lands and the same culture with the people of the region who also confess relations with the same God of revelation. This characterizes our witness and determines its emphasis on the uniqueness of Christ within the monotheistic religions. I hope therefore that you will recognize that Christian mission is fulfilled through the life and witness of the local churches and not necessarily through missionary activities originating outside the Middle East which may be more appropriate to the culture in which they were conceived. I do not assume that you will fully agree with me, but I trust at least you would see this is a fundamental issue that needs to be discussed further together. My major concern is to see that what Western evangelicals consider to be their mission in the Middle East does not ultimately become anti-mission. This could happen if it ignores the churches, their renewal movement, their vision of Christian or church unity, and their [own] particular call to witness.

Both of us are rooted in rich spiritual traditions. We need mutually to learn from them. Let us seek ways of sharing each other's gifts through dialogue and prayer. Let us conduct Biblical and theological dialogue which will help contribute to our understanding of the Bible, our witnessing, our evangelizing. Let us seek means of proclaiming the truth of our Lord in the search for peace and justice in the region.

I therefore appeal to you, as you are able, to visit the Middle East and to look not only at the stones and walls, but learn about the "living stones"—God's people here who have kept the light of Christ burning in these lands since Pentecost. Hundreds of thousands of Christians visit here every year, yet most of them remain unaware of our faith, our witness, even our very presence. In doing so, they miss the opportunity to experience the spiritual heritage of Christianity in the lands where it began and continues to witness on behalf of the church worldwide. Similarly, Middle Eastern Christians miss the opportunity for sharing and developing a greater sense of fellowship and unity with Christians of other lands and cultures within the worldwide Church of Christ.

I hope and pray that my words will speak to your heart and that you will respond to this urgent appeal. The historical moment is crucial, not only for the volatile politics of our troubled region, but for the future of Christian witness here. May the Holy Spirit help us mutually discern the signs of the times, understand our call and define our common responsibility in response to the Gospel of Jesus Christ in the Middle East today.

The solidarity I am appealing for is first and foremost a bond of love which should destroy all racial, cultural or confessional barriers between us, thus transforming mistrust or indifference into a common commitment in the search for our unity in witness to truth, love and hope in the resurrected Lord, Jesus Christ.

Yours in Christ,

Gabriel Habib
General Secretary

A Chronology of Middle Eastern Christianity

A.C.E. 34 Peter in Antioch
36 Paul (Paul) of Tarsus' conversion on the road to Damascus
43 Followers of Jesus first called Christians in Antioch
64 Nero's persecution, martyrdom of Peter and Paul
70 Destruction of Jerusalem by the Romans
90s Marcionism and Gnostic heresies challenge the church
135 Jerusalem temple and Holy Sepulchre desecrated, Massada
200 Emperor Septimus Severus issues edict against Christians; systematic persecution begins.
285 St. Antony begins monasticism and cenobitic life in western desert of Egypt.
301 Gregory the Illuminator converts King Tiridate, and Armenia becomes first Christian nation.
312 Emperor Constantine embraces Christianity.
317 Pachomius begins monastic life in Upper Egypt.
324 Constantine selects Constantinople as center of Empire.
325 First Ecumenical Council at Nicea condemns Arianism.
380 Emperor Theodosius declares Christianity religion of Empire.
381 Council of Constantinople
416 Church of Cyprus established.
431 Council of Ephesus condemns Nestorius.
451 Council of Chalcedon and split of Christianity.

486 Council of Seleucia, Church of Persia adheres to Nestorianism.
520 Church of Armenia (Etchmiadzine) excommunicates Constantinople and maintains autonomy.
610 Persians seize Antioch and Damascus
622 Prophet Mohammed leaves Mecca for Medina (Al Hijira)
632 Prophet Mohammed's night flight to Jerusalem, the prophet dies.
637 Muslims conquer Mesopotamia
638 Muslims take Jerusalem
642 Muslim armies seize Persia, Armenia, Alexandria.
681 Council of Constantinople condemns monothelitism.
685 Monks of St. Maron elect John Maron president.
1054 Schism between Rome and Constantinople
1096 Crusaders take Antioch
1099 Crusaders seize Jerusalem
1187 Crusaders defeated by Saladin and abandon Jerusalem.
1215 Maronites recognized by Rome as the Church of Antioch.
1221 Crusaders fail in march on Cairo
1268 Antioch destroyed.
1295 Armenian Catholicosate established in Cilicia.
1366 Damascus becomes seat of Patriarch of Antioch.
1400 Monguls invade Syria and seize Damascus.
1453 Fall of Constantinople; Greek Orthodox Patriarchate of Constantinople recognized by Ottomans as head of Christian churches.
1552 Founding of the Chaldean Catholic church
1724 Greek Catholic Church (Melkites) established.
1740 Armenian Catholic church established.
1820 First Protestant missionaries arrive in Smyrna and Syria.
1847 National Evangelical (Presbyterian) Church established in Syria and Lebanon; Latin Patriarchate begins in Jerusalem.
1851 Lutheran Church established in Jordan.
1863 Coptic Evangelical (Presbyterian) Church in Egypt.
1866 Syrian Protestant College founded in Beirut (later renamed American University of Beirut).
1888 Episcopal (Anglican) Bishopric established in Jerusalem.
1899 Coptic Catholic Church established in Egypt.

(Source: *MECC PERSPECTIVES*, "History of Middle East Christianity," Dr. Tarik Mitri, October 1986).

A MODERN MIDDLE EAST CHRONOLOGY (Emphasis on Lebanon, Israel-Palestine)

1891 William E. Blackstone, a Christian Zionist, organizes the first lobby effort in the United States calling for a Jewish state in Palestine.

1896   Theodor Herzl publishes *Der Judenstaat* calling for a Jewish state, Palestine one of many options.

1897   (August) Herzl convenes the First Zionist Congress (Basle)

1901   World Zionist Organization establishes the Jewish National Fund to finance and purchase land in Palestine for exclusively Jewish colonization. Population of Palestine approximately 500,000 with 94% Palestinian Arab (Christian and Muslim), Jews 5%.

1914   Arabs in Greater Syria (Syria, Lebanon, Palestine) protest Ottoman rule and demand independence. Outbreak of World War I.

1915   Sir Henry McMahon, British high commissioner in Egypt, writes six letters to the Sharif of Mecca, promising independent Arab states.

1916   Britain and France secretly sign the Sykes-Picot agreement providing for division of the Middle East between the two powers.

1917   Arab Legion and British Army enter Palestine; Palestinians request independence promised in MacMahon correspondence.

1917   (November) British foreign secretary Lord Arthur Balfour declares in letter to Lord Rothschild that Britain will use its influence to establish in Palestine "national home to the Jewish people." The population of Palestine is 700,000 of whom 574,000 are Muslims, 70,000 Christians, and 56,000 Jews.

1919   Palestinians convene their first National Conference with the goal of opposing the Balfour Declaration and establishing a Palestinian state.

1920   San Remo Conference grants Britain the mandate over Palestine; France receives the mandate for Syria and Lebanon.

1921   President Wilson of the United States sends the King-Crane Commission to investigate and report on the situation in Palestine; it recommends a secular democracy.

1922   British issue a white paper that rejects Palestinian independence and calls for a partition of the country. British census puts Palestinian Christian population in Jerusalem at 14,699 or 51% of Jerusalem's 28,607 inhabitants.

1926   Lebanon receives a constitution and becomes the Lebanese Republic.

1929   The Jewish National Fund purchases a large section of land from an absentee Lebanese landowner; rioting occurs with 116 Palestinian Arabs and 135 Jews killed.

1931 Britain investigates and publishes a new white paper, curbing land sales to Zionists and limiting immigration.

1936 Pogroms against Jews in Nazi Germany convinces British to raise quotas; full-scale Palestinian strikes lead to the outbreak of a rebellion that continues until 1939.

1937 British Royal (Peel) Commission concludes "the situation in Palestine has reached a deadlock" and calls for a partition of the country. Both sides reject the proposal.

1939 Britain again investigates and issues a white paper that calls for curbing Zionist immigration and establishing a single, bi-national democracy in Palestine with Jews and Arabs sharing an independent state. Zionists reject proposal.

1939-45 World War II and Nazi genocide against Jews. Massive Jewish immigration begins; many Western nations refuse to allow Jews to enter their countries.

1942 Zionist Biltmore Declaration calls for unlimited Jewish settlement; rejects Palestinian self-determination.

1943 Lebanon declares independence; National Pact confirmed.

1945-47 Zionist paramilitary groups (the Haganah, Irgun, and Stern Gang) launch bloody campaign against British and Palestinians.

1947 (November 29) The UN approves the Partition Plan. Palestinian Arabs own 92% of the land and represent 67% of population, but UN Partition Plan proposes 55% of state to Jews.

1948 British announce intent to leave Palestine on May 15. On April 8, an Irgun terror unit attacks the village of Deir Yassin near Jerusalem, where 254 Palestinians are killed. Red Cross investigator condemns the massacre. Eventually there are 750,000-770,000 Palestinian refugees.

1949 (December), UN Resolution 194 calls for the return of Palestinian refugees to their homes.

1951 Jordan's King Abdullah killed after leaving Jerusalem's Mosque of Omar. On December 25 (Christmas Day), Palestinian Christian villages Ikrit and Biram destroyed

1956 Israel, France, and Britain invade Egypt over Suez Crisis. U.S. President Eisenhower opposes invasion and war is averted.

1957 Arab League announces boycott of companies dealing with Israel until Palestinian rights are adopted.

1958 U.S. Marines land in Beirut to shore up presidency of Camille Chamoun as civil war breaks out in Lebanon.

1958 Gamel Abdel Nasser becomes president of United Arab Republic (Egypt, Syria, Yemen).

1964 (May 28) Palestine Liberation Organization, established in Jerusalem, joins Arab League. Charles Helou replaces Chamoun as president of Lebanon.

1967 (June) Israel defeats Egypt, Syria, and Jordan and occupies the Golan Heights, East Jerusalem, West Bank, Gaza Strip, and Sinai Peninsula. UN Resolution 242 adopted in November.

1969 From February 1 to 4, Palestine National Council (PNC) elects Yasir Arafat Chairman, reiterates call for secular, democratic state and equality for all citizens. Nineteen Palestinian forces withdraw from Jordan to establish bases in Lebanon.

1973 On January 12, the eleventh PNC calls for independent Palestinian state on any portion of historic Palestine. United Nations Resolution 338 adopted in October.

1974 PLO accepted as sole representative of Palestinians. Middle East Council of Churches (MECC) established in Beirut.

1975 On April 13, clash between Palestinians and Lebanese Phalangists at Ain al-Rummaneh marks beginning of Lebanese Civil War, convulsing the country for over 15 years. In November, UN passes Resolution 3379, equating Zionism with racism. Fighting breaks out in central Beirut in September and continues through the rest of the year.

1976 Lebanese Phalangist forces blockade Palestinian refugee camps; Palestinians retaliate in siege at Damour. In Israel on March 30, major demonstrations in the Galilee mark first Land Day protest of Israeli confiscation of Palestinian land. On April 12, first (and only) free municipal elections in occupied territories bring 25 nationalist candidates into office. Phalangists and Syrians shell Palestinian camp Tel al-Zataar for 53 days; Phalangists massacre inhabitants.

1977 Likud Party comes to power under Menachem Begin. On November 9, Egyptian president Sadat visits Israel. On December 25, Israel's Knesset declares it illegal to proselytize Jews.

1978 Israel invades South Lebanon on March 14 and occupies Lebanon to the Litani River, eventually withdrawing under significant international pressure. Israel turns remainder of South Lebanon to Major Saad Haddad who proclaims it "Free Lebanon."

1978 Soviet-U.S. peace talks, based on UN Resolutions 242 and 338 (land exchanged for peace) fail in Geneva.

1979 Camp David Peace Accords signed in Washington, D.C., between the United States, Israel, and Egypt.

1980 European Economic Community issues Venice Declaration calling for end to Israeli settlements and accepting Israel and Palestinian right to self-determination. International Christian Embassy-Jerusalem opens in September.

1981 On June 7, Israel bombs Iraq's nuclear reactor; Jerry Falwell defends the action.

1982 (June) Israel invades Lebanon in its "Peace for Galilee" campaign and attacks Palestinian institutions and population centers in Beirut and South Lebanon, leaving over 20,000 Lebanese and Palestinians dead. PLO withdraws on August 30th; Bashir Gemayal elected president of Lebanon and assassinated on September 14. Sabra-Shatila massacre, September 16-18. Approximately 400,000 Israelis protest in Tel Aviv. Amin Gemayel replaces brother as president of Lebanon.

1983 UN General Assembly adopts Resolution 38/58c, calling for international peace conference with Israel and PLO to negotiate self-determination and independent states for both, with Israeli withdrawal to pre-1967 borders in exchange for security guarantees.

1985 (February) The historic fourth General Assembly of the Middle East Council of Churches unites heads of churches in the Middle East who had not met since the Council of Nicea in A.C.E. 325.

1987 (December) Palestinian Intifada begins and spreads throughout occupied West Bank and Gaza Strip.

1988 Over 225 Palestinians killed in first five months of Intifada. On June 13, Palestinian pacifist Dr. Mubarak Awad expelled to the United States. On November 15, PNC declares independence and calls for Palestinian State beside Israel based on UN resolutions. On December 7 in Stockholm, Arafat meets delegation of five U.S. Jewish leaders and recognizes Israel.

1989 Palestinian Christian village Beit Sahur, after prolonged tax revolt, is sealed off by Israeli military. Official Israeli census notes Palestinian Christian population declines to 2.3% (35,000) of total in occupied territories. Jerusalem Christians at 15,000. In December, South African Bishop Tutu visits Jerusalem and calls for Palestinian state and compares their situation to apartheid.

1990 (February) The Middle East Council of Churches holds its fifth General Assembly in Cyprus, with Catholic churches of Rome and the Middle East becoming full members. In August, Iraq invades Kuwait.

1991 (January) Coalition of UN armies attack Iraq, forcing its defeat and withdrawal from Kuwait.

1992 Madrid peace talks begin. Israel receives $10 billion in loan guarantees from the U.S.

1993 U.S.-sponsored peace talks stall in Washington after ninth and tenth round. On September 13, Israel and PLO recognize each other and begin transitional Palestinian government in Jerico and Gaza.

1994   After repeated delays, an Israeli settler (Dr. Baruch Goldstein) massacres 29 Palestinians at prayer in Hebron's Ibrahimi Mosque. Hamas follows with a series of terrorist bombings. On May 4, 1994, the PLO and Israel sign an economic agreement for Gaza and Jericho. In November the Middle East Council of Churches holds its Sixth General Assembly.

Notes

Chapter 1

1. For those who might be wondering, I never did figure out what happened to the canary. I waited until Grandma brought the cage into the house and tried to come up with an explanation. Grandma never said a word about the subject because, lo and behold, to my utter delight, the canary reappeared safe and sound inside the cage.

Chapter 2

1. The adjective "holy" is often placed in lower case and in quotes because theologically, land is not holy in Scripture. Rather, God and God's people are holy.

2. Futurist premillenialism is a form of Western Protestant evangelical theology that developed in the nineteenth century, emphasized the future fulfillment of certain biblical prophecies, and divided history into dispensations (eras) according to God's dealings with the human race.

Chapter 3

1. For a brief description of each Eastern church, see Charles A. Kimball, *Angle of Vision* (New York: Friendship Press, 1992).

2. Fred J. Khouri, *The Arab-Israeli Dilemma* (Syracuse: Syracuse University Press, 1985), pp. 8-9.

3. For additional historical information on Lebanon, see David Gilmour, *Lebanon: The Fractured Country* (London: Martin Robertson & Co., Ltd., 1983), pp. 3-20, 34-51.

4. *Ibid.*, pp. 21-33; and Robert Fisk, *Pity the Nation* (New York: Simon and Schuster, 1990), pp. 55-91.

5. Gilmour, *Ibid.,* p. 9.

6. Fisk, *Ibid.*, pp. 74-99.

Chapter 4

1. Thomas Merton, *The New Man* (New York: Bantam Books, 1962), p. 2.

Chapter 5

1. The term *evangelical* is understood in the Middle East as applicable only to the churches of the Reformation, whose missionaries established sizable churches throughout the region during the previous 150 years. Today most of these churches are totally Arab in leadership and decision making. When discussing the evangelicals, products of the

eighteenth-century North American evangelical movements, it is more accurate to include the adjective "Western," which differentiates them from the indigenous Arab evangelicals in the Middle East.

2. *London Sunday Times*, October 5, 1986, p. 1ff.

3. See Seymour Hirsch, *The Samson Option* (New York: Random House, 1991), pp. 290, 307-315.

Chapter 6

1. The official United Nations position, as well as that of the United States and most U.S. churches since the mid-1970s, is that the West Bank, East Jerusalem, and the Gaza Strip are lands occupied by Israel in June 1967. According to UN Resolutions 242 and 338, a just and peaceful solution to the conflict must be based on Israel's withdrawal from these territories in exchange for a United Nations mediated peace, with security guarantees for both parties.

2. See W. F. Albright, *From Stone Age to Christianity*, (Baltimore: John Hopkins Press, 1967).

3. Ian Lustick, *For the Land and the Lord* (New York: Council on Foreign Relations, 1988), p. 142.

Chapter 7

1. Jan Willem van der Hoeven, in a lecture at the International Christian Embassy-Jerusalem, October 7, 1991 (taped by the author).

2. The term *Israelite* is used here and throughout the book to describe the tribe of Hebrew-speaking Jews who fled in the exodus, experienced the covenant at Sinai, and eventually settled as a loose tribe in part of ancient Canaan. They did not become a nation until Saul was king (approximately 920 B.C.E).

3. Malcolm Hedding, *Christian Zionism and Its Biblical Basis* (Jerusalem: International Christian Embassy, 1988), p. 8.

4. Michael Harper, "Israel—The Good, the Bad and the Ugly" (Renewal Magazine, April, 1988), pp. 6-7.

5. Several contemporary Jewish thinkers have advocated the justice position, but see especially Yehosophat Harkabi, *Israel's Fateful Hour* (New York: MacMillan, 1989); and the theological argument in *Marc Ellis, Toward a Jewish Theology of Liberation* (Maryknoll, N.Y.: Orbis Press), 1989.

6. Hendricus Berkhof, *Christian Zionism and Its Biblical Basis* (Jerusalem International Christian Embassy-Jerusalem, 1988); p. 7. The basis of the article was Berkhof's speech at the First International Christian Zionist Congress, Basle, Switzerland, 1985. ICEJ edited the speech and published its own edited version without authorization.

7. *Ibid.*.

8. Hedding, pp. 8-9.

9. John R. W. Stott, "The Place of Israel," unpublished sermon delivered at All Soul's Church, London.

10. Raymond Brown, *Birth of the Messiah* (Garden City, N.J.: Doubleday and Company, Inc., 1979), p. 74.

11. Stott.

12. John Nelson Darby, "The Hope of the Church of God," *The Works of John Nelson Darby*, vol. I, no. 1, William Kelly, ed. (Kingston on Thames: Stow Hill Bible and Trust Depot, 1962), p. 363.

13. Hedding, p. 8.

Chapter 8

1. For a brief overview of the history of millennial thought, see John H. Gerstner, *Wrongly Dividing the Word of Truth* (Brentwood, Tenn.: Wolgemuth & Hyatt, Inc., 1991). The best analysis of the biblical roots is D. S. Russell, *The Message and Meaning of Jewish Apocalyptic* (London: S.C.M. Press, 1964).

2. Barbara Tuchman, *Bible and Sword* (New York: New York University Press, 1956), p. 3.

3. Thomas Brightman, "Apocalypsis Apocalypseos," London: 1585.

4. Sir Henry Finch, *The World's Great Restauration or Calling of the Jews* (London: Edward Griffin for William Bladen, 1621), p. 6.

5. *Ibid.*, p. 3.

6. Gerstner, pp. 26-27.

7. John Nelson Darby, *The Collected Writings of J. N. Darby*, vol. I, no. 1, William Kelly, ed. (Kingston on Thames: Stow Hill Bible and Trust Depot, 1962), p. 94.

8. Nahum Sokolow, *History of Zionism*, vol. 1 (London: Longman, Green and Co., 1919), p. 127.

9. Albert M. Hyamson, *Palestine Under the Mandate* (London: Muthuen & Co. Ltd., 1950), p. 10, 12.

10. Regina Sharif, *Non-Jewish Zionism,* (London: Zed Press, 1983), p. 68. Sharif's important work is the first critical analysis of Tuchman's thesis on the Britain-Zion connection and offers useful analysis on both the political and religious aspects of Zionism.

11. Kenneth Young, *Arthur James Balfour* (London: G. Bell & Sons, Ltd., 1963), p. 256.

12. *Ibid.*, p. 256.

13. *The Question of Palestine* (New York: United Nations Press, 1979), p. 3.

14. Philip Guedalla, *Napoleon and Palestine* (London: G. Allen and Unwin, Ltd., 1925), pp. 48-49.

15. Christopher Sykes, *Two Studies in Virtue* (New York: Alfred A. Knopf, 1953).

Chapter 9

1. Edward W. Said, "Palestine, Then and Now," *Harper's Magazine*, December, 1992, p. 50.

2. Yitzhak Shamir, "Keynote Address," West Jerusalem: Second Christian Zionist Congress, April 10, 1988.

3. *News From Israel*, Jerusalem: June, 1985, p. 31.

4. *Jerusalem Post*, September 20, 1985, p. 15.

5. *A Christian Response to Israel* (Jerusalem: International Christian Embassy-Jerusalem, 1985). (Pamphlet)

6. *The Second Christian Zionist Congress* (Jerusalem: International Christian Embassy-Jerusalem, 1988).

7. *Ibid.*

8. *Declaration of the First International Christian Zionist Congress* (Jerusalem: International Christian Embassy-Jerusalem, 1985).

9. Jan Willem van der Hoeven in *A Christian Response to Israel.* (Pamphlet)

10. Jan Willem van der Hoeven, *Israel and the Nations* (audiotape) (Jerusalem: International Christian Embassy-Jerusalem, 1988).

11. *A Christian Response to Israel.* (Pamphlet)

12. *Prepare Ye the Way of the Lord* (brochure Jerusalem: International Christian Embassy-Jerusalem, 1991).

13. Pnia Pelli, *Jerusalem Post*, September 20, 1985, p. 15.

14. *Prepare Ye the Way of the Lord.*

15. *Ibid.*

16. *Ibid.*

17. *A Christian Response to Israel.* (Pamphlet)

18. *Newsletter* (Pittsburgh, Pa.: Christian Embassy Consulate, 1987).

19. Middle East Council of Churches, Limassol, Cyprus, "Statement of the Heads of Churches in Jerusalem," April 1988.

20. "Resignations Damage Christian Embassy Credibility," *Al-Fajr*, Jerusalem; March 21, 1885.

21. *Prepare Ye the Way of the Lord.*

22. *Ibid.*

23. *Ibid.*

24. *Jerusalem Post,* October 11, 1991.

25. *Jerusalem Post,* October 3, 1991.

26. "Jerusalem Christian Embassy Aids Contras," *Israeli Foreign Affairs,* (Sacramento: September, 1988).

Chapter 10

1. Joseph L. Ryan, "Refugees Within Israel," *Journal of Palestine Studies*, vol. II, no. 4, 1973, p. 9.

2. *Ibid.*

3. Author's interview with Canon Shehadeh, Chicago, Illinois, May 1992.

Chapter 11

1. Larry Collins and Dominique Lapierre, *O Jerusalem* (New York: Pocket Books, 1973), p. 444.

2. *Ibid.*, pp. 444-445.

3. Naim Ateek, *Justice and Only Justice* (Maryknoll, New York; 1989), p. 7.

4. *Ibid.*, p. 9.

5. *Ibid.*., p. 10,

6. Benny Morris, *The Birth of the Palestinian Refugee Crisis* (Cambridge: Cambridge University Press, 1987), p. 4.

7. Michael Palumbo, "What Happened to Palestine?" *The Link* (Batavia, Ill.: 1990) Americans for Middle East Understanding, p. 20.

8. Simha Flapan, *The Birth of Israel* (New York: Pantheon Books, 1987), p. 81.

9. Colin Chapman, *Whose Promised Land?* (Batavia, Ill.: Lion Publishing, 1983), p. 50.

10. Transcribed from a taped presentation by Audeh Rantisi at the Evangelical Home for Boys, Ramallah, West Bank, October 13, 1991.

11. *Ibid.*

12. Audeh Rantisi, *Blessed Are the Peacemakers* (Grand Rapids: Zondervan Publishing House, 1990), p. 26.

13. Ibrahim Abu-Lughod, *The Transformation of Palestine* (Evanston: Northwestern University Press, 1980), pp. 183-202.

14. David Hirst, *The Gun and the Olive Branch* (London: Futura, MacDonald and Company, 1983), p. 138.

15. Samuel Katz, *Battleground: Fact and Fantasy in Palestine* (New York: Bantam Books, 1977), pp. 23-24. For a contrast see the United Nations document, *The Question of Palestine* (New York: United Nations Division on Palestinian Rights, 1979), and *United Nations Conciliation Commission for Palestine: Report of the UN Economic Survey Mission for the Middle East*, document A/AC.25/6, p. 18; Director's report, *Annual Report of the Director General of UNWRA*, UN Doc. 5224/5223, Nov. 25, 1952. For Palestinian statistics see *Facts and Figures about the Palestinians*, published by the Center for Policy Analysis in Palestine (2435 Virginia Avenue NW; Washington, D.C. 20037).

16. Larry Ekin, *Enduring Witness* (Geneva: World Council of Churches, 1985). The subsequent quotes on page 130 are from the same source, pp. 8-9.

17. *Ibid.*, pp. 8-9.

Chapter 12

1. Edward W. Said, *Culture and Imperialism* (New York: Alfred A. Knopf, 1993), pp. 8-9.

2. David Fromkin, *A Peace to End All Peace* (New York: Henry Holt and Company, 1989).

3. Harold Wilson, *The Chariot of Israel* (New York: W. W. Norton, 1981), p. 54.

4. Wilson, *Ibid.*, p. 66; see also "The Question of Palestine," *United Nations, Division on Palestinian Rights* (United Nations, New York, 1979).

5. Alfred Koestler, *The Thirteenth Tribe* (New York: Random House, 1976), p. 223.

6. Quoted in "Seventy Years On" Editorial (London: Middle East International), October 24, 1987; p. 2.

7. Quoted in Thomas and Sally Mallison, *The Palestine Problem in International Law,* (Essex, England: Longman Group Ltd., 1986), p. 64.

8. *Ibid.*, p. 65.

9. Colin Chapman, *Whose Promised Land?* (Batavia, Illinois: Lion Publishing, 1981), p. 54.

10. Mallison and Mallison, *Ibid.*, p. 66.

11. Fromkin, *Ibid.*, p. 257.

12. *Ibid.*, pp. 258-259.

13. *Ibid.*, p. 159.

14. Fromkin, *Ibid.*, p. 397.

15. Wilson, *Ibid.*, p. 67.

16. *Ibid.*, p. 69.

17. *Ibid.*, p. 73.

18. *Ibid.,* p. 72.

19. Several publications document the villages and the procedures: Walid Khalidi, *All that Remains* (Washington: Journal of Palestine Studies, 1992), and Dr. Jamil Fayez, The Royal Committee on Jerusalem, Government of Jordan, (New York: Americans for Middle East Understanding), 1992.

20. Letter from Mansour Kardosh, Arab Association for Human Rights, June 15, 1994.

21. "Water, the Next War in the Middle East?" *New York Times* (March 17, 1991), p. 3.

22. Jonathan Kuttab, Editorial, *The New York Times* (June 5, 1994).

23. Naseer Aruri, Editorial (Middle East International, May 15, 1994), p. 16.

24. Pope John Paul II, Message Delivered at the Ecumenical Vigil for Peace, *Assisi, Italy, 1993.*

25. Dr. Afif Safieh, "A Palestinian Perspective on the Peace Process," (Washington: The Center for Policy Analysis on Palestine, November 12, 1991), p. 9.

Chapter 13

1. Jean Zaru, presentation at St. Georges Anglican Cathedral, East Jerusalem, October 8, 1992.

2. "Holy Land Christians Worry About Survival," *Christian Century* (April 14, 1991), p. 452.

3. *MECC Perspectives,* No. 8 (Limassol, Cyprus: Middle East Council of Churches, July 1990), p. 41.

4. *Christian Century*, April 14, 1991, *Ibid.*

5. "Israel Says It Helped Finance Settlers in Christian Quarter," *New York Times*, April 23, 1990; see also Anthony Lewis, "Israel Against Itself," *New York Times*, April 27, 1990.

6. Faxsimile from World Vision International, Jerusalem Office, May 5, 1993.

7. *Ibid.*

8. A letter by Avi Granot, Counselor for Church Affairs, Embassy of Israel, 3514 International Drive NE, Washington, D.C. 20009.

9. Naim Ateek, Marc Ellis, and Rosemary Ruether, eds. *Faith and the Intifada* (Maryknoll, New York: 1992), p. 61.

10. *Ibid.*, pp. 62-64.

11. Fr. Riah Abu-al Assel, speech to a Mercy Corps International delegation, Nazareth, Israel, August 18, 1991.

12. Kenneth Cragg, *The Arab Christian* (Louisville: Westminster Press, 1991), p. 247.

13. MECC New Report (May/June, 1993) vol. 3, p. 23.

14. *Ibid.*

15. *Ibid.*

16. The Lausanne Covenant, International Congress on World Evangelization, Lausanne, Switzerland, July 1974.

17. Leonard Rodgers, telefax letter to Ed Steele Agency, from Venture Middle East, Nicosia, Cyprus; February 13, 1993.

Chapter 14

1. Letter from Bob Seiple, president of World Vision, May 11, 1994 (919 West Huntington Drive, Monrovia, CA 91016).

2. James Wall, "South Africa Changes," *Christian Century*, May 11, 1994, p. 483.

3. For an illustration of the "AD 2000 Movement," see *Mission Frontiers*, vols. 1-16, published by the Center for World Mission, 1605 Elizabeth Street, Pasadena, CA 91104. The movement claims to have 20 million followers.

4. Address to the Signs of Hope Conference organized by the Middle East Council of Churches and Evangelicals for Middle East Understanding, October 7, 1991, Limassol, Cyprus.

5. Kenneth Cragg, *The Arab Christian* (Louisville: Westminster/John Knox Press, 1991).

6. Gabriel Habib, keynote address to the Evangelicals for Middle East Understanding Conference, February 4, 1994; Washington, D.C. (available from EMEU, 847 Chicago Avenue, 3C; Evanston, IL 60202).

7. Ibid.

8. Data taken from the Unified Arab Economic Report (1991), summarized by Rami Khouri in an address to the Signs of Hope Conference, 1992, Nicosia, Cyprus.

9. Ibid.

10. "Christian Mission in the Arab World: A Confidential Report," The Cooperative Strategy Group, Nicosia, Cyprus; 1993.

11. David Cooperrider and Suresh Srivasta, *Appreciative Management and Leadership: The Power of Positive Thought and Action in Organizations* (San Francisco: Jossey-Bass Inc., 1990), p. 93.

12. Ibid., p. 122.

13. Ibid., p. 122-123.

14. Jonathan Kuttab, lecture in Jerusalem to a Mercy Corps International Study-Tour Delegation, March 18, 1991.

15. Thomas Merton, "Letter to Jim Forest" (Reprinted flyer by Pax Christi of Illinois, 1988).

16. Gabriel Habib, "Open Letter to North American Evangelicals," Middle East Council of Churches, Limassol, Cyprus, July 1987.

Bibliography

The following works were used directly in the text or were consulted by the author as background material. This bibliography does not attempt to be exhaustive but will provide the reader with useful references for continued study.

Historical and General Overviews

Antonius, George. *The Arab Awakening.* New York: Capricorn Books, 1965.

Atiya, Aziz, S. *A History of Eastern Christianity.* Millwood, N.Y.: Kraus Reprint and Periodicals, 1980.

Carter, Jimmy. *The Blood of Abraham.* Boston: Houghton Mifflin, 1986.

Fromkin, David. *A Peace to End All Peace: The Fall of the Ottoman Empire and the Creation of the Modern Middle East.* New York: Avon Books, 1989.

Hitti, Philip K. *A History of the Arabs.* 10th ed. New York: St. Martin's Press, 1970.

Horner, Norman H. *A Guide to the Churches of the Middle East.* Elkhart, Ind.: Mennonite Board of Missions, 1989.

Hourani, Albert. *A History of the Arab Peoples.* Cambridge, Mass.: Harvard University Press, 1991.

Khouri, Fred. *Arab-Israeli Dilemma.* Syracuse, N.Y.: Syracuse University Press, 1988.

Kimball, Charles A. *Angle of Vision.* New York: Friendship Press, 1992.

Lamb, David. *The Arabs—Journeys Beyond the Mirage.* New York: Random House, 1988.

Mansfield, Peter. *The Arabs,* rev. ed. New York: Viking Penguin Books, 1992.

Quandt, William, Fuad Jabber, and Ann Lesch. *The Politics of Palestinian Nationalism.* Berkeley, Calif.: University of California Press, 1973.

Yergin, Daniel. *The Prize: The Epic Quest for Oil, Money, and Power.* New York: Simon and Schuster, 1991.

The Israeli-Palestinian Conflict

Abu-Lughod, Ibrahim, ed. *The Transformation of Palestine.* Evanston, Ill.: Northwestern University Press, 1971.

Ateek, Naim S. *Justice and Only Justice.* Maryknoll, N.Y.: Orbis Books, 1989.

Ateek, Naim, Marc Ellis, and Rosemary Ruether, eds. *Faith and the Intifada.* Maryknoll, N.Y.: Orbis Books, 1992.

Begin, Menachem. *The Revolt.* New York: Nash, 1977.

Beit-Hallahmi, Benjamin. *Original Sins: Reflections on the History of Zionism and Israel.* New York: Pluto Press, 1992.

Bergen, Kathy, David Neuhaus, and Ghassan Rubeiz, eds. *Justice and the Intifada.* New York: Friendship Press, 1991.

Birkland, Carol J., and Holly K. Einess, eds. *Two Peoples . . . The Same Land.* Minneapolis: Augsburg Fortress Publishers, 1987.

Cattan, Henry. *The Palestine Question.* New York: Croom Helm/Methuen, 1988.

Chacour, Elias, with David Hazard. *Blood Brothers.* Tarrytown, New York: Revell (Chosen Books), 1988.

Chacour, Elias, with Mary Jensen. *We Belong to the Land.* San Francisco: HarperCollins, 1990.

Chapman, Colin. *Whose Promised Land?* Batavia, Ill.: Lion Publishing, 1983.

Chomsky, Noam. *The Fateful Triangle.* Boston: South End Press, 1984.

Cobban, Helena. *The Palestinian Liberation Organization: People, Power, Politics.* Cambridge, Mass.: Cambridge University Press, 1984.

Collins, Larry, and Dominique Lapierre. *O Jerusalem!* New York: Simon and Schuster (Touchstone), 1988.

Dimbleby, Jonathan. *The Palestinians.* London: Quartet Books, 1979.

Eban, Abba. *Heritage: Civilization and the Jews.* New York: Summit Books, 1984.

Eban, Abba. *Personal Witness: Israel Through My Eyes.* New York: Putnam's, 1991.

Ekin, Larry. *Enduring Witness: The Churches and the Palestinians.* Vol. 2. Geneva: The World Council of Churches, 1985.

El-Asmar, Fouzi. *To Be an Arab in Israel.* Washington, D.C.: Institute for Palestine Studies, 1978.

Elon, Amos. *The Israelis: Founders and Sons.* London: Penguin Books, 1988.

Flapan, Simha. *The Birth of Israel.* New York: Pantheon Books, 1988.

Friedman, Thomas. *From Beirut to Jerusalem.* New York: Farrar, Straus, Giroux, 1989.

Fuller, Graham. *The West Bank of Israel: Point of No Return?* Santa Monica, Calif.: The Rand Corporation/Office of the Secretary of Defense, 1989.

Gilmour, David. *Dispossessed: The Ordeal of the Palestinians.* London: Sidgwick and Jackson, 1980.

Graham-Brown, Sarah. *Palestinians and Their Society 1880-1946.* London: Quartet Books, 1980.

Gresh, Alain. *The P.L.O.: The Struggle Within.* London: Zed Books, 1988.

Grollenberg, Lucas. *Palestine Comes First.* London: SCM Press, 1980.

Grossman, David. *The Yellow Wind.* New York: Delacorte Books, 1988.

Hadawi, Sami. *Bitter Harvest: Palestine 1914-79.* Delmar, N.Y.: Caravan Books, 1979.

Halsell, Grace. *Journey to Jerusalem.* New York: Macmillan and Company, 1982.

Halsell, Grace. *Prophecy and Politics.* Chicago: Lawrence Hill Books, 1986.

Harkabi, Yehosaphat. *Israel's Fateful Hour.* New York: Harper & Row, 1986.

Hart, Alan. *Arafat: Terrorist or Peacemaker?* London: Sidgwick and Jackson, 1984.

Hertzberg, Arthur, ed. *The Zionist Idea: A Historical Analysis and Reader.* Westport, Conn.: Greenwood Publishing Group, 1971.

Hirst, David. *The Gun and the Olive Branch.* London: Futura Press, 1981.

Irani, George. *The Papacy and the Middle East.* Notre Dame, Ind.: Notre Dame University Press, 1986.

Jiryis, Sabri. *The Arabs in Israel.* New York: Monthly Review Press, 1976.

Johnson, Paul. *A History of the Jews.* New York: HarperCollins, 1988.

Khalidi, Walid. *Before Their Diaspora.* London: St. Martin's Press, 1980.

Khalidi, Walid, ed. *From Haven to Conquest: Readings in Zionism and the Palestine Problem Until 1948.* Washington, D.C.: Institute for Palestine Studies, 1987.

Laqueur, Walter. *A History of Zionism.* New York: Schocken Books, 1972.

Laqueur, Walter and Barry Rubin, editors. *The Israeli-Arab Reader.* 4th ed. New York: Penguin Books, 1984.

Lustick, Ian. *Arabs in the Jewish State.* Austin: University of Texas Press, 1980.

Lustick, Ian. *The Land and the Lord.* New York: Council on Foreign Relations, 1988.

Mallison, Thomas and Sally. *The Palestine Problem in International Law.* London: Longmans, Ltd., 1986.

Mandel, Neville. *The Arabs and Zionism Before World War I.* Berkeley: University of California Press, 1976.

McDowell, David. *The Uprising and Beyond.* Berkeley: University of California Press, 1989.

Morris, Benny. *The Birth of the Palestinian Refugee Problem.* New York: Oxford University Press, 1987.

Nazzal, Nafez. *The Palestinian Exodus from Galilee, 1948.* Washington, D.C.: Institute for Palestine Studies, 1978.

Oz, Amos. *In the Land of Israel.* San Diego, Calif.: Harcourt Brace Jovanovich, 1983.

Palumbo, Michael. *The Palestinian Catastrophe: The 1948 Expulsion of a People from Their Homeland.* London: Faber and Faber, 1987.

Rantisi, Audeh, with Ralph Beebe. *Blessed Are the Peacemakers.* Grand Rapids, Mich: Zondervan Publishing House, 1991.

Rodinson, Maxime. *Israel and the Arabs.* New York: Pantheon Books, 1968.

Ruether, Rosemary and Herman. *The Wrath of Jonah.* San Francisco: Harper & Row, 1989.

Sacher, Howard. *A History of the Jews in America.* New York: Alfred A. Knopf, 1992.

Said, Edward. *After the Last Sky.* New York: Pantheon Books, 1986.

Said, Edward. *Culture and Imperialism.* New York: Simon and Schuster, 1993.

Said, Edward. *Orientalism.* New York: Pantheon Books, 1978.

Said, Edward. *The Question of Palestine.* New York: Pantheon Books, 1983.

Sayigh, Rosemary. *Palestinians: From Peasants to Revolutionaries.* London: Zed Press, 1979.

Segev, Tom. *1949: The First Israelis.* London: The Free Press, 1986.

Shahadeh, Raja. *Occupier's Law.* Washington, D.C.: Institute of Palestine Studies, 1985.

Shahadeh, Raja. *The Third Way: A Journal of Life in the West Bank.* New York: Quartet Books, 1982.

Shaheen, Jack. *The T.V. Arab.* Bowling Green, Ohio: Bowling Green University, 1984.

Sharif, Ragina. *Non-Jewish Zionism.* London: Zed Press, 1983.

Shipler, David. *Arab and Jew: Wounded Spirits in a Promised Land.* New York: Penguin Books, 1986.

Sykes, Christopher. *Two Studies in Virtue.* New York: Alfred A. Knopf, 1953.

Tivnan, Edward. *The Lobby: Jewish Political Power and American Foreign Policy.* New York: Simon and Schuster, 1987.

Viorst, Milton. *Sands of Sorrow.* London: I.B. Taurus, 1987.

Other Arab Countries and Regions

Ang, Swee Chai. *From Beirut to Jerusalem.* London: Collins (Grafton), 1989.

Ball, George. *Error and Betrayal in Lebanon.* Washington, D.C.: Foundation for Middle East Peace, 1984.

Cutting, Pauline. *Children of the Siege.* London: Heinemann, 1987.

Fisk, Robert. *Pity the Nation.* New York: Atheneum, 1990.

Hiro, Dilip. *Iran Under the Ayatollahs.* London: Routledge Chapman and Hall, 1990.

Al-Khalil, Samir. *Republic of Fear: The Inside Story of Saddam's Iraq.* New York: Pantheon, 1991.

Levin, Sis. *Beirut Diary.* Downers Grove, Ill.: InterVarsity Press, 1990.

Mackey, Sandra. *The Saudis: Inside the Desert Kingdom.* New York: Signet, 1990.

Mahfouz, Naguib. *Midaq Alley, The Thief and the Dogs, Miramar* (trilogy). New York: Quality Paperback Book Club, 1989.

Miller, Judith, and Laurie Mylroie. *Saddam Hussein and the Crisis in the Gulf.* New York: Random House (Times Books), 1991.

Nassib, Salim. *Beirut, Frontline Story.* New York: Africa World Press, 1983.

Randal, Jonathan. *Going All the Way.* New York: Vintage, 1984.

Seale, Patrick. *Asad.* Berkeley: University of California Press, 1989.

Wright, Robin. *In the Name of God: The Khoumeini Decade.* New York: Simon & Schuster, 1991.

Wright, Robin. *Sacred Rage: The Wrath of Militant Islam.* New York: Simon & Schuster (Touchstone), 1986.

Interfaith Issues

Betts, Robert B. *Christians in the Arab East.* Atlanta, Ga.: John Knox Press, 1982.

Cragg, Kenneth. *The Arab Christian.* Louisville: Westminster/John Knox Press, 1991.

Ellis, Marc. *Toward a Jewish Theology of Liberation.* Maryknoll, N.Y.: Orbis Books, 1987.

Ellis, Marc. *Beyond Innocence and Redemption: Confronting the Holocaust and Israeli Power.* San Francisco: Harper & Row, 1991.

Kimball, Charles. *Striving Together: A Way Forward in Christian-Muslim Relations.* Maryknoll, N.Y.: Orbis Press, 1991.

Moussalli, Ahmad S. *Radical Islamic Fundamentalism: The Ideological and Political Discourse of Sayyid Qutb.* Beirut: American University of Beirut, 1991.

242 Anxious for Armageddon

Christian Zionism and Other Christian Aspects

Baker, William. *Theft of a Nation.* Las Vegas, Nev.: Defenders Publications, 1982.

Barr, James. *Fundamentalism.* Philadelphia: Westminster Press, 1977.

Beegle, Dewey. *Prophecy and Prediction.* Ann Arbor, Mich.: Pryor Pettengill, Publisher, 1978.

Blackstone, William E. *Jesus Is Coming.* New York: Fleming Revell, 1986.

British Council of Churches. *Toward Understanding the Arab and Israeli Conflict.* London: British Council of Churches, 1982.

Burrows, Millar. *Palestine Is Our Business.* Philadelphia: Westminster Press, 1959.

Cox, William. *Amillennialism Today.* Phillipsburgh, Pa.: Presyterian and Reformed Publishing Co., 1966.

Davies, W. D. *The Gospel and the Land.* Berkeley: University of California Press, 1974.

Davies, W. D. *The Territorial Dimension of Judaism.* Berkeley: University of California Press, 1982.

Dayton, Donald. *Discovering an Evangelical Heritage.* New York: Harper & Row, 1976.

Falwell, Jerry. *The Fundamentalist Phenomenon.* New York, Doubleday, 1981.

Falwell, Jerry, *Listen America.* New York: Doubleday, 1980.

Froom, LeRoy E. *The Prophetic Faith of Our Fathers.* Vol. IV. Washington, D.C.: Review and Herald, 1954.

Gaspar, Louis. *The Fundamentalist Movement.* The Hague: Moulton and Company, 1965.

Handy, Robert, ed. *The Holy Land and American Protestant Life: 1800-1948.* New York: Arno Press, 1981.

Hunt, Dave. *Peace, Prosperity, and the Coming Holocaust.* Eugene, Ore.: Harvest House Publishers, 1983.

Hunter, James Davison. *American Evangelicalism.* New Brunswick, N.J.: Rutgers University Press, 1983.

Kraus, Norman. *Dispensationalism in America.* Richmond, Va.: 1958.

Ladd, George Eldon. *The Blessed Hope.* Grand Rapids: William B. Eerdmanns Publishing Company, 1956.

Lewis, David. *Magog 1982 Cancelled.* Harrison, Ark.: New Leaf Press, 1982.

Lindsay, Hal. *The Late, Great Planet Earth.* Grand Rapids: Zondervan Press, 1971.

Lindsay, Hal. *The 1980s: Countdown to Armageddon.* New York: Bantam Books, 1980.

Lindsay, Hal. *The Promise.* Eugene, Ore.: Harvest Publications, 1982.

Malachy, Yona. *American Fundamentalism and Israel.* Jerusalem: Hebrew University Press, 1978.

Marsden, George. *Fundamentalism and American Culture.* New York: Oxford University Press, 1980.

Nijim, Bashir, ed. *American Church Politics and the Middle East.* Belmont, Mass.: AAUG Press, 1982.

Noe, John. *The Apocalypse Conspiracy.* Brentwood, Tenn.: Wolgemuth and Hyatt Publishers, Inc. 1991.

Packer, J. I. *Fundamentalism and the Word of God.* Grand Rapids: William Eerdmans Publishing, Co. 1972.

Rausch, David. *A Legacy of Hatred: Why Christians Must Not Forget the Holocaust.* Grand Rapids: Baker Book House, 1990.

Rausch, David. *Zionism Within Early American Fundamentalism.* New York: Edwin Mellen Press, 1982.

Robertson, Pat. *The Secret Kingdom.* Nashville: Thomas Nelson and Sons, 1982.

Sandeen, Ernest. *The Roots of Fundamentalism.* Chicago: The University of Chicago Press, 1970.

Schissel, Steve with David Brown. *Hal Lindsay and the Restoration of the Jews.* Edmonton, Alberta: Still Waters Revival Books, 1990.

Simon, Merrill. *Jerry Falwell and the Jews.* Middle Village, N.Y.: Jonathan David Publishers, Inc., 1984.

Tuchman, Barbara. *Bible and Sword.* New York: Ballantine Books, 1984.

Weber, Timothy. *Living in the Shadow of the Second Coming.* (Grand Rapids: Zondervan Publishing House, 1983).

Weir, Benjamin and Carol. *Hostage Bound, Hostage Free.* Philadelphia: Westminster Press, 1987.

Wilson, Dwight. *Armageddon Now.* Tyler, Tex.: Institute for Christian Economics, 1991.

Index

105, 107, 109, 112, 119, 127-129, 152, 155, 160-161, 163, 166, 168
Jewish National Fund, 138, 141, 145-146
Jordan, 51, 53, 59-60, 74, 125, 136, 150, 160, 164, 228
Jordan River, 133, 140
Judaism, 175, 177, 182
Judaism/Jews, 184

K
Kafity, Bishop Samir, 92, 164, 169
Khouri, Bishop Elia, 148
King-Crane Commission, 140, 226
Knesset, 97, 103
Koestler, Arthur, 136
Kuttab, Jonathan, 191
Kuwait, 135

L
Labor, 64, 107
Labor Party, 125
Land, 60-64, 66, 69, 71-76, 79-81, 83, 86-87, 91-92, 101, 103, 105-106, 111, 120-121, 130, 162, 216-217
Lausanne Committee for World Evangelization, 48, 108, 236
Lausanne Covenant, 170
Lausanne Executive Committee for World Evangelization, 77
Lawrence of Arabia, 135
League of Nations, 135-140, 154
League of Nations Covenant, 137, 139-140, 147, 154
Lebanon, 30-32, 34, 36-39, 42, 59, 62, 73, 103, 116-117, 120, 129, 136, 150, 160, 164, 171, 213, 226-228, 232
Likud, 64, 105, 107
Likud Party, 100-101, 228
Lindsey, Hal, 86
Lloyd-George, David, 134-135
Lloyd-Jones, David, 94

M
MECC, 181, 186-187, 192
Madrid Peace Process, 148
Magnes, Judah, 142
Mahfuz, Nagib, 185
Mandate, 135, 137-140, 155
Mandate (British), 135, 137, 141, 143, 155
· Mandela, Nelson, 179

Maronites, 36, 38-39, 41-42, 225
McMahon Correspondence, 226
McMahon, Sir Henry, 135
Meir, Golda, 146
Melkite Catholic, 34
Melkites, 36
Mercy Corps, 42
Merton, Thomas, 47, 192
Mid-tribulationists, 90
Middle East Council of Churches, 58, 98, 106, 229, 234
Middle East Council of Churches (MECC), 32, 34, 39, 160, 211, 213, 225, 228, 236
Middle Eastern Christians, 106
Millennial, 25, 90
Mohammed, 61
Muslim, 105, 112, 159, 163
Muslim (Islam), 192

N
Nasser, Dr. Hanna, 148
Nazis, 27, 69, 132, 227

O
O'Neill, Dan, 42
Open Door, 171
Oslo Agreements (DOP), 147, 154-155
Ottoman Empire, 36, 51, 226
Ottoman Empire (Turks), 134, 136, 147, 207, 225

P
PLO, 28, 41, 44, 51, 56, 65-66, 108, 131-132, 148, 150-151, 153-154, 164, 179, 188, 227-229
Palestine National Council (PNC), 28
Paris Peace Accords, 138
Paris Peace Conference, 137, 141
Paris Peace Treaty, 155
   proposals, 137
Partition, 144
Peele Commission, 125, 141, 143, 227
   report, 141
Phalangists, 38-41, 228
Plan Dalet, 124, 126, 128
Plymouth Brethren, 88-90
Post-tribulationists, 90
Pre-tribulation, 90, 111
Premillennial (futurist), 24
Premillennial dispensationalist, 26, 81, 113
   eschatology, 87

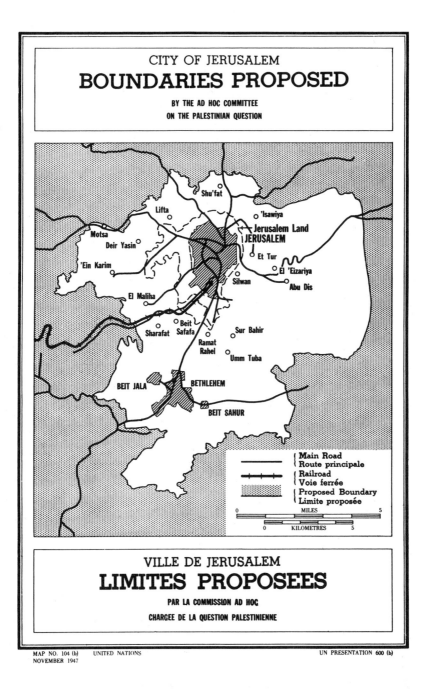

CITY OF JERUSALEM
BOUNDARIES PROPOSED
BY THE AD HOC COMMITTEE
ON THE PALESTINIAN QUESTION

Shu'fat

Lifta

'Isawiya

Jerusalem Land
JERUSALEM

Motsa

Deir Yasin

Et Tur

'Ein Karim

El 'Eizariya

Silwan

Abu Dis

El Maliha

Beit Safafa

Sharafat

Sur Bahir

Ramat Rahel

Umm Tuba

BEIT JALA

BETHLEHEM

BEIT SAHUR

Main Road
Route principale
Railroad
Voie ferrée
Proposed Boundary
Limite proposée

MILES
0   5

KILOMETRES
0   5

VILLE DE JERUSALEM
LIMITES PROPOSEES
PAR LA COMMISSION AD HOC
CHARGEE DE LA QUESTION PALESTINIENNE

UN PARTITION PLAN – 1947
AND
UN ARMISTICE LINES – 1949

—·—·— Boundary of Former Palestine Mandate

PLAN OF PARTITION, 1947

Arab State
Jewish State
Jerusalem

– – – Armistice Demarcation lines, 1949
(Shown where at variance with Mandate boundary.)

MAP NO. 3067   UNITED NATIONS
SEPTEMBER 1979

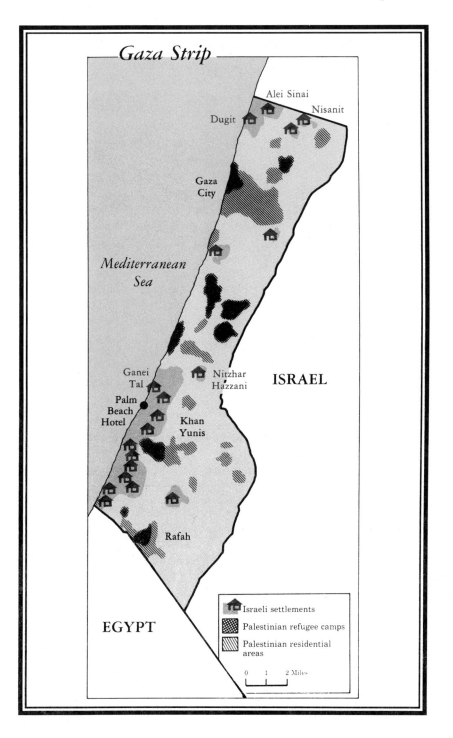

Gaza Strip

Alei Sinai

Nisanit

Dugit

Gaza
City

Mediterranean
Sea

Ganei
Tal

Nitzhar
Hazzani

ISRAEL

Palm
Beach
Hotel

Khan
Yunis

Rafah

EGYPT

🏠 Israeli settlements

Palestinian refugee camps

Palestinian residential
areas

0   1   2 Miles

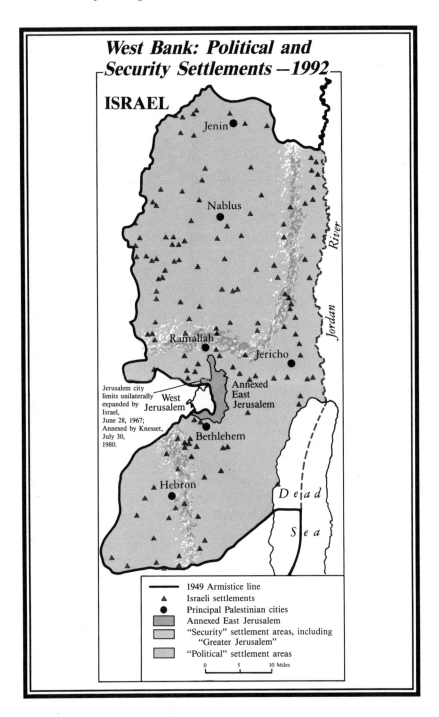

West Bank: Political and Security Settlements — 1992

ISRAEL

Jenin

Nablus

Ramallah

Jericho

Jerusalem city limits unilaterally expanded by Israel, June 28, 1967; Annexed by Knesset, July 30, 1980.

West Jerusalem

Annexed East Jerusalem

Bethlehem

Hebron

Jordan River

D e a d

S e a

——	1949 Armistice line
▲	Israeli settlements
●	Principal Palestinian cities
▨	Annexed East Jerusalem
▢	"Security" settlement areas, including "Greater Jerusalem"
▨	"Political" settlement areas

0   5   10 Miles

The Author

Donald E. Wagner has served pastorates in three Presbyterian churches. For ten years he was national director of the Palestine Human Rights Campaign. Since 1990 he has been director of Mercy Corps International's Middle East Program.

Wagner has led over twenty tours to the Middle East and has organized over fifteen national conferences. In 1987-1988 he lived in the Middle East with his family and worked for the Middle East Council of Churches as a liaison with Western evangelicals. He is the editor (with Hassan Haddad) of *All in the Name of the Bible* (Amana Press, 1986); coauthor (with Dan O'Neill) of *Peace or Armageddon: The Unfolding Drama of the Middle East Peace Accords* (Zondervan, 1993), and author of several political and Christian articles on the Middle East.

Wagner and his wife, H. Drew McAllister, live in Evanston, Illinois. They are parents of Matthew (1983), and Anna (1984). Don's older son Jay (1970) lives in Toledo with his wife Tracy.